Law and the Exception

This book proposes a paradigm shift in the way that 'the state of exception'—as it is usually named in legal and political theory—is to be understood. Building on the assumption that the exception is a heuristic idea that is still a relevant category for a critical deconstruction of law, this book argues that it needs to be rethought outside the boundaries of its traditional understanding. To this end, the book offers two strategies. First, it develops the ideas of 'exceptionality' and 'exceptionalisation' in order to grasp how measures, norms and mechanisms that clearly have an exceptional character are no longer confined within the boundaries of classic institutions such as the state of exception, martial law, the state of emergency and so on. As demonstrated recently during the COVID-19 pandemic, legal systems may dissimulate the exceptional as the normal, avoiding the use of formal states of exception and adopting measures that are of exceptional nature. This book maintains that it is necessary to think of 'exceptionality' outside of its usual legal footholds. Emergency laws are considered here as part of a more general sphere of exceptionality that must be understood as the product of a process of the accumulation of symbols, practices, notions and images that are only partially expressed through law, despite having long populated the legal imagination. Second, the book offers an analysis of the inner exceptional life of liberal constitutionalism: the subterranean authoritarian drives dissimulated by the rule of law.

This book will interest scholars and researchers in legal and political theory, as well as continental philosophy.

Gian-Giacomo Fusco is a lecturer in law at Kent Law School (University of Kent, Canterbury). He obtained his doctoral degree in law at the University of Kent. His research interests include jurisprudence, critical theory, history of ideas and urban studies. His more recent monograph, *Form of Life: Agamben and the Destitution of Rules* (2022), engaged with and developed further Agamben's concept of destituent potential as a critique of the law.

Przemysław Tacik is Assistant Professor at the Institute of European Studies of the Jagiellonian University of Kraków, Poland, and Director of the Nomos: Centre for International Research on Law, Culture and Power. A philosopher, lawyer and sociologist by education, he holds PhDs in philosophy (2014) and international law (2016), as well as habilitation in law (2024). He has been a visiting scholar at numerous universities. In his academic work, he combines both philosophical and legal perspectives, attempting to approach them from an interdisciplinary angle. His current research is focused on critical legal theory and contemporary philosophy. He has authored five books as well as over 60 articles and two translations of a poetry volume (from French to Polish). His most recent monographs are *A New Philosophy of Modernity and Sovereignty: Towards Radical Historicization* (2021) and *Deconstructing the Right to Self-Determination in International Law: Sovereignty, Exception, Biopolitics* (2023).

Part of the
NOMOS STUDIES IN LAW, CULTURE AND POWER
Series

A GlassHouse book

Law and the Exception

Towards a New Paradigm

Gian-Giacomo Fusco
and Przemysław Tacik

Routledge
Taylor & Francis Group
a GlassHouse Book

First published 2026
by Routledge
4 Park Square, Milton Park, Abingdon, Oxon OX14 4RN

and by Routledge
605 Third Avenue, New York, NY 10158

a GlassHouse book

Routledge is an imprint of the Taylor & Francis Group, an informa business

British Library Cataloguing-in-Publication Data
A catalogue record for this book is available from the British Library

ISBN: 978-1-032-79084-8 (hbk)
ISBN: 978-1-032-79086-2 (pbk)
ISBN: 978-1-003-49044-9 (ebk)

DOI: 10.4324/9781003490449

Typeset in Sabon
by Apex CoVantage, LLC

Contents

Acknowledgments

The authors would like to express their gratitude first to the other members of the Nomos Centre, with whom they have spent many times discussing issues related to exceptions. For the last five years, as a research community, we have been trying to address intellectually the ongoing processes—the expansion of the executive, spread of crisis narratives, abuse of power in the name of security and protection and suspension of individual liberties. This book certainly owes much to these common reflections. In particular, the authors would like to thank Cosmin Cercel, Tormod Johansen and Alexandra Mercescu for all our talks, inspirations and friendship.

Our thanks also go to Colin Perrin and Naomi Round Cahalin from Routledge, who offered us invaluable help and support in the publication process.

Przemysław Tacik's research for this publication has been supported by a grant from the Priority Research Area (Foreign Research Visits) under the Strategic Programme Excellence Initiative at Jagiellonian University. The author would like to thank Max-Planck-Institut für ausländisches öffentliches Recht und Völkerrecht in Heidelberg for the hospitality offered during his research stay in 2023.

Introduction

Despite the upheavals of recent years, marked by revolts, a global pandemic, wars and coup d'états, the concept of the state of exception seems to have lost the prominence it once held at the turn of the last century. The distress that has accompanied the awareness of the political and social risks embedded in the spillover of exceptional measures into the ordinary legal system during the two-decades-long war on terror has been overshadowed by a more optimistic (and somehow realist) narrative of the state of emergency, which highlighted the 'resilience' of the legal and political mechanisms of liberal democracies and portrayed acute moments of crisis not as authoritarian moments for the suspension of law and rights, but as a field of normopoietic intervention and institutional adaptation.

Since at least the second half of the 20th century, the exception has undergone a normalisation process, becoming a highly regulated form of government. This is for factual/historical and institutional reasons. Liberal democracies, traditionally equipped with emergency measures designed to address severe social and political crises like wars or uprisings, found themselves inadequately prepared to manage the wide range of critical events shaping the global political landscape. The need to respond to emergencies that deviate from the traditional war-like framework led to the establishment of numerous legislative measures, both ordinary and extraordinary, tailored to each specific crisis. Unforeseeable critical events cannot be totally excluded from the horizon of our political orders, but 'the more we increase our knowledge on the capabilities' of a legal system, 'as well as on the hazards threatening it, the unforeseeable, and thereby the need for legal exceptionalism, is constantly pushed'.[1]

The growing juridification of crisis management has made the exceptional government of emergencies less exceptional and more the outcome of enforced rules. But this logically implies that the dichotomy norm/exception upon which the very category of emergency laws has been thought and

1 Kristian Cederval Lauta, *Disaster Law* (Routledge 2014) 71.

DOI: 10.4324/9781003490449-1

shaped is somehow dissolved or displaced. When crises are no longer occasions for a simple suspension of rights and delegation to the executive of broad extra-legal powers but become a field of norm production, the exception seems to become a category of normality and, as a concept, loses its heuristic potential. This is the kernel of a narrative of emergency that has been gradually established in the last two decades, which has shifted the focus from the exceptional nature and scope of the growing network of legal instruments and institutions involved in the management of emergencies to the normative and political means for the containment of the transformative potential embedded in exceptional circumstances.

But what are the theoretical implications of shifting or decentering the dichotomy between normality and exception? Can we truly move beyond the exception/normality framework as a legal epistemic category? What does it mean for liberal democracies and liberal law to suspend rights and the normal rule of law while still preserving their liberal essence? With this book, we seek to offer a critical response to these questions, pushing legal theory toward new paradigms that can more effectively engage with the theoretical conundrums of the relationship between norm and exception within liberal legalism and the liberal theory of the state.

Our starting point is the conviction that although surrounded by uncertainty and conceptual imprecision, the category of exception is still useful for the comprehension of the specific legal reaction to the emergencies constellating the current global scenario, but it needs further crucial development and clarification. We believe it necessary to reconsider the traditional Schmittian perspective that envisaged the state of exception as something essentially extra-legal, which is invoked when necessity calls and discharged when necessity ceases to be. To this purpose, this book offers an attempt to construct a general theory of exception; that is a generalisation and reconceptualisation of the field of exception or emergency studies. In times of blurred lines between the legal and the political, when various exceptional states appear in disguise, in creeping and unobvious forms, we desperately need to go beyond the safe cabinet of operative legal concepts. Given that the law seems to gradually weaken in its power not only to curb exceptions but also to record them and keep them visible, we cannot rely on legal terminology but require a broader conceptual framework. Its founding assumption is the need to go beyond the distinction between normality and exception, this being relative to a given legal order.

Emergency laws, from our perspective, must be considered as part of a sphere of exceptionality, which lives an autonomous life within the legal, assuring the primordial guarantee of the triumph of power that underpins the law over the reality it wants to inform. Such a sphere of exceptionality, which is only partially expressed in the words of the law, is the product of a process of accumulation of symbols, practices, notions and images that, throughout history, populated the legal imagination. The concept of exceptionality allows us to identify the character of legal measures and practices regardless of whether the legal system formally records them as exceptional or normal. Especially during the COVID-19 pandemic, it became clear that effectively exceptional measures can pass off as 'normal' ones. What we, therefore, need to gain is a sufficient analytic distance from the normality/exception distinction that each legal order establishes.

Such a new conceptuality is acutely needed in our times, when the tension between juridification of universalist ambitions and anti-nomic and often authoritarian forms of exercising power disturbs the very relation of the rule and the case. It seems that after years of liberal solidification of the rule of law, power is again getting out of hand, being exercised shamelessly, with the invocation of crisis narratives and sometimes in blatant disregard of rules. Under such circumstances, we can no longer rely on the distinction between the normal and the exceptional as conveyed by legal systems, but we need more potent conceptual tools.

1

The book sets out, in Chapter 1, by questioning the very nature of the state of exception as a legal category, and this is because of its essential semantic instability. Indeed, as a concept, it lacks precision and definitive focus, functioning instead as a general term encompassing various legal and factual phenomena associated with social and political crises where ordinary legal measures prove inadequate. Asking, 'What is the state of exception?' risks, therefore, becoming an exercise in merely cataloguing the forms of its occurrence. Moreover, one might question the utility of such an inquiry: in the realm of law and legal phenomena, focusing on the 'what' often proves limiting. Since the legal field is shaped not by tangible objects but by categories and terms, ontology inevitably overlooks the essence of normativity—its effectuality. Nevertheless, this does not mean that the nature of the state of exception in law cannot be meaningfully analysed.

As banal as it might seem, the state of exception depends on the existence of legal norms. To the extent that an exception is an exception to a norm, the state of exception arises essentially as an epiphenomenon of legal systems. It refers to moments when specific rules and procedures are suspended, rendered ineffective, or altered without actual changes in the status of their validity. In this regard, the state of exception brings to the fore the fundamental tensions that exist between the formal validity of norms and their practical-concrete application by exposing how the two can be decoupled without infringing on the foundation of the edifice of the law. As a legal construct, the state of exception exists within a critical zone: between the law's existence as form and the practical institutions enforcing it.

The exceptional deviation from the normal application of the law is often necessary to address unforeseen events, where rigid adherence to legal norms could result in suboptimal outcomes or harm to the social body, allowing at the same time the preservation of the broader continuity of the legal system, through a misapplication of specific norms. Although general and aiming for absolute applicability, the text of the law cannot account for the infinite potentiality of the contingency of human social life. This is because of the inherent weakness of language, that is, its openness and interpretability and its incapacity to provide a full account of the world it relates to. The capacity to make exceptions, therefore, constitutes itself as a supplement helping legal normativity to cope with the limits of law.

As such, the state exception shares a common ground with other mechanisms for the adaptation of the law to unique circumstances without fundamentally altering the core structures of legal normativity; more specifically, as we shall see, it shares foundational discourses with the legal concept of equity. Indeed, the state of exception and equity are not only genealogically linked to that excess of authority that has characterised legal-sovereign power throughout time but share the same rationale as suspension of the law on the grounds of a specific limit of the law itself. The existence of equity (pretty much in all its forms) is justified as a corrective to the potential 'injustice' of a strict application of the law since the language of the law cannot account for the potentiality of the world's contingency. Such a rationale has been regularly used to legitimise the infringement of the law in case of emergency. Exemplary in this regard is John Locke's analysis of the King's prerogative—that power to act discretionary for the common good, outside and at times against the law. There are many things, he writes, which elude the law's provision 'for since many accidents may happen, wherein a strict and rigid observation of the laws may do harm'; inasmuch that it is impossible for the law to 'provide for all accidents and necessities that may concern the public good . . . there is a latitude left to the executive power, to do many things of choice with the laws do not prescribe'.[2]

The logical consequence of this argument is that the original locus of both the state of exception and equity is never the norm itself, but it is the institutional apparatus applying it. One of the theses that this work aims to advance is that the possibility of making exceptions (from the equitable overriding of norms by judges to the discretion of the executive in a state of emergency) is never inscribed in the norm but originates in the moment of law's application as the prerogative of the legal institutional apparatus. By suspending or deviating from a norm while preserving its validity, exceptions reveal the fundamental duality within the legal system. To the extent that the law cannot apply itself to the reality it aims to regulate, the formal linguistic expression of the law's norm necessitates its concrete enforcement: an authoritative decision by agents empowered to render those norms effective. And it is the

2 John Locke, *Two Treaties on Government* (Hackett Publishing Company 1980) §§ 159–160.

very possibility of the law's enforceability that produces a sphere of exceptionality, which we claim is what can ultimately grant unlimited application of the law.

The remnants of exceptionality in a legal system is, in this sense, the marker of law's acknowledgement of its occasional inoperativity and self-insufficiency with respect to the contingency of reality, which is remedied with exceptions. Therefore, although closely related to the pragmatic sphere of law's application, exceptionality remains an essential element but irreducible to legal forms; by allowing suspension of the norms, it provides effective instruments to ensure the continuity of law's effectuality circumventing the limits of the legal system in its relation to reality. But exceptionality is more than simply responding to challenges of contingency—it involves the overriding of the supposed structural infelicities of the legal system.

2

Chapter 2 lays the foundations for a general theory of exception, which aims to reconceptualise basic notions and ideas of exception/emergency studies. It begins by identifying their current insufficiencies. The chief one seems to be the dependence of the exception/normality distinction on the existing legal systems, which, especially currently—when they tend to dissimulate effectively exceptional measures as normal ones—is deceiving. The theory propounded here calls for a deep philosophical reconsideration of the field. The age-old debate between those who seek the foundation of the legal order in the exception (like Carl Schmitt) or normality (like Hermann Heller) casts a long shadow on exception studies. Much as the general theory of exception sides with Schmitt's dialectical approach, it aims to move beyond the binary concepts of 'the sovereign' and 'the exception' towards a more nuanced and dynamic theorisation, based on new philosophical engines. It does so by introducing and expounding the concept of exceptionality, construed as an energy that traverses a legal system. Exceptionality can be fixed in particular points and bulwarked by procedural devices, like states of exception, but maintains an excess in relation to them. In other words, instead of treating exceptional institutions as problems in themselves, we should rather approach them as partial attempts to bind an energy—exceptionality—that inevitably permeates each legal system.

Given that the relation between the normal and the exceptional is established by each legal system, the concept of exceptionality allows for distancing from how a certain measure or practice is recorded formally in a legal order. In this respect, the general theory of the exception encounters paradoxes well-known to psychoanalysis: the problem of the symbolic metaorder, which would record what happens in an order of the first level. The concept of exceptionality inherits part of the internal impossibility of what Jacques Lacan calls the Big Other of the Big Other. It thus demonstrates the deep entanglement not only between normality and exception but precisely between the legal order and the normative version of reality that it establishes. Exceptionality is reconstructable either as bound in an exceptional device, as its excess, or as a trace that haunts the legal system. Eventually, Chapter 2 provides an overview of the basic themes of the general theory of the exception as revised through the concept of exceptionality. First, it discusses possible philosophical engines of thinking about the exception. Then, it investigates the relations between the political and the legal, the rule and the case, as well as the temporality that exceptions contain and produce.

3

Chapter 3 addresses the process that in exception studies usually appears as the greatest scare: the exception getting out of hand, prolonging itself and blurring lines with normality. The concept that the general theory of the exception offers to grasp it is exceptionalisation. What it describes is the reallocation of exceptionality within channels of the legal system, often with a release of stray exceptional energy that traverses the legal. Yet, upon closer scrutiny, exceptionalisation is not just a shift in how exceptionality is distributed and spent; it also entails perturbations of its visibility. Indeed, exceptional devices have often been theorised as necessitating a transparent and certain process of *recording* what kind of normative and factual changes happen under their rule. Meanwhile, exceptionalisation destabilises this recording and thus renders in certain areas the normal and the exceptional indifferentiable.

As a result, exceptionalisation provokes an effective change of the constitutional regime outside its own registration. What it does is blur the division between *pouvoir constituant* and *pouvoir constitué*: while exercising the latter, the former is effectively engaged. For this reason, exceptionalisation corresponds to a profoundly fetishist transformation: a regime is both preserved as to its symbolic organisation (esp. main principles) but effectively modified through invisible incremental changes. Exceptionalisation is thus not just a legal or political problem but also an epistemological one of what is seen and recorded. Chapter 3 enquires into how this process can be analysed. To this purpose, it also re-adapts Ernst Fraenkel's theory of the dual state in order to demonstrate the fluidity of exceptionality in exceptionalised systems like the one of the Third Reich. The problem with such systems is not that they completely blend the political and the legal; they preserve their separation and binding but make their quilting point extend over the entire system with privileged organs, such as the Gestapo or the NSDAP, deciding on the very boundaries for legality. As argued in Chapter 3, nowadays legality displays a particular tendency towards exceptionalisation, which results in constitutional fetishism: the overall politico-legal structures seem untouched in their principles but are effectively hollowed out by exceptionality traversing the body of the legal system.

4

Chapter 4 brings together both terms coined in the two previous ones—exceptionality and exceptionalisation—in order to understand how they reframe the concept of (modern) sovereignty. First of all, sovereignty demonstrates its profound links with both legality as such and the exceptionality present within: indeed, it is sovereignty that offers the final push for the law to contact and mould reality. Drawing upon Agamben's recognition, it can be noticed that the law requires sovereignty for its very applicability. If so, exceptionality—as the presence of sovereignty within the law—is a price paid for the fact that the law can effectively work. There is, consequently, a deep affinity between exceptionality and the mediating work of sovereignty, which assures the day-to-day functioning of the law.

In order to account for it, Chapter 4 engages in a deeper historical exploration of modern sovereignty as built on the idea of survival: the sovereign being the position of always having the upper hand and assuring—biopolitically—survival of 'its own' population. The law, in contrast, risks its status with every application. Therefore, there is a peculiar entanglement between modern sovereignty and the law, the former guaranteeing the survival of the latter, its applicability. Various exceptional measures demonstrate that the same force which assures law application finds itself compelled to sometimes raise the upper hand in order to assure the survival of polity and its legality. As a consequence, the presence of exceptionality in the law is inherently linked to the modern biopolitical construction of the relationship between 'the people' and 'its' state. When exceptional measures are invoked, they produce their own deformed version of history, in which the emergence of the modern state through a biopolitical link between the state and the people becomes clearly discernible. Exceptionality is, at the same time, a necessary remainder of the process of normalisation, which eventually produces democracies based on the rule of law. It remains within the legal as the deferred presence of the ultimately recurring sovereignty. In this role, it allows for grasping the legal system as a palimpsest of exceptionalisations and normalisations.

Finally, Chapter 4 investigates exceptionality and sovereignty as two fields of energy which can be bound in cathexes—respectively, exceptional devices and nominal sovereigns—but retain an excess vis-à-vis their fixed points. The relation between exceptionality and sovereignty is not a full overlap; in their reduced forms—as bound in exceptions and sovereigns—the relation between them is described by Schmitt's famous theorem about the sovereign deciding on the exception. The role of legality is to distribute exceptionality and sovereignty, but in case of exceptionalisation, both are released. The era we are entering again now is marked by this process, blurring the lines between the legal and the illegal, law and politics, normal and exceptional.

5

The volume, then, in Chapter 5, tries to make sense of the normalisation of the exception from the point of view of liberal legalism. In its historical development, liberal constitutionalism accommodated the discrepancy between law and exception by erecting a boundary between normal constitutional order and crisis government while, at the same time, electing the law as the primary tool for organising social and political life in almost their totality. The outcome of these somewhat opposing drives is the logical growing juridification of emergency regimes: its normalisation. But this means that what was intended to be a specific power exceeding legalisation—the duty and prerogative to act for the common good outside and against the law—has become disembedded from the executive function, becoming a proper legal doctrine. What was acknowledged as mainly an extra-legal, political and, to a certain extent, moral issue has become, in this way, a legal question through the legalisation of the law's excess.

Faced with its own excesses, the reaction of liberal legalism is that of denial through internalisation. As a system of norms, the law lives in a strange paradox; it is capable of regulating its other only by internalising it and transforming it through its categorisation as legal. This is, in a sense, very clear in the relationship the law entertains with violence. For the law, punishment represents a form of revenge that 'succeeds in limiting and isolating its effects in accordance with social demands',[3] through its own subsequent limitation and nullification. The acquisition of a decisive faculty of limiting violence (and of pursuing justice) is, for the law, determined by the possibility of implementation of specific forms of legal violence. But this means that it is the law itself that must 'determine and eliminate violations of the law' through the internalisation and legalisation of what is ultimately eternal to the boundaries of legality. This paradox, as Niklas Luhmann claims, 'is evident in the anomaly of the self-defence/emergency law. There remain residual and borderline cases where the law permits the violation of law in legally defined terms and conditions'; in cases where illegality and violence are permitted, 'the paradox of legal coding shows up—but in a form which is immediately unfolded within the legal system through setting conditions which make the paradox invisible'.[4] The normalisation and internalisation of

3 René Girard, *Violence and the Sacred* (Bloomsbury 2013) 24.
4 Niklas Luhmann, *Law as Social System* (OUP 2004) 265.

exceptionality do not resolve the problem (an exception remains such even if it's legal) but make it invisible by translating it into a problem of legality and conformity to laws.

Although paradoxical, the internalisation of its own excesses serves the ultimate goal of legalism. One of the stated aims of the liberal paradigm is 'the attempt to legally programme state practice' through law: statutes and constitutional law are in this light assigned the function of 'regulating all essential aspects of life in society'.[5] This logically implies that in the liberal political paradigm, all forms of power that substantially exceed the legal remit must be replaced or put under control. To put it in other words, the 'law-rule is meant to banish the nightmare of the state of exception',[6] through its ultimate regulation. The outcome of such an operation cannot but be paradoxical: on the one hand, the law internalises instruments that allow for its self-destruction; on the other hand, it is through the legalisation of exceptionality that the law can sustain its sovereign illimited application. Ultimately, exceptionality allows the law to reach outside its limits and constantly expands its remits. The internalisation of the exception, thus, serves the ultimate goal of legalism, granting the law's claim for universal illimited applicability.

6

What type of liberal democracies and liberal law can normalise the exception, with all the consequences that this entails, while still maintaining their liberal character? Chapter 6 explores this question by placing the idea of a normalisation of the exception in relation to the concept of state form. As Carl Schmitt clearly understood, the state of exception is not simply a label to be loosely attached to emergency powers but is 'a general concept in the theory of the state'.[7] The theoretical understanding of the normalisation of exceptionality, therefore, cannot elude a reflection of such an issue. If anything, abstracting legal concepts from historical political practices to which they belong always risks becoming an essentialist enterprise destined to irrelevance to existing social reality. The normalisation of exceptionality, in this regard, should not be seen as a temporary deviation from the trajectory of a 'normal' liberal state form but is the manifestation of a historical process of transformation of bourgeois democracy, which in its current form has assumed the hybrid form of a liberal authoritarian state.

5 Günter Frankenberg, *Political Technology and the Erosion of the Rule of Law* (Cheltenham, UK: Edward Elgar Publishing 2014) 97.

6 Frankenberg, *Political Technology and the Erosion of the Rule of Law.*

7 Carl Schmitt, *Political Theology, Four Chapter on the Concept of Sovereignty* (Chicago: The University of Chicago Press 2005) 6.

The modern bourgeois state form has appeared as a composition of related antithetical elements. The legal framework and the law rule serve as foundational elements of the liberal state, ensuring fundamental socio-economic freedoms. However, the apparent neutrality and universality of the bourgeois state are repeatedly undermined by its inherent need to intervene coercively. The modern liberal state, constituted as it is of a sovereign legal power and executive/governmental authorities, is formed as a supposedly balanced double structure, according to which 'the law regulates the administration and the administrative apparatus applies and implements the law', through coercive means.[8] For the liberal governmental paradigm, the supposed consistency of general laws must be sustained by governmental actions necessary to foster economic stability, the functioning of the markets, maintain production and limit all those factors interfering with economic freedoms. The protection of the rules structuring economic relations goes, in this light, hand in hand with the direct exercise of the means of force and power of the state for the specific purposes of ensuring the reproduction and self-expansion of capital and the domination of the bourgeoisie.

There is a growing consensus, spanning the whole political spectrum, that the liberal state, in the last few decades, has undergone a structural mutation, manifested in a growing centrality of the executive and the administrative apparatus, which has caused an imbalance in the structure of powers. As Nikos Poulantzas has somehow presciently observed, since the 1970s, a new state form emerged, characterised by 'intensified state control over every sphere of socio-economic life combined with the radical decline of the institutions of political democracy and with draconian and multiform curtailment of so-called "formal" liberties'.[9] Such a state form – which he called authoritarian statism – is characterised by a sustained transfer of powers and authority from the legislative to the executive, the weakening of the rule of law and a decreasing importance of political parties as the main social and political actors for the construction of hegemony. As parliaments lost relevance in shaping political and economic strategies, the decisional authority shifted to the networks of powers of governmental apparatuses, bypassing the formal/traditional majoritarian institutions. This determined the irresistible rise of the state administration, which by definition does not have a representative function and therefore is to a certain extent sealed off from democratic intervention, with the consequent politicisation of the supposedly neutral and formal bureaucratic apparatus and the depoliticisation of majoritarian institution.

8 Giorgio Agamben, *The Kingdom and the Glory* (Stanford: Stanford University Press 2011) 143.

9 Nikos Poulantzas, *State, Power, Socialism* (Verso 2000) 203.

The form of the state of late capitalism joins, therefore, two opposed souls: there is an authoritarian aspect more manifest in the prominent role of the executive, the decline of democratic institutions and the tendency to strengthen security (with the normalisation of the exception included); and this is accompained by the maintenance of economic liberalism, the protections of markets and economic freedom from political interferences. Authoritarian practices are here functional to the depoliticisation of the economic sphere. In this authoritarian-liberal state, we see the resurfacing of the foundational tension at the heart of the modern state between the rule of law and exception, government of rules and government of men. By promoting legalism and a vision of the human for which essential liberties are defining character, liberalism tried to distance itself from authoritarian practices. And yet, the liberal mind had come to terms with the fact that to realise its own vision of society and social life, a constant recourse to the main planks of authoritarian ruling was needed.[10] The liberal use of authoritarian strategies is, in this sense, functional to the creation and protection of an order of economic security consistent with the liberal view of what liberty means. The normalisation of exceptionality, its entrenchment into 'normal' law and its constant expansion are consistent with the dominant liberal state form, for which the rule of law and the liberal vision of society go hand in hand with the strengthening of state power.

The present volume is variegated but united by a common purpose of reconceptualisation of the current exception/emergency paradigms. As such, it is probably opening a door—or doors—rather than making a finishing act. But given how the field of exceptions makes reality precede the law, there will be a lot to learn from how exceptionality will develop in the coming decades.

10 Mark Neocleous, *Critique of Security* (Edinburgh: Edinburgh University Press 2008) 31.

Chapter 1

What Is (State of) Exception the Name of?

Gian-Giacomo Fusco

1.1 Introduction

Like objects of everyday use, words deteriorate, lacerate and undergo fractures as they glide through the flow of their usage. They lose precision, refusing to remain fixed to their supposedly assigned signified, especially if their coinage is not particularly strong. The term 'state of exception' falls into this category: an inherent semantic instability marks its conception. Nevertheless, this has not prevented it from becoming one of the more popular terms in the juridico-political vocabulary of the last century. Theorists have consistently exploited this denotative weakness. From the implementation of emergency measures in the never-ending war on terror to the (legal) creation of legal black holes, such as Guantanamo, and pandemic lockdowns, the concept of the 'state of exception' has been crucial for critically examining the effects of legal crisis-response mechanisms on the social and individual lives of people during prolonged emergencies. This single term, state of exception, articulated the intellectual anxiety provoked by the normalisation of illiberal—and at times openly repressive—measures that were initially intended to be temporary in a time pervaded by a long, uninterrupted series of crises. The state of exception served as evidence (and embodiment) of the fundamental disconnection between form and force perpetuated by legal systems by exposing the misalignment of legal norms and the unspoken force of the law and by challenging the optimistic narratives that naturally connect the safety of democracies with the rule of (whatever) law.

Differently from its cognate categories such as state of emergency, necessity, state of siege and urgency, state of exception appears as a generic term encompassing all the diverse legal and factual phenomena related to situations of severe crises,[1] which cannot be solved recurring to ordinary legal instruments. Its semantic character is more that of a floating signifier,

1 Marie Goupy, *L'état d'exception ou l'impuissance autoritaire de l'État à l'époque du libéralisme* (Paris: CNRS Éditions, 2016).

DOI: 10.4324/9781003490449-2

potentially applicable to several different referents: loose enough to mean many things yet still specific to a not-so-large set of phenomena. For some, the exception represents the 'no-man's-land between public law and political fact, and between the juridical order and life';[2] while for others, it is a specific legal object that 'lies squarely within the field of public law'.[3] The state of exception has also been defined as a mindset that 'hides in a dogmatics of the borderline situation', which regularly tends to justify 'extraordinary violence and killings implemented by the state' in the worst-case scenario.[4] More recently, in the context of the recent global pandemic, the state of exception has been conceptualised as a notion that should be at best applied to characterise cases in which emergency powers are purposefully implemented to bring about radical changes to the legal and political settlements of polities.[5]

While certainly contributing to the success of the notion, such ambiguity is a conceptual limit with disorienting effects. At the root of this semantic inconsistency most likely lays the treatment that Carl Schmitt (the godfather of the notion) dedicated to the concept. Throughout his works (especially those of the 1920s), Schmitt has seldom characterised the state of exception [*Ausnahmezustand*] in an oscillatory manner, as both a question of fact and a question of law. In the book *Dictatorship* (1921)—his first serious intervention on the issue—the term state of exception appears as a juridical category referring to the specific normative reaction that modern states undertake to bring situations of crises back to normality. Here, while discussing the establishment and the historical evolution of the *état de siège* in 19th-century France, Schmitt maintains that 'the state of siege was an administrative and technical device akin to the state of exception', according to which authorities 'could do what turned out to be necessary in a specific situation'.[6] Moreover, in the appendix discussing art. 48 of the Weimar Constitution (which is absent from the first edition of the volume), he openly speaks about 'the implementation of the state of exception' and its regulation. In *Dictatorship*, thus, the state of exception is portrayed

2 Giorgio Agamben, *State of Exception* (Chicago and London: The University of Chicago Press, 2005) 1.

3 Martin Loughlin, *Foundations of Public Law* (Oxford: Oxford University Press, 2010), 402.

4 Günter Frankenberg, *Political Technology and the Erosion of the Rule of Law* (Cheltenham, UK: Edward Elgar Publishing, 2014) 132–133.

5 See Gustavo Zagrebelsky, 'Emergenza ed Eccezione', in AA.VV. *Il Mondo dopo la Fine del Mondo* (Roma-Bari: Laterza, 2020), 500–515; Mariano Croce and Andrea Salvatore, *Cos'è lo stato di eccezione* (Milano: Nottetempo, 2022). See also: Rafał Mańko, Przemysław Tacik and Gian-Giacomo Fusco, 'The Return of the Exception', *Acta Universitatis Lodziensis. Folia Iuridica*, vol. 96, 2021.

6 Carl Schmitt, *Dictatorship. From the Origin of the Modern Concept of Sovereignty to Proletarian Class Struggle*, transl. Michael Hoelzl and Graham Ward (Cambridge and Molden, MA: Polity Press, 2014) 167.

mainly as a legal-technical device according to which an agent, in case of emergency, is appointed with the authority to do whatever it takes to bring back the social and political situation to normality.

Not long after the publication of *Dictatorship*, Schmitt returned to the question of the state of exception in his *Political Theology*, enriching the notion of several semantic layers. Here, he writes that the state of exception 'can at best be characterized as a case of extreme peril, a danger to the existence of the state'.[7] The exception, he goes on,

> is that which cannot be subsumed; it defies general codification, but it simultaneously reveals a specifically juristic element the decision in absolute purity. The exception appears in its absolute form when a situation in which legal prescriptions can be valid must first be brought about. Every general norm demands a normal, everyday frame of life to which it can be factually applied and which is subjected to its regulations. The norm requires a homogeneous medium. This effective normal situation is not a mere 'superficial presupposition' that a jurist can ignore; that situation belongs precisely to its immanent validity. There exists no norm that is applicable to chaos. For a legal order to make sense, a normal situation must exist, and he is sovereign who definitely decides whether this normal situation actually exists.[8]

Thus, in *Political Theology*, the state of exception is defined as a factual condition of abnormality that a legal order, designed to govern normal times, cannot regulate. The exception is an anomaly that disrupts the normal flow of life in a political community, interrupting the continuity of the legal system's effective normativity.

Being part of the realm of contingency, exceptions are not all of the same kind; different intensities have different impacts. A single event that disrupts public order or even a series of such events—breaks in the fabric of the law—are qualitatively and quantitatively distinct from war. According to Schmitt, only when the essential effectiveness of a norm is compromised in its regulative function by a specific event do we encounter a true state of exception. In its factual dimensions, an event materialises as a (state) of exception when it can render the rules of a legal system ineffectual. This occurs when the established legal standards, previously effective in governing social interactions, can no longer maintain proper order.

But things, for Schmitt, are even more complicated. What makes a fact into an anomaly capable of giving rise to a state of exception is not dependent on

7 Carl Schmitt, *Political Theology. Four Chapter on the Concept of Sovereignty*, transl. by George Schwab (Chicago: The University of Chicago Press, 2005) 6.

8 Schmitt, *Political Theology*, 13.

the fact itself—on the objective evidence of the lost effectivity of norms—but is the outcome of a decision over the same fact. And according to his notorious definition of sovereignty, the one that has the authority (and power) to decide whether we are in front of the exceptional case is the sovereign. A state of exception, Schmitt suggests, exists as long as a sovereign agent decides it exists. The sovereign decision depends on some facts, but they do not bind it: the decision on the exception, he claims, is in 'the true sense absolute'[9]—neither deduced by the norm nor simply coerced by the concrete situation, but on the contrary, producing both the exception (as a fact) and the normal conditions necessary for the law to be effective. Giorgio Agamben captured this ambiguity when he wrote that the exception's primary effect is to create a situation that can be defined neither in factual terms nor in legal ones: the exception 'institutes a paradoxical threshold of indistinction between the two. It is not a fact, since it is only created through the suspension of the rule . . . it is not even a juridical case in point, even if it opens the possibility of the force of law'.[10]

It is worth noting that Schmitt developed his theory of the state of exception as a polemical stance against what he calls normativism (i.e., Kelsen's positivism) and to expose the limits—and perhaps the hypocrisy—of liberal legalism, which attempts to reduce the entire political life of the state to predictable sets of norms. Schmitt argues that certain practices, such as the state of exception and concrete decision-making processes, as well as certain entities (like sovereign power), belong to the juridical sphere but cannot be fully reduced to pure norms. This claim is central to demonstrating the inherent openness and non-uniformity of legal systems. Yet, while effectively exposing this jurisprudential position, Schmitt's conceptualisation of the exception failed to unambiguously explain the nature of the exception itself. Perhaps the theorisation of the *Ausnahmezustand* in *Political Theology* should be seen more as an attempt to develop a polemic against the positivism that dominated European jurisprudence—highlighting its inability to grasp the uncertain nature of law—rather than as a direct answer to the question: 'What is the state of exception?' Yet, one might question the usefulness of even asking such a question. As Yan Thomas poignantly argued, 'any investigation undertaken from an ontological point of view, that is through the question "What is a thing?" would halt the access to legal matters'.[11] The law is fundamentally based on operations, procedures and effectuality. Legal norms and categories do not possess the ontological

9 Schmitt, *Political Theology*, 12.

10 Giorgio Agamben, *Homo Sacer. Sovereign Power and Bare Life* (Stanford: Stanford University Press, 1998) 18–19.

11 Yan Thomas, 'La Valeur Des Choses: Le Droit Romain Hors La Religion', *Annales. Histoire, Sciences Sociales*, vol. 57, no. 6, 2002, p. 1435.

status of (physical) 'things'; rather, they exist as legal norms and categories through the effects they produce in the reality they seek to regulate. The only pertinent question from this perspective would be: what are the effects of the state of exception?

However, this does not preclude the possibility of addressing the nature of the state of exception as a legal object, beginning with the simple observation that, since an exception is always an exception to a norm, the state of exception arises as an epiphenomenon of a legal order. The state of exception brings to the fore the fact that there are situations where the law's norms, although valid, are not and should not be effective. The existence of a valid norm is a prerequisite for any exception, which, in its concrete application, suspends the norm's effect without undermining its formal validity. Furthermore, as we have seen, a defining characteristic of the state of exception is that it transcends the boundary between facts and norms; it emerges as the result of a decision regarding what the state of affairs should be. After all, what else could the meaning of an exception be if not a specific, conscious deviation from a valid, existing norm?

As a specific object within the sphere of law, the state of exception arises from the rift that both separates and connects the formal existence of norms with their concrete application. This rift exists in a critical zone essential to the law positioned between the boundaries of the law's letter and the institutions responsible for enforcing it. The state of exception, as a discrete and limited alteration of the law, does not create a new law but instead preserves the existing legal framework and ensures its continuity. While the generality of rules should not be mistaken for absolute universality, the strict application of legal rules to specific facts, especially in unforeseen circumstances, may lead to unjust or harmful outcomes that contradict the broader purposes of the rules. Therefore, the state of exception represents a specific deviation—whether through suspension or alteration—of a norm, enacted when the normal application of the law is deemed detrimental to the legal system or the community's well-being. It shares the nature of other legal mechanisms that adapt the law to unforeseen circumstances without fundamentally altering it. More specifically, this chapter will argue that the state of exception shares foundational discourses with the legal concept of equity. Examining this shared territory makes it possible to explore the nature of exceptionality in law as a distinct sphere of normativity.

1.2 A Kind of Exclusion

Giorgio Agamben is perhaps the thinker who has most intensely explored the concept of the state of exception. Through a deep engagement with legal theory, history, metaphysics, theology and politics, he has developed an original philosophy centred on this idea. For Agamben, the 'logical structure' of the exception constitutes the kernel (the *archè*) of the various cultural and social phenomena that underpin how the West has historically conceived of itself.[12] In *Homo Sacer. Sovereign Power and Bare Life*, he defines the exception in this way:

> The exception is a kind of exclusion. What is excluded from the general rule is an individual case. But the most proper characteristic of the exception is that what is excluded in it is not, on account of being excluded, absolutely without relation to the rule. On the contrary, what is excluded in the exception maintains itself in relation to the rule in the form of the rule's suspension. The rule applies to the exception in no longer applying, in withdrawing from it. The state of exception is thus not the chaos that precedes order but rather the situation that results from its suspension. In this sense, the exception is truly, according to its etymological root, taken outside (*ex-capere*), and not simply excluded.[13]

As for the law, Agamben suggests that the logic of the exception operates by including, within the formal sphere of the norm, what is, by definition, excluded by the law's normativity: the possibility of its transgression. The illegal (or abnormal) case, the one that must be sanctioned, is logically the product of the normative aim of rules and the legal system as a whole. What counts as abnormal, therefore, is determined only after the normal has been defined. However, within the logical structure of the norm, the set of cases to be sanctioned is already included as part of the factual premise whose occurrence triggers the application of the sanction. The normative function of the law manifests itself in the fact that legal norms have a regulative character, that is to say that they are capable of creating the sphere of their own 'reference in real life and make that reference regular'; legal norms, Agamben writes, 'stabilizes and presupposes the conditions of this reference' and for this reason the originary structure of the rule is always of this kind: 'If (a real case in point, e.g.: *si membrum rupsit*), then (juridical consequence, e.g.: *talio esto*)', in which a fact is included in the juridical order through its exclusion, and transgression seems to precede and determine the lawful case.[14]

Here, in a Kelsenian fashion, Agamben points out that the real case to be sanctioned is ultimately presupposed as the first reference for the juridical consequence, yet it is simultaneously excluded as a result of its inscription into the law. Within the legal norm, the abnormal fact—what is excluded—stands in 'relation of exception' to the legal sphere. The process of normalisation, which is generally embedded in the very function of the

12 Giorgio Agamben, *The Use of Bodies* (Stanford: Stanford University Press, 2014) 264–265.
13 Agamben, *Homo Sacer*, 17.
14 Agamben, *Homo Sacer*, 25–26.

law, presupposes that what it must externalise and exclude as abnormal (or illegal) as a necessary condition for the norm. This means that the formal structure of the law is built upon a fundamental exception, wherein something is both included (an abnormal fragment of life) and excluded (as a transgression of the normal). It is through this simultaneous exclusion and inclusion of the abnormal that the normal can be defined as opposed and different. To the extent that an exception is the product of the suspension of a norm, exceptions in law could be seen, in this context, as the liberation of what is caught within the norm: the abnormal, once excluded, no longer serves as the negative condition of the norm but becomes the positive affirmation of the negative.

A paradigmatic example of the law's capture of the outside is, for Agamben, the *lex talionis*. In its historical manifestation, such legal formulation has been considered as capturing the simple and banal idea that when a wrong is committed, there must be some sort of punishment: it is the offence that dictates the necessity of an appropriate punishment. Present in the major ancient legal tradition (The Code of Hammurabi, Mosaic law and Roman law had their specific formulation of such law), the talion does nothing more than set the principle of 'exacting retribution': the value of a limb for the loss of a limb, the value of an eye for the loss of an eye.[15] The *lex talionis*, thus, should be read figuratively as expressing an axiom of general limitation of violence through a criteria of proportionality: the punishment should fit the crime. In the Twelve Tables, for instance, the *lex talionis* seems to provide an alternative when in a dispute, other forms of pacifications failed: *si membrum rupsit, ni cum eo pacit, talio esto*—If he destroys a limb, unless they reach an agreement, let there be retribution/retaliation[16]—in the same form (*talio*: from *talis*, the same) of the act to be sanctioned. Therefore, as Agamben points out, in the *lex talionis*, 'the juridical order does not originally present itself simply as sanctioning a transgressive fact but instead constitutes itself through the repetition of the same act without any sanction, that is, as an exceptional case'.[17] And this, he goes on, represents something like an original inclusion in the law of the same violence it sanctions.

For jurisprudence, the *lex talionis* has long been a disturbing presence: something archaic that does not belong to our modern scale of values, which at the same time seems to expose formal elements of the present state of the law, that is, 'what counts as an appropriate punishment'.[18] This is well

15 Gunther Plaut, *The Torah: A Modern Commentary* (New York: Union of American Hebrew Congregations, 1981) 571.

16 William Ian Miller, *Eye for an Eye* (Cambridge: Cambridge University Press, 2006) 47.

17 Miller, *Eye for an Eye*, 26.

18 Jeremy Waldron, 'Lex Talionis', *Arizona Law Review*, vol. 34, 1992, pp. 25–51.

summarised by H. L. A. Hart in his discussion of the principle of retribution. As he points out, the notion that 'what the criminal has done should be done to him . . . the killer should be killed, the violent assailant should be flogged'[19] represents a crude form of proportionality or fittingness. However, he goes on, 'this idea is incapable of generalisation without absurdity . . . . Theft cannot be punished by theft, defamation by defamation, forgery by forgery, adultery by adultery'.[20] To make the idea of appropriateness or proportionality that the principle of retribution involves a viable one, Hart tried to rephrase such principle by including another criterion that of 'wickedness', to establish a generalisable relationship between crime and punishment with equal uncertain results:

> the suffering imposed by the punishment should be in some sense equal to or proportionate to the wickedness of the crime. But in what sense? How measure either wickedness or suffering in the absence of units of either?. . . there is no natural relationship to be discerned between wickedness and punishment of a certain degree or kind, so that we can say the latter naturally 'fits' the former.[21]

At stake in the principle of the *lex talionis*, thus, is, on the one hand, the question of the appropriateness of the punishment and, on the other hand, the ontological difference between crime and the necessary (legal) consequence. The idea of retribution exposes in this way the unnatural and artificial relationship that connects and separates crime and punishment, facts and norms. 'The talion', as William Ian Miller rightly claims, 'is about measuring':[22] 'how to measure value and then how to find an appropriate means of payment once value had been determined'.[23] But this necessarily involves mastering a technique, an art: establishing the exact measure between opposites, evaluating consequences and making exceptions—practices necessary to the structuring of the artificial relation between facts, norms and sanctions.

In *Homo Sacer. Sovereign Power and Bare Life*, Agamben considers the *exceptio* in Roman Law as a further paradigmatic example of the logic of exception at work. In the classical period (3rd century BC–2nd century AD), the *exception* emerged out of the adjudication procedure as an instrument in the hands of the defendant to neutralise the conclusiveness of the grounds proffered by the plaintiff and thus to render the normal application of the

19 H. L. A. Hart, *Punishment and Responsibility* (Oxford: Oxford University Press, 1968) 161.
20 Hart, *Punishment and Responsibility*.
21 Hart, *Punishment and Responsibility*, 161–162.
22 Miller, *Eye for an Eye*, xii.
23 Miller, *Eye for an Eye*, 25.

ius civile impossible. At that time, the Roman civil trial was essentially built upon a 'formulary system', organised in two separate phases: the first before the praetor (the magistrate who had the authority to administer justice) and the second before a 'private judge', essentially a layman who was to verify the facts of the case. A legal dispute began with the plaintiff acquiring a *formula*, summarising the core elements of the disagreement between the parties from the praetor.[24] This first phase required the presence of the defendant. Once the *formula* had been composed, the praetor sent it for trial before a judge. In building the formula, the defendant had the right to include an *exceptio* (as a form of defence), which was a clause including an assertion that, without denying the plaintiff's claim, opposes it, adducing a fact not alleged by the plaintiff. For example, in a proceeding to recover property, the defendants might claim that they owe the property claimed by the plaintiff, but that, for instance, 'according to a special agreement (*pactum de non petendo*) the plaintiff assumed the obligation not to sue for the money'.[25] The *exceptio* works as a negative condition, to wit, the judge may condemn the defendant if there has not been an agreement that the plaintiff will not bring an action.[26]

In the case of the basic form of contract, the *stipulatio*, the highly formalised ritual granting its validity, required the parties to conclude the binding promise through a question (*interrogatio*: i.e., do you promise to pay) followed by an affirming answer using exactly the same verb (*spondeo*: I promise to pay). The answer should strictly respond to the question since any variation or inclusion of conditions made the contract void. The formal perfection of the ritual was the only element granting the efficacy of the contract, and this made the promise actionable on the simple ground of the performance of the oral exchange of question and answer, irrespective of the fact that other circumstances might have made the obligation impossible to comply with or the contract formed fraudulently. For the one asking the question it was enough to demonstrate that the *stipulatio* had taken place, and this gave a decisive advantage in case of dispute. However, over time, the praetorian law developed the instrument of the *exceptio doli*, which granted the debtor the possibility of opposing the *stipulatio*, showing that the obligation was not based on a just cause. The praetor could use his own authority to include an additional clause (*exceptio*) in the relevant formula that enabled the defendant to render the plaintiff's claim ineffective by showing grounds for denying

24 Examples from Gaius.

25 Adolf Berger, *Encyclopedic Dictionary of Roman Law* (The Lawbook Exchange, 2002) 458. See also Reinhard Zimmermann, *The Law of Obligations. Roman Foundations of the Civilian Tradition* (Cape Town, Wetton, Hohannesburg: Juta & Co, Ltd, 1992) 657–682; Ulrike Babusiaux et al. (eds), *Handbuch des Römischen Privatrechts* (Tübingen: Mohr Siebeck, 2023) 2874–3052.

26 Berger, *Encyclopedic Dictionary of Roman Law*, 458.

judgment in the plaintiff's favour. When the *exceptio* was based on the allegation that the plaintiff had acted fraudulently (*dolo*), it was designated *exceptio doli*.[27]

The Roman *exceptio*, for Agamben, is a paradigmatic example of how the law can internalise the 'exclusive' moment of its own self-procured suspension. Indeed, the *exceptio* is not outside of the law but, he maintains, is rather the outcome of a 'contrast between two juridical demands, a contrast that in Roman law refers back to the opposition between *ius civile* and *ius honorarium*'.[28] While the first included 'statutes (leges), plebiscites, decrees of the senate (*senatus consulta*), enactments of the emperor and the authority of the jurists' (D. 1.1.7) and was formal and strict, the second was the law introduced by the magistrates (especially the praetors) during the Republican time and the early Empire, to temper, supplement or amend rules and procedures of the civil law, 'in the interest of the public utility (*propter utilitatem publicam*, D. 1.1.7.1.)' by taking into consideration the exigency of an everchanging social and economic life. The *exceptio*, thus, was part of those procedural remedies established by the operation of the praetors that eventually developed into a system that ran in parallel and supplemented the *ius civile*. The praetor by 'imaginative approaches to the situations in which he would grant an established remedy or when he might refuse it' has been capable of bringing

> about remarkable changes in the shape of the civil law. The praetor came to admit claims that he regarded as equitable although they were not recognized under *ius civile*, and to reject claims that he viewed as unjust although they were legitimate at civil law. In doing this he presided over the formation of a new body of law in which some quite radical departures from tradition were made.[29]

The granting of exceptions, in this regard, 'was an ingenious device that enabled the praetor to deliver appropriate relief in individual cases without questioning the validity of the relevant legal rule'.[30] Such a form of exception, thus, emerges out of the necessity to avoid results that contrast with the very purpose of the law, which is the production of some good, in the rift that connects and separates the source of the law, its word and letters, and the concrete application to individual cases. Thus, the requirements of form and

27 Zimmermann, *The Law of Obligations*, 93–94.
28 Agamben, *Homo Sacer*, 23.
29 David Johnston, 'Succession', in D. Johnston (ed), *Cambridge Companion to Roman Law* (Cambridge University Press, 2015) 200.
30 George Mousourakis, *Roman Law and the Origins of the Civil Law Tradition* (Springer, 2015) 51.

the rigour and restrictiveness of the *ius civile* did not prevent the equitable results demanded by the progress of civil life.[31]

While the *exceptio* in Roman law, as Agamben claims, is the outcome of a clash between two juridical exigencies (to preserve the continuity and the formality of the *ius civile* and to prevent unfair outcomes in individual cases), the sovereign exception instead 'represent[s] a further dimension', in which a relationship between two juridical exigencies is displaced into the 'limit relation between what is inside and what is outside the law'.[32] Here, what distinguished the *exceptio* in adjudication and the sovereign (state) of exception is not a matter of quality—in both cases, we are faced with an exception to a rule or rules—but is here a question of (both qualitative and quantitative) intensity: on the one hand, the *exceptio*, involves the suspension of a norm; on the other, the sovereign exception regards the limit of the law itself. Indeed, the sovereign exception, in the philosophical vocabulary of Agamben's philosophy, is a 'zone of indistinction between nature and right', that marks the always mobile threshold between the inside and the outside of the law, that is presupposed by juridical normativity. It is such a delimitation that, in the end, determines the space in which the law can have validity. However, the outside of the law is never totally exterior to the law; rather, it is the byproduct of the sovereign decision, and the exception, therefore, represents an interior threshold that establishes an exteriority immanent to the juridical order.

1.3 The Exception of Equity

In his *Political Theology: Four New Chapters on the Concept of Sovereignty*, Paul W. Kahn writes:

> Equity and revolution are outside of law but not illegal. They mark the point at which judgments of legality lose their hold on the imagination. Even though both equity and revolution make reference to law—both hold forth law as the norm—neither is an application of law. The norm . . . requires ordinary circumstances for its operation; the exception occupies those circumstances that are less—or more—than ordinary. The quality of the exception is always one of self-limitation: the exception cannot become normal. Nevertheless, the nature of norms is such that the exception is always subject to normalization: law will seek to extend to the exceptional decision.[33]

31 Salvatore Riccobono and Edward Nathan. 'Outlines of the Evolution of Roman Law', *University of Pennsylvania Law Review and American Law Register*, vol. 74, no. 1, 1925, pp. 3–4.

32 Agamben, *Homo Sacer*, 23.

33 Paul W. Kahn, *Political Theology: Four New Chapters on the Concept of Sovereignty* (New York: Columbia University Press, 2011) 34.

Equity and revolution, Kahn argues, are specific instances of the exception, but with different intensities. 'Equity', he claims, 'reveals on the smallest scale' the 'possibility of political decisions evoking meanings set against the ordinary legal norm', while revolution 'a paradigmatic instance of the Schmittian exception—does so on the largest scale'.[34] The parallel between equity (here intended as equity in English law) and revolution is not simply limited to their formal aspect of being an exception to the law. For Kahn, they seem to share the same nature and origin: sovereignty in its more sacral dimension. Equity and revolution are indeed 'linked to each other as the miracle of creation is linked to the miraculous answer to a singular prayer'.[35] However, this implies that sovereignty is more than the entity embodying it. As a principle, it permeates the legal system as a source of legitimacy for the spectrum of decisions based on the law and beyond. As long as the partition of powers of the state finds in sovereignty its source, it is, in the end, the sovereign that grants the existence of both the rule of the law and the exception.

The nature and origin of the body of principles and rules that, in English law, fall under the label of 'equity' present a highly vexing question—one that is of utmost interest from our perspective, as it reveals the logic of exceptionality as few other legal issues do. When F. W. Maitland famously defined equity as 'that body of laws administered by our English courts of justice which, were it not for the operation of the Judicature Acts, would be administered by courts known as Courts of Equity',[36] he openly (and somewhat polemically) admitted that the only proper and unifying ground for the multitude of doctrines and remedies commonly categorised as equitable is the fact that they were produced and administered by the Chancery—a court that, for centuries, constituted a fundamental part of the dual legal system of English law, until it was eventually dissolved by statute in the 19th century. While essentially undisputable, Maitland's statement, reducing equity to a historical accident, does not effectively address decisive questions related to the justification for the very existence and persistence of equitable principles or the exceptional nature of the foundation of the Court of Chancery itself.

In the history of English law, equity—in its mundane embodiment, the Chancellor—emerged as a form of intervention when Common Law rules (and rulings) were deemed insufficient or unjust. After the Norman invasion and the introduction of a new legal system, the common law and its courts, the King retained the authority to make decisions in individual cases where the strict application of the law led to unfair outcomes.

34 Kahn, *Political Theology*, 33–34.
35 Kahn, *Political Theology*, 34.
36 Frederick Maitland, *Equity: A Course of Lectures* (CUP, 1936) 1.

This helped the Monarchy maintain a decisive grip on the power of the courts, ensuring that ultimate control over the administration of justice remained with the Crown. However, a side effect of this retained power was that the King became overwhelmed with a growing number of petitions, necessitating the establishment of a distinct system to manage them. The Lord Chancellor (who, in medieval Europe, was the chief bureaucrat responsible for government administration, and in England up until the reformation, he was also regularly a member of the clergy) was thus empowered to hear petitions on behalf of the monarch. By the 13th and 14th centuries, submitting petitions to the Chancellor had become standard practice, making the Chancery to evolve into a permanent court system parallel to the common law courts, and sanctioning the beginning of the body of rules known as equity.[37]

In its early development, equity represented an alternative tool for resolving legal disputes in cases where common law rulings were deemed inadequate.[38] As a logical consequence, equity had to provide remedies different from those typically offered by the common law. For instance, equity might recognise an interest in property where none exists under common law or render a contract non-binding by considering circumstances and facts that fall outside the scope of common law. Ultimately, equity did not aim to reform or change legal norms; rather, it emerged as a corrective mechanism, addressing unjust outcomes produced by the rigid application of law. Equity, Larissa Katz suggests, is 'the practice of allowing for exceptions where a particular application of a general rule produces results at odds with the purposes or normative ideals to which that rule is committed'.[39] When legal norms produce unjust results in individual cases, the logical response might be to reform the law; however, equity creates exceptions while affirming the validity of the underlying norm.[40]

37 On the history of equity and the chancery, see John Baker, *An Introduction to English Legal History* (Oxford University Press, 2002); Gary Watt, *Equity Stirring: The Story of Justice Beyond Law* (Hart Publishing, 2009); Dennis Klinck, *Conscience, Equity and the Court of Chancery in Early Modern Law* (Ashgate, 2010).

38 The parallel between the operation of equity and that of the ius honorarium is obvious and the object of a few investigations; i.e., W. W. Buckland and Arnold McNair, *Roman Law and Common Law. A Comparison in Outline* (Cambridge: Cambridge University Press, 1936) 3–4.

39 Larizza Katz, 'Pathways to Legal Rights. The Function of Equity', in Dennis Klimchuk, Irit Samet and Henry E. Smith (eds), *Philosophical Foundations of the Law of Equity* (Oxford University Press, 2020) 168.

40 Kahn, *Political Theology*, 35. See on this point: Geoffrey Samuel, 'Equity and Legal Reasoning', *Pólemos*, vol. 11, no. 1, 2017, 41–53.

Perhaps there is no more explicit and authoritative explanation of why the exception of equity is needed than that offered by Lord Ellesmere in the foundational *The Earl of Oxford's Case*.[41] Here we read:

> [T]he cause why there is a Chancery is, for that men's actions are so diverse and infinite, that it is impossible to make any general law which may aptly meet with every particular act, and not fail in some circumstance. The office of the Chancellor is to correct Mens consciences for frauds, breach of trust, wrongs and oppressions, of what nature soever they be, and to soften and mollify the extremity of the Law, which is called Summum Jus. . . . Law and Equity are distinct, both in their courts, their judges, and the rules of justice; and yet they both aim at one and the same end, which is to do right; as Justice and Mercy differ in their effects and operations, yet both join in the manifestation of God's glory.[42]

The very possibility of an equitable exception to the normal ruling of the courts of common law, which is what legitimises the existence of the Chancery as a separate institution, has come to be traditionally justified by reference to what could be defined as 'the argument of contingency': the generality of the law is never so general as to encompass every possible circumstance. It is, in a sense, the very essence of the law that involves the necessary possibility of making exceptions to it—and this logically implies the recognition of a defect, a breach, in the fabric of the law itself, faced with the contingency of human life. Although such argumentative lines were first advanced by Plato in *Statesman*,[43] throughout time, the discourse about the necessity of delivering corrections to the 'imperfect' results of a strict application of general rules has become associated with Aristotle—and Lord Ellesmere in *The Earl of Oxford Case* is no exception.[44] In the *Nicomachean Ethics*, while examining the most appropriate way of applying the law, Aristotle observed how, because of its generality/universality, the law is not capable of providing the best outcomes in all circumstances and, therefore, an instrument of

41 On the history of this judgment, see David Ibbetson, '*The Earl of Oxford's Case* (1615)', in Charles Mitchell and Paul Mitchell (eds), *Landmark Cases in Equity* (London: Hart Publishing, 2012) 1–32.

42 Ibbetson, '*The Earl of Oxford's Case* (1615)', 1 Ch Rep 1, 6–7.

43 '[L]aw can never issue an injunction binding on all which really embodies what is best for each: it cannot prescribe with perfect accuracy what is good and right for each member of the community at any one time. The differences of human personality, the variety of men's activities and the inevitable unsettlement attending all human experience make it impossible for any art whatsoever to issue unqualified rules holding good on all questions at all times', Plato, *Statesman 294a-b*, transl. J. B. Skemp (Bristol, England: Bristol Classical Press, 1952).

44 Nick Piška in this regard has offered an interesting reading of the Aristotelean 'equity' as a *pharmakon*. See Nick Piška, 'Aristotle's Pharmacy', *Pólemos*, vol. 11, no. 1, 2017, pp. 5–21.

rectification is at times needed. *Epieikeia* [equity] is the name he gave to this corrective. As we read in an oft-cited passage:

> [A]ll law is universal but about some things it is not possible to make a universal statement which will be correct. In those cases, then, in which it is necessary to speak universally, but not possible to do so correctly, the law takes the usual case, though it is not ignorant of the possibility of error. And it is none the less correct; for the error is not in the law nor in the legislator but in the nature of the thing, since the matter of practical affairs is of this kind from the start. When the law speaks universally, then, and a case arises on it which is not covered by the universal statement, then it is right, when the legislator fails us and has erred by over-simplicity, to correct the omission—to say what the legislator himself would have said had he been present, and would put into law had he known . . . . And this is the nature of the equitable, a correction of law where it is defective owing to its universality.[45]

Such assertions are not isolated in the corpus of Aristotle's work. Indeed, he affirms pretty much the same idea in *Rhetoric*, where he writes that what is

> equitable seems to be just, and equity is justice that goes beyond the written law. These omissions are sometimes involuntary, sometimes voluntary, on the part of the legislators; involuntary when it may have escaped their notice; voluntary when, being unable to define for all cases, they are obliged to make a universal statement, which is not applicable to all, but only to most, cases; and whenever it is difficult to give a definition owing to the infinite number of cases . . . for life would not be long enough to reckon all the possibilities.[46]

According to Aristotle, there are generally two cases in which the generality/universality of law might be defective. The first is an 'error in the nature of the thing', which is when the nature of the case to be decided according to law is so peculiar that the application of a norm is either difficult or produces an unfair outcome. The second is when the law appears defective since it is not carefully crafted. In both cases, equity can provide an exceptional, justice-oriented corrective that goes beyond the law. Of course, these two eventualities are not mutually exclusive: the fact that an event, although

45 *Nicomachean Ethics*, V.10, 1137b13–27. The translation is from Jonathan Barnes (ed), *The Complete Works of Aristotle: The Revised Oxford Translation*, vol. 2 (Princeton University Press, 1984) 1795–1796.

46 Aristotle, *The "Art" of Rhetoric 1374a*, transl. John Henry Freese (Cambridge, MA: Harvard University Press, 1947).

similar to those ruled by a norm, cannot be decided by the norm without doing injustice might be a signal of the legislator's fault; and conversely, we could reasonably foresee that a norm that appears composed of vague terminology will require exceptions.

How, in early modern times, the Aristotelean *epieikeia* was made the foundational theory and justification for the very existence of equity is as much a historical accident as the emergence of the Chancery itself. The matching of the Aristotelean discussion over the limits of law was already firmly established in Christopher St. Germain's seminal treatise *Doctor and Student*, where we read,

> And for the plainer declaration what equity is, you shall understand, that since the deeds and acts of men, for which laws have been ordained, happen in diverse manners infinitely, it is not possible to make any general rifle of the law, but that it shall fail in some case and therefore makers of law take heed to such things as may often come, and not to every particular case, for they could not though they would. And therefore, to follow the words of the law were in some case both against justice and the commonwealth. Wherefore in some cases it is necessary to love the words of the law, and to follow that reason and justice requires, and to that intent equity is ordained; that is to say, to temper and mitigate the rigor of the law. And it is called also by some men *epieikeia*.[47]

The peculiarity of the operation of establishing an equivalence between 'equity' and the Aristotelean *epieikeia* is due principally to the fact that the roots, history and meaning of the two words are essentially different. Equity comes from the Latin *aequitas*, which has a specific legal meaning and history. Already before the 2nd century BC, *aequum* constituted a technical element of juridical vocabulary: it represented one of the characters of the application of the law (*ius*) and not something separated, opposed or ultimately different. For the Romans, the *ius* to be just needed to be equitable.[48] Furthermore, the meanings of *epieikeia* and *Aequitas* are substantially different: the first comes from the verb ἔποικα, which means 'to resemble', and expresses what is convenient and adequate in a situation that requires regulation; the second instead conveys the 'condition of being *aequus*' that is 'equal', 'uniform' and 'that does not present differences'.[49] While, therefore, the two words are certainly similar in some of their meanings, their

47 Christopher St Germain, *The Doctor and The Student* (Cincinnati: Robert Clarke & Co, 1886) ch. 16.

48 Dario Mantovani, *La Aequitas Romana: una Nozione in Cerca di Equilibrio* (Istituto Lombardo—Accademia Di Scienze E Lettere. Incontri Di Studio, November 2017), 24. Add literature on this.

49 Mantovani, *La Aequitas Romana*, 42.

equivalence is somewhat difficult to establish. And, indeed, the stated identity between equity and *epieikeia* is, in the end, a historical accident probably due to a renowned interest in Aristotle's works that emerged in early modern times under the influence of Medieval scholasticism.[50] Indeed, one of the earlier evidence of the equivalence between equity and *epieikeia* can be found in Aquinas, when in discussing cases in which following the law would produce unfair outcomes, he wrote that 'on these and like cases it is bad to follow the law, and it is good to set aside the letter of the law and to follow the dictates of justice and the common good. This is the object of "*epikeia*" which we call equity'.[51]

In the history of English law, the existence of the exceptions of equity is genetically linked to the exceptional nature of sovereignty. As we have seen previously, in its early stages, equitable reliefs were accessed by appealing to the King; although a system of courts was already in place, Maitland writes, 'there is still a reserve of justice in the king. Those who cannot get relief elsewhere present their petitions to the king' who is 'asked to find a remedy for the love of God and in the way of charity'.[52] Equity emerged virtually with no mediation from the King's authority to act outside and against the law: while common law courts applied the norm, speaking in his name, they were the mediated voice of the King. The immediate presence of the King, however, 'was located in the Chancery and the Star Chamber—the civil and criminal sites of equity'.[53] The logical consequence of its dependence on the sovereign conscience is the assumption that equity operates 'outside' or 'beyond' the Common law as a form of discretionary and somewhat informal justice. And this is well summarised in the renowned speech of 20 June 1616 by King James I, when he stated that the Chancery is

> a Court of Equity, and hath power to deal in Civil causes: It is called the dispenser of the Kings Conscience, following always the intention of Law and Justice; not altering the Law nor making black which other Courts made white, nor vice versa; But in this it exceeds other Courts, mixing Mercy with Justice, where other Courts proceed only according to the strict rules of Law: And where the rigour of the Law in

50 See in this regard: Lorenzo Maniscalco, *Equity in Early Modern Legal Scholarship* (Brill, 2020).

51 Aquinas, Summa Theologica II.II, Q120, art 1. Statements like: 'Following Aristotle, the first sentence of Justinian's Digest began with Celsus's statement that *ius est ars boni et aequi* ('law is the art of the good and the equitable'), borrowing the *aequitas* from Aristotle's *ἐπιείκεια* ('equity')' by James Edelman are very controversial in nature. See James Edelman, 'The Equity of the Statute', in Dennis Klimchuk, Irit Samet and Henry E. Smith (eds), *Philosophical Foundations of the Law of Equity* (Oxford University Press, 2020) 361.

52 Frederick Maitland, *Equity: A Course of Lectures* (CUP, 1936) 3–5.

53 Kahn, *Political Theology*, 36.

> many cases will undo a Subject, there the Chancery tempers the Law with equity, and so mixes Mercy with Justice, as it preserves men from destruction. And thus is the Kings Throne established by Mercy and Justice.[54]

The source of the authority to implement the exception of equity in the Chancery is the King's 'sacral character', without which 'the exception could look like nothing more than a failure of law, that is, as an instance of injustice'.[55] The authority (or we might even say the 'jurisdiction') of the sovereign, here, exceeds that of any courts (and the law itself), and the reference to the theological notion of Mercy and the capacity to do justice is what makes this excess legitimate and not simply an exercise of raw/arbitrary power.[56]

While the development of the multitude of equitable doctrines and remedies is the product of judicial operations, the actual emergence of equity is an operation ascribable to sovereign power, more specifically to that part of the state/sovereign authority that exceeds the jurisdiction and control of law and parliament. As Katz argues, the institution of equity in common law emerged not from 'the judiciary's understanding of its role (eg to do justice first), but from the executive's understanding of its role within the constitutional order'.[57] Equity, she goes on, 'was one of a bundle of prerogative powers that constitute the executive (or the Crown) as the fountain of justice and honour'; and 'prerogative power—or reasons of state, as it is sometimes called—is often described as an arbitrary power to decide the exception, shielded from review by courts or the legislature'.[58] The exception of equity and what has been termed 'state of exception' are genealogically linked to that excess of authority that has characterised sovereign power throughout time: the right to pardon that is still retained by specific authorities and executive power to act outside the limits of law are, in a sense, scores and reminders of such an excess. Considered under this light, the reference to a limit in law's universality, the legal production of injustice through a literal (strict) application of the law and the need for flexibility

54 King James VI and I, *Political Writings* (Cambridge: Cambridge University Press, 1995) 214.

55 Kahn, *Political Theology*, 36.

56 While theological themes play a central role in defining the King's authority to grant exceptions to the law—and, by extension, equity—a deeper analysis of these arguments lies beyond the scope of this work. For further discussion, see Zofia Rueger, 'Gerson's Concept of Equity and Christopher St. German', *History of Political Thought*, vol. 3, no. 1, 1982, pp. 1–30; Richard Hedlund, 'The Theological Foundations of Equity's Conscience', *Oxford Journal of Law and Religion*, vol. 4, no. 1, 2015, pp. 119–140; Cristina Costantini, 'Millenaristic Equity. Theological Order and Legal Faith', *Pólemos*, vol. 10, no. 2, 2016, 329–355; Mark Fortier, *The Culture of Equity in Early Modern England* (Abingdon: Routledge, 2016).

57 Katz, 'Pathways to Legal Rights', 172.

58 Katz, 'Pathways to Legal Rights'.

that the law requires faced with the contingency of human social living appear more as a discourse developed to legitimise the sovereign's authority to act outside the boundaries of the law, rather than a genuine exposition of a flaw in the law.

It should not come as a surprise, then, that the arguments that have been advanced to sustain the legitimacy—and the ultimate legality—of the state of exception and equity's jurisdiction involve similar lines of reasoning. This is clearly evident in Jonh Locke's analysis of the King's prerogative—that power to 'act according to discretion for the public good, without the prescription of the law, and sometimes even against it'. There are 'many things . . . which the law can by no means provide for', he writes,

> for since many accidents may happen, wherein a strict and rigid observation of the laws may do harm . . . because also it is impossible to foresee, and so by laws to provide for all accidents and necessities that may concern the public, or to make such laws as will do no harm, if they are executed with an inflexible rigour on all occasions, and upon all persons that may come in their way; therefore there is a latitude left to the executive power, to do many things of choice which the laws do not prescribe.[59]

In the chapter on prerogative, thus, Locke extends the rationale for the need for equitable exceptions to the sphere of public law (public good): it is the impossibility of providing for all the circumstances and accidents that make the strict application of the law harmful (to the common good) when applied inflexibly on all occasions. It is part of the executive's authority to act exceptionally outside the boundaries of legal determinations.

A clear precedent for such an argument can be found in Aquinas' *Summa Theologiae*, in the analysis of the principle of 'necessity' as a justification of the authority to suspend laws in time of emergency. All laws, Aquinas writes, are aimed at some common good, and we can call them 'laws' because of this. However, there are cases in which 'the observance of some point of law . . . is very harmful', and this is due to the fact that the 'lawgiver' when laying down rules 'cannot have in view every single case', he, therefore 'shapes the law according to what happens most frequently, by directing his attention to the common good'. In cases where the following the law strictly would be 'hurtful to the general welfare', it is necessary not to observe the law. Aquinas gives as an example an endangered city:

> For instance, suppose that in a besieged city it be an established law that the gates of the city are to be kept closed, this is good for public welfare

59 Locke, *Two Treaties on Government*, §§ 159–160.

> as a general rule: but, it were to happen that the enemy are in pursuit of certain citizens, who are defenders of the city, it would be a great loss to the city, if the gates were not opened to them: and so in that case the gates ought to be opened, contrary to the letter of the law, in order to maintain the common good, which the lawgiver had in view.[60]

Here, the limits of law's generality, central to the discourse of equity, are directly applied to a problem of the security of a besieged city—which is coincidentally the event that gave the name to one of the most renowned forms of state of exceptions.

A similar argumentative line could be found in Alexander Hamilton, who, while discussing the extent of governmental authority to protect the nation, claimed that

> These powers ought to exist without limitation, because it is impossible to foresee or define the extent and variety of national exigencies, or the Correspondent extent and variety of the means which may be necessary to satisfy them. The circumstances that endanger the safety of nations are infinite, and for this reason no constitutional shackles can wisely be imposed on the power to which the care of it is committed. This power ought to be coextensive with all the possible combinations of such circumstances.[61]

And Schmitt, too, sustains that the cause why the sovereign has (unlimited) authority to act outside the limits of the legal order is because cases of 'extreme peril' and 'danger to the existence of the state' cannot be codified pre-emptively in 'the existing legal order': the 'precise details of an emergency cannot be anticipated, nor can one spell out what may take place in such a case, especially when it is truly a matter of an extreme emergency and of how it is to be eliminated'.[62]

The analogy between the justification of the need for equity and that of the broad (and unlimited) sovereign authority in the context of emergencies is rather stringent. In both cases, the recourse to an argument *ad contingentiam* constitutes the ground upon which the powers of acting by suspending a norm are considered legitimate. The generality and universality of law's words cannot account for the infinite potentiality of the world's contingency. In this sense, the sovereign capacity to make exceptions appears as the outcome of a discrepancy between language and the world, or better,

60 *Summa Theologiae*, Prima secundae, q. 96, art. 6*: utrum ei qui subditur legi, liceat praeter verba legis agree.*

61 Alexander Hamilton, *The Federalist Papers* (Palgrave MacMillan, 2009) 61–62.

62 Schmitt, *Political Theology*, 6–7.

as the appropriation of the power to decide the limit and extent of such a discrepancy.

1.4 Law's Defeat

In analytical jurisprudence, the question of the potential presence of exceptions to rules is often addressed through the concept of *defeasibility*.[63] Such a notion has been circulating at least since H. L. A. Hart discussed it in the essay 'The Ascription of Responsibility and Rights',[64] and refers to the phenomenon whereby a norm allows for exceptions that cannot be fully specified or predicted in advance and are instead determined by particular circumstances that 'defeat' the application of the norm. If, for instance, we make a promise to visit a friend, and on the day of the visit, it turns out that 'keeping the promise would involve neglecting someone dangerously ill', the 'fact that this is accepted as an adequate reason for not keeping the promise surely does not mean that there is no rule requiring promises to be kept, only a certain regularity in keeping them'. The fact that, in this situation, 'defeating' the rule represents the accepted 'right' thing to do, Hart claims, does not provide us with discretion to infringe rules when it suits us.[65] A norm retains its capacity to be a norm in the presence of invalidating, defeating conditions and 'even when the list of such conditions cannot be stated in advance. This last qualification appears to capture the distinctive claim of defeasibility'.[66] Exceptions, in other words, defeat but do not destroy rules.

A fundamental characteristic of law is its attempt to guide future decisions by referencing the past, making it continuously vulnerable to the uncertainties of human social experiences. The legal field is thus defined by a tension between the need for continuity and stability and the necessity to adapt to new circumstances. Exceptions serve as tools that enable adaptation and change while preserving the continuity of the law. The concept of defeasibility captures this delicate balance, where the law must be preserved in a state of constant precarity; therefore, far from being something negative—as the

63 On defeasibility, see Marshall Swain, 'Epistemic Defeasibility', *American Philosophical Quarterly*, vol. 11, 1974, p. 15; Donald Nute (ed), *Defeasible Deontic Logic* (Dordrecht: Kluwer Academic Publisher, 1997); Jordi Ferrer Beltrán and Giovanni Battista Ratti, 'Deafeasibility and Legality: A Survey', in J. Ferrer and G. B. Ratti (eds), *The Logic of Legal Requirements* (Oxford: Oxford University Press, 2012); Luís Duarte D'almeida, *Allowing for Exceptions. A Theory of Defences and Defeasibility in Law* (Oxford: Oxford University Press 2015).

64 H. L. A. Hart, 'The Ascription of Responsibility and Rights', *Proceedings of the Aristotelian Society*, vol. 49, 1948, pp. 171–194.

65 H. L. A. Hart, *The Concept of Law* (Oxford, 1961) 136.

66 Frederick Schauer, 'On The Supposed Defeasibility of Legal Rules', *Current Legal Problems*, vol. 51, no. 1, 1998, p. 224.

word 'defeat' naturally suggests—the defeasibility of law exposes the plasticity of the norms' formality in front of the contingent; the possibility of their being bent and suspended to achieve a specific result.

In modern jurisprudence, the problem of the fallibility of rules has always been a central part of the discussion of the nature of law and its limits. One popular example reported by Pufendorf[67] (and referred to by Blackstone),[68] is that of a statute in Bologna which enacted that 'Whoever drew blood in the streets should be severely punished', and that was determined as not extending to a barber who mistakenly opened the vein of a person while working. The strict application of the law, in such a case, would produce an outcome opposing the very spirit of the law. In like manner, William Blackstone refers to a law passed by Edward III which 'forbids all ecclesiastical persons to purchase provisions at Rome': such a rule seems

> to prohibit the buying of grain and other victual; but when we consider that the statute was made to repress the usurpations of the papal see, and that the nominations to benefices by the pope were called provisions, we shall see that the restraint is intended to be laid upon such provisions only.[69]

For Blackstone, these examples are cases exemplifying the need for equitable exceptions to rules, which he frames as discovering the true spirit of a law and applying it according to the actual reason for its own creation.[70]

Defeasibility is such a ubiquitous phenomenon in law that, for some, it represents an essential trait of the very application of legal norms. A popular explanation of this fact is that the law, by making use of natural language, incorporates the same limits (and vagueness) of language itself.

67 Samuel Pufendorf, *De jure naturae et gentium libri octo* (Oxford: Clarendon Press, 1688), book V, ch.12 §8.

68 William Blackstone, *Commentaries on the Laws of England* (Philadelphia: J. B. Lippincott Co., 1893), Introduction, section 2, §4.

69 Blackstone, *Commentaries on the Laws of England.*

70 Blackstone, *Commentaries on the Laws of England*, §5. A case that has come to exemplify law's defeasibility in the context of contemporary legal theory is *Riggs v. Palmer* (22 N.E. 188 N.Y. 1889). Rendered popular by Ronald Dworkin, this judgment concerns the right of Elmer Palmer—the defendant—to inherit under his grandfather's will. Elmer, eager to claim his inheritance, murdered his grandfather before he could alter or revoke his will. After his conviction, Elmer argued that under New York state law, the will remained valid, entitling him to inherit. Although the statute technically permitted Elmer to inherit even after committing murder, the New York Court of Appeals ruled otherwise, invoking the maxim 'no man shall profit from his own wrong'. A strict application of the law in this case would have led to a morally unacceptable outcome: allowing a murderer to benefit from his own wrongdoing. Here, the judges asserted that they were not bound by the literal interpretation of the law and deemed the most immediately applicable legal rule defeasible in the pursuit of justice.

Hart famously spoke of the *open texture* of language. 'Whichever device, precedent or legislation, is chosen for the communication of standards of behaviour', he writes, 'however smoothly they work over the great mass of ordinary cases, will, at some point where their application is in question, prove indeterminate; they will have what has been termed an open texture'.[71] The explanation Hart provides for the existence of such an open texture (which aligns with that of Friedrich Waismann,[72] the author from which he took the notion) is what we have previously termed the 'argument of contingency':

> the reason is that . . . we are men, not gods . . . If the world in which we live were characterized only by a finite number of features, and these together with all the modes in which they could combine were known to us, then provision could be made in advance for every possibility. We could make rules, the application of which to particular cases never called for a further choice. Everything could be known, and for everything, since it could be known, something could be done and specified in advance by rule. This would be a world fit for 'mechanical' jurisprudence. Plainly this world is not our world; human legislators can have no such knowledge of all the possible combinations of circumstances which the future may bring. This inability to anticipate brings with it a relative indeterminacy of aim.[73]

To explain what he means by the open texture of law, Hart made use of the renowned example of the rule 'that no vehicle may be taken into the park'—the underlying intent of which is to maintain peace in the part. This rule applies with no complications to the paradigmatic cases, such as 'motor-cars, the bus, and motor-cycles'. While in the case of a 'toy motor-car electrically propelled', the application of the rule becomes somehow cumbersome, as it seems not to contradict the intent of the rule itself. 'When the unenvisaged case does arise', Hart claims,

> we confront the issues at stake and can then settle the question by choosing between the competing interests in the way which best satisfies us. In doing so we shall have rendered more determinate our initial aim, and shall incidentally have settled a question as to the meaning, for the purposes of this rule, of a general word.[74]

71 Hart, *The Concept of Law*, 128.
72 Friedrich Waismann, 'Verifiability', *Proceedings of the Aristotelian Society (Supp.)*, vol. 19, 1945, pp. 119–147, and in A. G. N. Flew (ed), *Logic and Language* (Oxford: Basil Blackwell, 1951) 117–144.
73 Hart, *The Concept of Law*, 128.
74 Hart, *The Concept of Law*, 129.

For Hart, the law is inherently prone to uncertainty because language itself is essentially uncertain. And to the extent that legal rules are normally expressed in natural languages and are typically interpreted and applied through natural language, they embody the same limits and virtues of language in general. In Hart's account, this open-textured fabric of (legal) language appears as the reason for the very phenomenon of law's defeasibility, as the cause of the always present possibility of making exceptions to the law. 'The open texture of law', he sustains, 'means that there are, indeed, areas of conduct where much must be left to be developed by courts or officials striking a balance, in the light of circumstances, between competing interests which vary in weight from case to case'.[75] However, ascribing defeasibility to the rules of the law looks like a counterintuitive enterprise. In the end, the words of the law become open-textured only when an authority decides so, when the practical application of the law breaks the immaculate inoperativity of the law's textual existence. Indeed, as Frederick Schauer claims:

> Defeasibility is thus not a property of rules at all, but rather a characteristic of how some decision-making system will choose to treat its rules. The Wittgensteinian maxim that rules do not determine their own applications reminds us that how a rule will be treated is not something inherent in the rule itself. If the plain or literal (but not necessarily the ordinary language) meaning of a rule can indicate an outcome, it is a function not of the rule but of how the rule will be treated whether that indicated outcome is to be taken as conclusive, presumptive, or even, at the extreme, as having no weight in itself, being but a totally transparent (to its background justification, or to the all-things-considered best outcome) heuristic or rule of thumb. The question of defeasibility is not a question about what is in a rule, but is rather a question about how what is in a rule, or about how what a rule says, is to be treated, and this is not, and can never be, something that can be determined by the rule itself.[76]

In their formal existence—as a text—the rules of the law stand in a realm of perfection, as a signifying system abstracted from the reality they must regulate. Only in their operativity do defeasibility and exceptions become potential eventualities. This is because the sphere of the norms and that of the legal decisions are somehow ontologically different—one belonging

75 Hart, *The Concept of Law*, 132.

76 Frederick Schauer, 'Is Defeasibility an Essential Property of Law?', in Jordi Ferrer Beltrán and Giovanni Battista Ratti (eds), *The Logic of Legal Requirements: Essays on Defeasibility* (Oxford: Oxford University Press, 2012) 87.

to the sphere of the semiotics, the other to that of practice—and cannot be placed in a relation of deduction. As Schmitt has poignantly noted, in the decision-making process, even in adjudicating whether the facts for a crime have been fulfilled or not, there is an element of 'pure' decision, which cannot be deduced from the content of the norm.[77] In every legal decision, Schmitt says, there is something like an *auctoritatis interpositio*, which makes it irreducible in its totality to legal principles and rules: the 'constitutive, specific element of a decision', he goes on, 'is from the perspective of the content of the underlying norm, new and alien. Looking at it normatively, the decision emanates from nothingness'.[78] And this becomes manifest in the faulty/wrong decision, which, until further determination, remains a valid one.

What seems to be at stake in the concept of defeasibility of legal norms—and of exception more generally—is the ultimate irreducibility of rules and ruling, of laws and decisions. Far from being a logical operation, the application of (general) norms to a specific individual case necessarily involves the passage from the abstract realm of commands to the dimension of concrete/practical decision: a passage that, by bridging two ontologically different spheres, cannot be characterised in pure inferential terms. In the application of juridical norms, Agamben writes, at issue is

> first and foremost the passage from a generic proposition endowed with a merely virtual reference to a concrete reference to a segment of reality (that is, nothing less than the question of the actual relation between language and world). This passage from langue to parole, or from the semiotic to the semantic, is not a logical operation at all; rather, it always entails a practical activity, that is, the assumption of langue by one or more speaking subjects and the implementation of that complex apparatus that Benveniste defined as the enunciative function, which logicians often tend to undervalue. In the case of the juridical norm, reference to the concrete case entails a 'trial' that always involves a plurality of subjects and ultimately culminates in the pronunciation of a sentence, that is, an enunciation whose operative reference to reality is guaranteed by the institutional powers.[79]

When legal norms are 'defeated' or when authorities determine an exception to the law, the ontological separation between norms and decision emerges, making visible how an anomic 'force' is capable of applying and realising a norm by suspending (and infringing) its dictates. The source or 'place' of

77 Carl Schmitt, *Der Hüter der Verfassung* (Berlin: Duncker & Humblot, 1996) 45–46.
78 Schmitt, *Political Theology*, 31–32.
79 Agamben, *State of Exception*, 39–40.

defeasibility is, therefore, to be ascribed to that sphere of practical anomie that is what ultimately grants law's operativity.

1.5 Exceptionality

According to what we have seen so far, exceptions, as legal incursion beyond the boundary limits of the law, are an exercise of true authority (which is what makes them a legitimate event and not an arbitrary infringement of the law). Either in the form of a deviation from a single norm, in adjudication or as the temporary suspension of a set of rights, with the usual alteration of the separation of powers, in an emergency, exceptions—we argue—appear as a constant feature to the legal design, which, however, have an essentially antagonistic relationship to norms. They signal that there are situations in which the application of the law is 'made' defective—all based on the evaluation that, in those circumstances, the most appropriate decision is to not apply legal norms. In this sense, exceptions are the product of different legal rationality that favours the authoritative decision and discretion over normative correctness, based on adherence to specific other principles (necessity, equity, fairness, etc.); and this is what makes them antagonistic to law's text.

Exceptions are also moments in which the ontological difference between the text of the law and its application (between norms and decisions) emerges with extreme clarity. The fact that an exception manifests itself in a decision that operates a suspension, or a deviation, from a norm without altering the validity of that norm is indeed evidence of the radical alterity of the elements composing the legal system. While the possibility of the linguistic expression of norms is a necessary validating element of the law, its force depends ultimately on the pronunciation of agents whose status grants them the necessary authority to make that pronunciation an effective one.[80] Decisions, to be legally valid, need the presence of both procedural, formal-normative elements and authoritative ones. As Agamben has poignantly claimed in the closing of *State of Exception*, the juridical system in its manifold manifestation seems to be built on a double structure formed by two heterogeneous yet coordinated elements:

> one that is normative and juridical in the strict sense (which we can for convenience inscribe under the rubric *potestas*) and one that is anomic and

80 The relevant issue here is that of legal hermeneutics and interpretation, as all legal agents approach the law from a background of a specific conception of the law. While such a question is relevant, a deeper analysis of it lies beyond the scope of this work. For further discussion, see Duncan Kennedy, *A Critique of Adjudication (fin de siecle)* (Cambridge: Harvard University Press, 1997); Gregory Leyh (ed), *Legal Hermeneutics: History, Theory, and Practice* (University of California Press, 2021).

metajuridical (which we can call by the name *auctoritas*). The normative element needs the anomic element in order to be applied.[81]

In the moment of the 'performative' taking place of the law, these two elements, albeit irreconcilable, seem to enter into a zone of indistinction, and it is in this space that 'exceptions' are nested. And to the extent that the possibility of its enforcement and application is what determines its existence and validity, the law involves (and produces) necessarily a sphere of *exceptionality*.

Exceptionality is an epiphenomenon of law's normativity—the product of the operation of an authoritative reminder that is always present in the decision-making process. As we have seen previously, the possibility of exceptions (which are the manifestation of exceptionality) is never inscribed in the law's norm but is the byproduct of how the text of the law is considered and interpreted by the institutional apparatus entitled to apply it. The locus of exceptionality (from the micro level of judges and official discretion to the executive power in a state of emergency) is the legal institutional apparatus itself. And to the extent that enforceability is an essential character of valid law, exceptionality seems to be a constant dimension of legal normativity, which stands in a relatively autonomous relationship with the text of the law, since exceptions, although cannot be subsumed totally, can become (or already are) expressions of law's design. The remnants of exceptionality in a legal system is, in this sense, the marker of law's acknowledgement of its own occasional inoperativity and self-insufficiency, with respect to the contingency of reality, which is remedied with exceptions. Therefore, although closely related to the pragmatic sphere of law's application, exceptionality remains an essential element but irreducible to legal forms; by allowing suspension of the norms, it provides effective instruments to ensure the continuity of law's effectuality circumventing the limits of the legal system in its relation to reality. But, exceptionality is more than simply responding to challenges of contingency, it involves the overriding of the supposed structural infelicities of the legal system.

In this regard, exceptionality assumes the form of a recession of the norm with the overall goal of its own application. This is an operation of liberation of a force that 'destroys' the norm to reinstate its most proper spirit. The legal system processes real conflictual stances through specific linguistic and categorial re-framing and can anticipate potential new contradictions by incorporating the possibility of its negation in the form of exceptionality. Indeed, what the contingency of the real mainly does is disrupt the normal adherence of the legal system to the real; the function of exceptionality is,

81 Agamben, *State of Exception*, 86.

in this sense, that of feeding, expanding and transforming the law with new inputs. This is, in a sense, the logical outcome of the narrative of contingency that has been deployed to justify the operation of exception: to the extent that the whole realm of contingency cannot be grasped by language, the law—being a linguistic practice—must remain open to the possibility of being defeated in order to maintain an effective regulatory function. Exceptionality, therefore, dissolves the security of legal expectations, revealing the potential indeterminacy of their already-achieved meaning and, in so doing, greatly expands the possibilities for intra-legal contradictions—to prevent the escalation of conflictuality between the normative sphere and the real. In exceptionality, the discrepancy between the norm (with its overall goal) and the realm of facticity is captured and recruited as a legal conflict: the one that dialectically binds the legal and the extra-legal. Exceptionality, in this sense, gives a legal structure to insecurity—by transforming contingency into expectable consequences; for this reason, the exception is not aimed at the eradication of external danger but more about expanding the law's receptivity of societal evolution—with all the risk that this includes. To the extent that exceptionality is ultimately independent of the sphere of the norm, the possibility of the destruction of the normative is always present in bringing the real to the normative.

The law tends to extend its reach to include and regulate exceptionality by constituting it as a kind of internal limit. This tendency is the outcome of the growth and evolution of the state form, with its juridical/bureaucratic apparatuses, and the decisive influence of the liberal tradition, which has envisaged the law as the core medium to inform political decisions and social conflicts. Prime examples here are those of equity and the state of exception. For the first, the initial exceptional-corrective incursion into the common law's business became, throughout time, a broad and structured body of principles and remedies that eventually have been integrated into the operation of the system of courts. As for the latter, the gradual encoding into the law text began with the emergence of constitutional and statutory provisions giving the executive-wide emergency powers to solve national crises and evolved with the emergence of a more limited and ad-hoc legislative model. But with the expanding juridification of reality, implicit in the historical evolution of positive law, exceptionality becomes a stream running through the governmental, administrative and judicial apparatuses in the form of a normalised and integrated discretion. If anything, exceptionality is that sphere of normativity that, by clashing with the limits of legal norms, exposes the very legal necessity to act outside the law's boundary to 'creatively' forge the condition for the application of the law itself. Exceptionality begins when and where the law ends, but chaos and disorder are still far from the horizon of events.

Chapter 2

Exceptionality

Towards the General Theory of Exception

Przemysław Tacik

2.1 Introduction: On the Need for the General Theory of Exception

Emergencies and exceptional measures have had a polarising effect on legal scholarship. On the one hand, they have drawn the attention of curious and suspicious theorists who rightly sensed that the exception—in all its ramifications—can guide us to the foundational level of modern legality and statality. Carl Schmitt can be rightly credited as the patron of such attempts;[1] however, he gave them a clear right-wing political spin.[2] Ernst Fraenkel's classic theory of the dual state provides a stunningly dynamic theory of flexible, dispersed exceptional interventions.[3] François Saint-Bonnet offered a thorough historical study elegantly encased in a theory of necessity and exception.[4] Most recently, a great theory of the exception was delivered by Giorgio Agamben,[5] who made it part of his multi-dimensional thought.[6] On the other hand, there has been a plethora of more 'normalised' or local theories of the exception that focus either

1 Carl Schmitt, *Political Theology. Four Chapters on the Concept of Sovereignty*, George Schwab transl. (MIT Press 1985); Carl Schmitt, *On Dictatorship. From the Origin of the Modern Concept of Sovereignty to Proletarian Class Struggle* Michael Hoelzl and Graham Ward transl. (Cambridge, Polity, 2014 [1921]) 119–127.

2 Oren Gross, 'The Normless and Exceptionless Exception: Carl Schmitt's Theory of Emergency Powers and the Norm-Exception Dichotomy' (2000) 21 *Cardozo L Rev* 1825, 1827–1829.

3 Ernst Fraenkel, *The Dual State. A Contribution to the Theory of Dictatorship* E. A. Shils, Edith Lowenstein and Klaus Knorr transl. (The Lawbook Exchange 2010).

4 François Saint-Bonnet, *L'état d'exception* (PUF 2001).

5 Giorgio Agamben, *State of Exception (Homo Sacer II, 1)* Kevin Attell transl. (The University of Chicago Press 2005); Giorgio Agamben, *Homo Sacer* Daniel Heller-Roazen transl. (Stanford University Press 1998) 1–29.

6 See Giorgio Agamben, *L'uso dei corpi. Homo sacer, IV, 2* (Neri Pozza 2014) 9–10; Giorgio Agamben, *The Sacrament of Language. An Archeology of the Oath (Homo Sacer II, 3)* Adam Kotsko transl. (Polity Press 2010) 46; Giorgio Agamben, *The Highest Poverty. Monastic Rules and Form-of-Life* Adam Kotsko transl. (Stanford University Press 2013) xi–xiii, 26, 62, 84–86, 115, 143–145.

DOI: 10.4324/9781003490449-3

on empirical studies of exceptional measures, their classification or legal challenges of containing exceptional powers.[7] Most valuable of these studies, especially by Oren Gross (both alone[8] and with Fionnuala Ní Aoláin),[9] Ninon Grangé,[10] Karin Loevy[11] and Tristan Barczak,[12] demonstrate the complexity of the exception and allow for nuance in Schmitt's legacy. But, between these two paradigms, there is not much communication. Great theories remain chiefly on the abstract level, separated from empirical research. More concrete ones—with their practical focus—often mystify the ability of the law to contain the political and omit the fascinating philosophical role of the exception.

The general theory of exception, which I will attempt to introduce in this chapter, strives to join the two sides of this hiatus. It aims to provide a conceptual field that would muster key concepts related to the exception, the law and the political. The new concepts that it proposes are meant to be operational in concrete analyses. This chapter will introduce and expound on the term 'exceptionality'; in the following one, I will focus on 'exceptionalisation'. Finally, the fourth chapter will use both concepts to rethink the idea of sovereignty.

The general theory of exception requires new methodological foundations in a twofold sense. First, what we need is a new scheme of concepts and their internal relatability: a new philosophical engine, so to speak. Schmitt's theory works with a Hegelian engine; Agamben has its own philosophical machine informed by Hegel, Heidegger, Benjamin and Foucault. The general theory is in need not only of a new engine but also a new way of its functioning. Accordingly, firstly, philosophical structures and gestures of thinking about the exception need to be updated, taking into account the legacy of Derrida,

7 See, for example, Jean-Claude Monod, *Penser l'ennemi, affronter l'exception. Réflexions critiques sur l'actualité de Carl Schmitt* (Editions de la découverte 2006); David Dyzenhaus, *The Constitution of Law. Legality in a Time of Emergency* (CUP 2006); Giacomo Delledonne, 'Crises, Emergencies and Constitutional Change' in Xenophon Contiades and Alkmene Fotiadou (eds), *Routledge Handbook of Comparative Constitutional Change* (Routledge 2021) 245–260; John Ferejohn and Pasquale Pasquino, 'The Law of Exception: A Typology of Emergency Powers' (2004) 2:2 *ICON* 210.

8 Oren Gross, 'The Normless and Exceptionless Exception', 1825; Oren Gross, 'Providing for the Unexpected: Constitutional Emergency Provisions' (2003) 33 *Isr YB Hum Rts* 13; Oren Gross, 'Extra-Legality and the Ethic of Political Responsibility' in Victor Ramraj (ed), *Emergencies and the Limits of Legality* (CUP 2008) 60–93.

9 Oren Gross and Fionnuala Ní Aoláin, *Law in Times of Crisis. Emergency Powers in Theory and Practice* (CUP 2006).

10 Ninon Grangé, *L'urgence et l'effroi. L'état d'exception, la guerre et les temps politiques* (ENS 2018).

11 Karin Loevy, *Emergencies in Public Law. The Legal Politics of Containment* (CUP 2016).

12 Tristan Barczak, *Der nervöse Staat. Ausnahmezustand und Resilienz des Rechts in der Sicherheitsgesellchaft* (Mohr Siebeck 2021).

Foucault and Žižek. In particular, deconstruction requires to be rethought in this context.

Secondly, we need *radical dynamisation* of conceptual tools with which we analyse the exception. So far, theoretical attempts have been oscillating around ossified and all-too-stable categories of the exception and the sovereign, which do not explain the complexity of exceptional measures and their effective work, especially when seen historically. The general theory of exception offers a chance of expanding the field. Here, some conceptual strategies from the field of particle physics will be of help. One of the greatest revolutions in 20th-century physics consisted in understanding particles (such as the electron) in terms of fields. Accordingly, so should the exception and the sovereign be conceived as particular points of allocation—cathexes, to borrow a psychoanalytical term—of two other concepts that should be understood as fields: exceptionality and sovereignty. As we will see, both exceptionality and sovereignty traverse and permeate the politico-legal system. Their concentration in particular points—the exception and the sovereign, operated by the legal—does not exhaust their work elsewhere and does not stop paradoxes stemming from their spillover from these positions. Such a switch dynamises the conceptuality of the exception.

The term 'general theory' will also hark back to Einsteinian understanding of the term. Einstein's general relativity is a development of special relativity, which grasped bindings between certain physical categories. In particular, it bound time dilation and contraction of space with the observer's position or established the equivalence of mass and energy. General relativity explains them by a broader framework, that is, by introducing the category of curved spacetime (which also corresponds to gravity). What I will undertake here is an analogous gesture of generalisation. So far, the exception has been bound with other politico-legal categories by particular postulates. For example, Schmitt's famous claim '[s]overeign is he who decides on the exception'[13] establishes a foundational link between the exception and the sovereign. Analogously, Agamben postulates a relation between the state of exception and ordinary law-application;[14] a claim I will analyse in greater detail. With both of these observations, despite their groundbreaking novelty, we remain at the level of special theories of the exception. But what we need is the invention of a general conceptual space in which they will appear as special incarnations of general relations.

What this chapter strives to found is, therefore, a general theory of exception, focused on theoretical investigations and a shot at explicating profound relations between main exception-related categories of legal and political

13 Schmitt, *Political Theology*, 5.
14 Agamben, *Homo Sacer*, 17–18.

scholarship. I will thus skip classic mid-level problems of emergency studies, such as finding practical ways to curb the abuse of exceptional powers.[15] Theories of exceptional devices and their effects need to be inscribed into a greater totality. Moreover, this theoretical venture will try not to explain the exception by inscribing and explaining it with legal categories. On the contrary, the exception will appear as a peculiar but inherent excrescence within the legal which can be explained only when the whole legal order is put within the new conceptual universe, alongside the political, sovereignty, biopolitics and modern historicity. Most importantly, the analysis needs to perform a strategic *epoché* on internally normative qualifications of exceptional measures: the distinction between the normal and the exceptional, established by the legal systems, is not the explanation of the problem but an *explanandum* itself. We thus need to sever the exception from the obfuscating grip of normative categories and make them relative to deeper concepts in the field.

The chapter will be structured as follows. First, I will expound on the need and sense for the general theory of exception. Second, the concept of exceptionality will be proposed and explained through a comparison with the state of exception. Then, I will proceed to building preparatory elements of the general theory of exception, focusing on its philosophical engines as well as axes and temporality of the exception.

2.2 From the State of Exception to Exceptionality

The vast field of studies on exceptional forms in law—in all their variegation, from emergency measures, through states of exception up to commissarial dictatorships—do not seem to offer a general term that would be able to take upon itself the burden of proper theorisation. In Agamben's theory, which is perhaps the most eloquent and in-depth analysis achieved so far, preference is given to the 'state of exception',[16] although 'exception'[17] as such occurs as well, even if more rarely. The relations between these two concepts in Agamben—for whose analysis there is no place in this chapter—is complex,[18] but definitely, the Italian philosopher plays out for his own philosophical purposes the polysemy of the term 'state of exception'. It connotes both a

15 On this topic see Dyzenhaus, *The Constitution of Law*.

16 Agamben, *State of Exception*.

17 Agamben, *Homo sacer*, 15–18.

18 See Stephen Humphreys, 'Legalizing Lawlessness: On Giorgio Agamben's State of Exception' (2006) 17:3 *EJIL* 677; Daniel McLoughlin, 'The Fiction of Sovereignty and the Real State of Exception: Giorgio Agamben's Critique of Carl Schmitt' (2016) 12 *L, Cult & Human* 509, 525–528; Paul A. Passavant, 'The Contradictory State of Giorgio Agamben' (2007) 35 *Pol Theory* 147, 153–157; Susan Dianne Brophy, 'Lawless Sovereignty: Challenging the State of Exception' (2009) 18 *Soc & Legal Stud* 199–207.

concrete legal device, triggerable and proclaimable,[19] and a *status* of exception, whose normative registrability is inseparable from the sphere of factuality.[20] Although this double connotation is exactly what Agamben's wants to prove to exist nowadays, such confusion is not conducive to building a precise conceptual framework.[21]

Equally, this conceptual work cannot be done by the term 'emergency', although it frequently appears in this scholarly field. By emergency I will understand here a socially interpreted constellation of facts, such as natural disasters or military actions. As such, it does not describe the dynamics of the law itself, its inherent processes, but the facts that the law constructs outside of itself. Emergency is produced as *Sein*, not *Sollen*, to use the Kantian formula; the term we are looking for must belong to the normative and the meta-normative, that is, to *Sollen*.

If we want to give this field a proper general theory—one that will pass from amassing multifarious phenomena to building a proper self-standing conceptual network—we require a term that will fully abstract from *particular incarnations* of exceptional forms. The state of exception—representing here the generic form of what can be called *exceptional devices*[22]—is a privileged scene of exceptional acts and practices, but surely not the only one. Not only does it compete with various states of emergency or urgency (however flamboyant a lawgiver's imagination turns out to be in a given jurisdiction),[23] but it also retains an anchoring in concrete normative regulations, often on the constitutional level.[24] The latter quality makes it cumbersome to talk about a state of exception if a proper normative device has not been triggered.

Distinguishing between the state of exception *de jure* (that is, formally proclaimed according to valid legal rules) and *de facto* (unregistered formally in the symbolic tissue of the law but producing the same factual results) may seem to relieve the dilemma, but only to a certain degree. The term itself is not general enough, but it also retains a direct relation to a particular legal device, either already triggered or—perhaps regrettably—not used when a need for it had occurred. Even more importantly, the state of exception melts law and facts in a way that may suit Agamben's philosophy but cannot make it a foundational concept for a general theory. As a more promising avenue appears 'the exception', if only it were not too substantialising and centring. Another complication is the fact that

19 Agamben, *State of Exception*, 1–24.

20 Agamben, *State of Exception*, 65–73.

21 Cf. Barczak, *Der nervöse Staat*, 82–84.

22 See Monod, *Penser l'ennemi, affronter l'exception*, 73–74.

23 For examples, see Barczak, *Der nervöse Staat*, 22–26, 79; Gross and Ní Aoláin, *Law in Times of Crisis*, 37–47.

24 For an overview of emergency clauses in constitutions, see Christian Bjornskov and Stefan Voigt, 'The Architecture of Emergency Constitutions' (2018) 16 *ICON* 101–125.

what the exception remains relative to a given legal order at a particular moment in time. Meanwhile, legal systems can attempt to dissimulate exceptional measures by labelling them as normal. The exception remains relative to this labelling. It has, therefore, important conceptual value but does not allow for abstracting from a here and now of a given legal order. The exception will be retained here for philosophical purposes, to connote a particular aspect of relatability between exceptional forms and the whole politico-legal framework to which they belong. In a more concrete sense, the exception is a correlate and the opposition to *normality*.[25] But, precisely for this reason, it cannot be used to explain the whole framework in which it is embedded. This calls for a different concept.

The term which offers a sufficient degree of flexibility and explanatory power is *exceptionality*.[26] It takes precedence before all particular incarnations in which it can appear, whatever name they bear and however they mix normativity and factuality. In other words, they can be related to the framework that it constitutes rather than give material from which induction would produce a generalised term. Moreover, exceptionality marks the fact that no exceptional device can ever channel it fully and exhaustively, excluding the possibility of measures that are exceptional but not named as such. Equally important is the power of this term to encompass *various philosophical engines* that may be installed in the theory that strives to explain exceptional forms.

Crucially, it allows for leaving the confinements of a given legal order—in which the exception and exceptional devices are defined—in a more general way than through a comparative study of particular legal devices. Exceptionality can describe both the state of exception proper (understood as a normative device triggered in extraordinary consequences) and all kinds of

25 See Bjornskov and Voigt, 'The Architecture of Emergency Constitutions', 98–103; Gross, 'The Normless and Exceptionless Exception', 1833–1834; Heinrich Oberreuter, *Notstand und Demokratie. Vom monarchischen Obrigkeits-zum demokratischen Rechtsstaat* (Ernst Vögel 1978) 12; Markus Kotzur, 'Die Weltgemeinschaft im Ausnahmezustand?' (2004) 42:4 *AVR* 353, 357. As noticed by Marie-Laure Basilien-Gainche, this opposition condenses other ones (such as power/violence, liberty/order, etc.). Marie-Laure Basilien-Gainche, *État de droit et états d'exception. Une conception de l'État* (PUF 2013) 38. On exception as 'everything *but*', see Rebecca Gould, 'Laws, Exceptions, Norms: Kierkegaard, Schmitt, and Benjamin on the Exception' (2013) 162 *Telos* 1.

26 The term itself is not new. It was used, for example, by Marie-Laure Basilien-Gainche to grasp border conditions of states of exception (like conditions of triggering them, methods in which they operate and their objectives). Basilien-Gainche, *État de droit et états d'exception*, 24. Other uses of the term can be found, for example, in: Gould, 'Laws, Exceptions, Norms', 16; Vojtěch Belling, 'The State of Exception and Limits of the Rule of Law' in Jakub Jinek and Lukáš Kollert (eds), *Emergency Powers. Rule of Law and the State of Exception* (Nomos 2020) 53; Jan Kysela, 'Exceptionality in Law' in Jinek and Lukáš (eds), *Emergency Powers. Rule of Law and the State of Exception* (Nomos 2020) 108. Nonetheless, 'exceptionality' used here has a distinctly precise and new theoretical meaning.

situations that may be normatively dubbed as 'normalised' or 'normal', but preserve an exceptional quality. It can identify the *exceptional content* both in official devices meant to make it visible and public and in apparent normality which aims to dissimulate it. For this reason *exceptionality precedes the distinction between the exception and normality*: naturally, it is crucial whether the legal system recognises a measure marked by exceptionality as exceptional or normal, but the latter distinction is relative to this system itself.

In other words, a particular form of exceptionality can be labelled by the legal system either as the exception (in which case we can say that the law performs proper registration) or as normality (when the law obfuscates effectively exceptional measures under the guise of business as usual). The COVID-19 pandemic demonstrated clearly that in many countries where states of emergency had not been declared, properly exceptional measures passed off as normal ones.[27] This means, in turn, that the general theory of exception cannot take the label that the legal system attaches to a certain act for a definitive determination of its exceptional or normal character. Surely, the normative qualification is significant, but by no means can it shut the door to theoretical recognition. Nor should it be misled by the factuality of emergency: a legal system can react to emergency through exceptionality, but this link is not necessary. In fact, emergencies can be addressed perfectly well within the 'normal' dimension of the legal order, without involving exceptionality. Moreover, not every rule needs to be explicitly suspendable in the light of the legal order to carry exceptionality.[28] This fact is particularly discernible in the construction of the US Constitution. Designed from the beginning as non-suspendable with a very limited scope of exception, it is exceptionality primarily through the strong executive and the special role of the President,[29] with flexible legislative delegations when necessary.[30]

What we now stumble upon is the old debate, incarnated most conspicuously in the dispute between Carl Schmitt and Hermann Heller, whether the law is best explained by—respectively—the exceptional or by the normal.[31] Beyond all practical political consequences of a choice in such an opposition,

27 See Przemyslaw Tacik, 'The Blizzard of the World: COVID-19 and the Last Say of the State of Exception' (2021) 96 *Folia Iuridica* 17.

28 Therefore, explicit derogation of a rule may be a definitional element of the state of exception or an emergency measure (see Saint-Bonnet, *L'état d'exception*, 25–27), but not of exceptionality as such.

29 See Clinton Rossiter, *Constitutional Dictatorship. Crisis Government in the Modern Democracies* (Routledge 2017) x–xix, 208–218; Michael Stokes Paulsen, 'The Constitution of Necessity' (2004) 79 *Notre Dame L Rev* 1257, 1282–1291.

30 Paulsen, 'The Constitution of Necessity', 218–220, 242.

31 Barczak, *Der nervöse Staat*, 138–149. Ernst-Wolfgang Böckenförde, 'Der verdrängte Ausnahmezustand. Zum Handeln der Staatsgewalt in außergewöhnlichen Lagen' (1978) 38 *NJW* 1881, 1884.

it is crucial to notice that this difference is, in fact, philosophical. When Schmitt defends the claim that it is the exception that reveals the contours of the entanglement between the political and the legal,[32] he sides with Hegel and the whole post-Hegelian tradition of thinking (including Kierkegaard).[33] In this paradigm, no entity exists tranquilly through its own self-constitution; on the contrary, every being is constituted by its differentiation from others and the totality within it ultimately subsists through negation. *Omnis determinatio est negatio*,[34] writes Hegel after Spinoza: negation is here a creative force, a new *hypokeimenon*, that brings things into being and upholds them in subsistence. The overwhelming role of this paradigm is visible especially today, when—rejuvenated by de Saussurian vision of *signifiants* determining themselves through negative references to other *signifiants*[35]—it became the daily bread of poststructuralism. Schmitt stands for the Hegelian side of philosophy: he looks for what appears as margins, special situations and excrescences, knowing that they hold a key to explaining the whole totality. It is thus of no surprise that he has been so often read by Marxists and poststructuralists;[36] his account of the exception is properly dialectical. The exception functions as a secret thread, by the pull of which the whole *theatrum* of the law embedded in the political is laid bare.

Meanwhile, Heller stands for the non-dialectical approach, deploring that 'all realization of law remains imprisoned by the demonic element of power'.[37] The price to be paid for disjoining the exception from the position of a key symptom vis-à-vis the legal order is a proper legal idealism: the belief in the self-standing quality of the law, which is only *factually* haunted by power. The religious imagery only underlines the foreignness of power in relation to legality. Whereas for the dialectical Schmitt politics is the proper hidden god of the law, Heller casts it in the role of the devil. His non-dialectical approach makes him convinced by how things declare themselves to exist rather than by the secret pattern of negative dependencies that determines them from within.[38]

32 Schmitt, *Political Theology*, 1–5.

33 Hasso Hofmann, 'Souverän ist, wer über den Ausnahmezustand entscheidet' (2005) 44:2 *Der Staat* 171, 173; Gould, 'Laws, Exceptions, Norms', 3–12.

34 Georg Wilhelm Friedrich Hegel, *The Science of Logic* George di Giovanni transl. (CUP 2010) 87.

35 Ferdinand de Saussure, *Cours de linguistique générale* (Payot 1995) 97–191.

36 See Chantal Mouffe, *The Challenge of Carl Schmitt* (Verso 1999).

37 Hermann Heller, 'The Nature and Structure of the State' (1996) 18 *Cardozo L Rev* 1139, 1163.

38 This trait is well recognisable in how Heller theorises the state as a natural order based on cooperation: 'the organization, as a fabric of conduct, possesses its effective (to be precise) actual unit by no other means than through the participants' cooperation, which is actualized unitarily through the organs. The unit of the objective order is the ideal unit of a normative structure of meaning, the unit of the organization is the actual unit of a cooperation

Still, the general theory of exception—although certainly closer to Schmitt than to Heller, with a caveat to be developed later—should not declare whether the exception or normality 'really' holds the key to the truth.[39] What seems far more important is how a given legal system itself produces, reproduces and upholds the difference between the exceptional and the normal—and what functions it serves. In this sense, exceptionality is a term that serves as a buffering and mediating matrix from which the legal system develops its *internal* distinction between the exceptional and the normal.

Importantly, exceptionality—as an apparent redoubling of the exception (understood as inherent to a given legal system)—corresponds to the inherent binding between norms and facts that every exceptional device displays. Suffice it to remark here, before further analysis, that part of exceptional devices is the normative dissimulation of the real effects that their application entails. Once a state of exception is proclaimed to be over, 'normality' is normatively reinstated with all effects of the special period obfuscated. Exceptionality is precisely a concept that allows of grasping the changes which happened effectively, even if they have not been registered legally and symbolically. In this sense, its existence is more of a structure in a conceptual scheme rather than an actually occupiable position. To borrow a Lacanian term, it offers a Big Other to the normality/exception distinction: its place of registration. But ultimately, it leads to an underlying lack—there is no ultimate and objective qualification of a measure, act or practice as 'properly' exceptional. Lacan's remark about the inexistence of the Big Other for the Big Other applies here as well: exceptionality can be approached from the normality/exception distinction, but it neither exists *in itself* nor has its own registering point. What can be done, however, is *correlating the exceptional changes registered in the law and outside of it.*

Exceptionality can also be posited as the dimension from which normality/exception originates through normalisation. Thus, a general theory of exception cannot work without *an understanding of legal normalisation* as its component. Normalisation is a procedure executed by the law and through the law, from which a given constellation of the exceptional and the normal emerges. It can be seen not only ontogenetically as occurring in a given legal

that has been brought about. Certainly no enduring organization is possible, much less the fabric of conduct that is the state, without the objective order in its characteristic as a concrete disposition of unit-formative conduct . . . . As soon as one understands by 'order' an actual hierarchy of normative propositions of obligation, one can certainly define the state like any other organization as a unit of order'. Analogically, sovereignty is for him just 'the highest power as the subject of sovereignty because it is elevated above all other powers in its territory and promulgates the highest legal norms. Hence, the sovereignty of the state is nothing more than the necessary consequence of its social function'. Heller, 'The Nature and Structure of the State', 1169, 1181.

39 Schmitt is often lambasted for giving the exception the priority which, in the words of Oren Gross, 'destructs the normal'. See Gross, 'The Normless and Exceptionless Exception', 1829.

system, but also phylogenetically—that is, as a historical process in which modern statality based on the rule of law was constituted.

The general theory of exception should thus correspond to the demand of Walter Benjamin to make the exceptional state seen as normality proper[40]—also, if not predominantly, from the historical perspective. The essence of Benjamin's recognition is that normality is a construct whose establishment and official affirmation do not jar with its perception only for the privileged classes. The oppressed live in a permanent state of exception not only because state violence is applied to them more freely and invisibly but also because they perceive the social reality as abnormal while being fed with ideological self-assertions of normality. Within the general theory of exception, there should be no normality before—or non-relative to—normalisation.

This does not mean, however, that the exception gains absolute priority. On the contrary, exceptionality is a negative matrix of politico-legal constitution, from which the exception—in its opposition to normality—emerges. The boundary between these two is shifting and flexible, operating to some extent due to political demands. The general theory of exception thus opens a space for functionalising the exception/normality distinction and for its empirical use.

Consequently, it also goes against the theory that normality can be defined sociologically as a 'normal state of society',[41] or just as natural regularity.[42] Typical awkward delegations of this matter to the domain of (usually imaginary) 'sociology' only conceal the Derridean logic of a supplement.[43] Tautological as it may sound, no normality can be defined without a normative level:[44] normality is a shadow that a particular legal order casts on the perception of factuality. It is a retroactive establishment of factual reality that supposedly confirms its legal counterpart. Therefore, expecting that identifying normality can be delegated outside of the realm of the law to some imagined scientific authority or a general feeling does not solve the problem. In fact, it

40 'The tradition of the oppressed teaches us that the "state of emergency" in which we live is not the exception but the rule. We must attain to a conception of history that is in keeping with this insight'. Walter Benjamin, 'Theses on the Philosophy of History' in *Illuminations* Harry Zohn transl. (Schocken Books 2007) 257. See also Monod, *Penser l'ennemi, affronter l'exception*, 33.

41 Barczak, *Der nervöse Staat*, 109; Böckenförde, 'Der verdrängte Ausnahmezustand', 1884.

42 Ferejohn and Pasquino, 'The Law of Exception', 221; Steffen Augsberg, 'Denken vom Ausnahmezustand her. Über die Unzulässigkeit der anormalen Konstruktion und Destruktion des Normativen' in *Freiheit—Sicherheit—Öffentlichkeit. 48. Assistententagung Öffentliches Recht* (Nomos 2009) 34–35.

43 Jacques Derrida, *Of Grammatology* Gayatry Chakravorty Spivak transl. (John Hopkins University Press 1997) 155.

44 See Heller, 'The Nature and Structure of the State', 1189–1192; Jasper Finke, 'Funktion und Wirkung der Ausnahme im Recht' (2015) 140:4 *AöR* 514, 523; Josef Isensee, 'On the Validity of Law with Respect to the Exceptional Case' in Jakub Jinek and Lukáš Kollert (eds), *Emergency Powers. Rule of Law and the State of Exception* (Nomos 2020) 11–12.

is rather part of the problem, a self-obfuscation of the whole construction of the legal—with very concrete violence concealed within normalisation. If so, the distinction between the exception and normality is not explicable solely *within* the legal order because it requires a broader framework of which this order is just a part.[45] In particular, foreign affairs of a state typically preserve a large component of exceptionality (visible in frequent invocations of necessity and increased role of the executive[46]), which demonstrates a short circuit between the construction of sovereignty, domestic normalisation and framing the international as a structural threat. The general theory of exception is designed precisely in order to gain the perspective from which the distinction between the exception and normality can be grasped functionally.

By imposing an *epoché* on how a given legal order drives the difference between the exception and normality, the concept of exceptionality grasps better the relations between the political and the legal. The exception is where the political seems to intervene directly in the legal. Still, it does so in the *theatrum* of normativity through channels that the legal system itself tries to determine. By allowing ourselves to be lured by exceptional institutions, such as the state of exception, we are mired in the internal ideology of the law. Meanwhile, if we relativise the distinction between the exception and normality to the operation of a given legal system—being itself a politico-legal entanglement—we are able to desubstantialise these terms and see their operations.

The exception is neither stable nor eternal; it does not have a firmly ontological or metaphysical status. It is rather permanently produced and reproduced by allocating exceptionality in particular loci. In turn, exceptionality can be seen as a quantum of energy that each legal system contains, which can be differently spread between various incarnations of 'exceptional' or 'normal' institutions and acts. These can be described by a term borrowed from psychoanalysis that we will elaborate further: cathexis. But there is no cathexis of exceptionality that would not produce an excess, a surplus outside its binding. Perhaps in modernity, Horace's maxim *naturam expelles furca, tamen usque recurret* should apply to exceptionality more than to nature. This return is visible in typical categorisations of exceptional measures. What they usually try to grasp is how much the law records and binds exceptionality—and how much remains outside. For example, Gross and Ní Aoláin distinguish between three models: extra-legal measures, accommodation and business as usual—construed according to the degree to which the

45 Therefore, if we define exceptionality only from within a given legal order, we will not recognise a great part of its work outside of the intra-normative distinction between normality and the exception. On the attempts to find a definition of exceptional measures, see Saint-Bonnet, *L'état d'exception*, 6–7; Loevy, *Emergencies in Public Law*, 48–53.

46 See Clement Fatovic, *Outside the Law. Emergency and Executive Power* (Baltimore: The Johns Hopkins University Press 2009) 2; Gross and Ní Aoláin, *Law in Times of Crisis*, 8, 59–60, 65.

law makes exceptionality visible (extra-legal measures suspend the law in the name of necessity, business as usual connotes using exceptionality within regular rules and accommodation is the middle way: exceptional devices).[47] What this categorisation demonstrates is that exceptionality permeates the law while remaining its *extime* (to use Lacan's term[48]) other, both most internal and always excessive.

The colonisation and distribution of exceptionality within the legal system is its permanent expenditure. One thing remains unquestionable for the general theory of exception: *there is no legal system without exceptionality.* The reason for this is structural. *Exceptionality preserves—within the legal system—the politico-legal substratum on which this system depends.* In other words, the existence of exceptionality corresponds to the primordial lack of autonomy of the legal system and its external dependence, which casts an excrescent shadow on this system itself. Exceptionality can be obfuscated, masked, diluted or dissimulated, but it remains within the legal just as cosmic microwave background in the universe after the Big Bang: *a trace of its both founding and ongoing event.* The legal system is born in a non-legal way and this act produces an excess of energy—exceptionality—that the legal system needs to normalise, compartmentalise and manage.

For this reason, the status of the exception cannot be satisfyingly explained only on normative grounds. Not only because the exception is declared by the sovereign, whose belonging to the normative system is at best partial; not only because the exception is a window through which the political appears as directly acting within the legal; but most importantly because a concrete form of the exception is an incarnation of exceptionality that the legal system inherits—both epochally and concretely. The persistence of exceptionality is a token that the legal system is fundamentally dependent on forces of a different nature than its own. This external otherness is cast upon the normative tissue—hence exceptionality becomes trapped and colonised within legal institutions and apparatuses—but contains a referential trace of the non-legal. Consequently, the position of exceptionality within the legal system can be seen in an immunological paradigm developed by Roberto Esposito:[49]

47 Gross and Ní Aoláin, *Law in Times of Crisis*, 12–17, 86, 110–111.

48 *Extime* in Lacan's thought connotes something 'ce qui nous est le plus prochain, tout en nous étant extérieur'. Jacques Lacan, *Le Séminaire. Livre XVI—De l'Autre à l'autre* (Seuil 2006) 224.

49 Esposito diagnoses the immunological logic as based on a negation of negation, a paradoxical, elusive way of absorbing what is harmful: 'la logica immunitaria rimanda a una non-negazione, alla negazione di una negazione. Il negativo non soltanto sopravvive alla cura, ma ne costituisce la condizione di efficacia. . . . [I]l carattere strutturalmente aporetico della procedura immunitaria: non potendo raggiungere direttamente il proprio obiettivo, è costretta a perseguirlo rovesciato. Ma, cosí facendo, lo trattiene nell'orizzonte di senso del proprio opposto: può prolungare la vita solo facendole di continuo assaggiare la morte'. Roberto Esposito, *Immunitas. Protezione e negazione della vita* (Einaudi 2002) 10–11.

the law is colonised through self-produced neoplasmic tissue, created by the reaction of the legal against its external anchoring. As Karen Loevy noticed, emergency (in her nomenclature) represents a field of *reactions* of the legal system.[50] Therefore, in a broad sense, the general theory of exception sides with Schmitt rather than Heller[51] because it construes 'normality' as a *normalised* state, produced and permanently supported by negative forces of resistance against the non-legal roots of the legal. But, admittedly, the law is itself on the side of normality precisely because it strives to extricate itself from the non-legal. It is in this context that we should read the never-ending discussion on whether the law can or cannot regulate necessity through exceptional measures.[52] This dilemma has no answer: in modern legal systems, as we will see, exceptionality remains an irremovable remainder that the law can distribute and manage but not eradicate.

If so, then the old adage *necessitas non cognoscet legem*[53] should be rather read in the context of its obverse supplement: *lex cognoscet necessitatem.* Not only does the legal know the non-legal, but it aims to brace itself against it and produce normative-factual devices to cushion the blow that comes from the outside.[54] The law, as such, can thus be seen as both a process and product of normalisation, then awkwardly delegated to underdetermined 'social sciences' for investigation. The law is thus never a 'normality' as such—which constitutes just a phantasmatic goal of the normative

50 Loevy, *Emergencies in Public Law*, 10–13.

51 Heller meanwhile assumes a rather tranquil entwinement between the constitution in a broad sense (*Verfassung*) and legal as well as non-legal norms permeating social life and making possible social life. Normality is a starting point, although it needs to be 'strengthened and completed' (*'verstärkt und ergänzt'*) by normativity. Heller assumes a double-layer binding: the normalising power of normativity (*'die normalisierende Kraft der Normativen'*) corresponds to the bottom-up normative power of the factually normal (*'die normative Kraft des faktisch Normalen'*). Hermann Heller, 'Staatslehre' in Christoph Müller (ed), *Gesammelte Schriften. Dritter Band* (Mohr Siebeck 1992) 363–365.

52 See Agamben, *State of Exception*, 17–28; Saint-Bonnet, *L'état d'exception*, 362; Loevy, *Emergencies in Public Law*, 25–33, 258–271; Barczak, *Der nervöse Staat*, 149–172; Dyzenhaus, *The Constitution of Law*, 34–53; Gross, 'Providing for the Unexpected' 17–21; Ferejohn and Pasquino 'The Law of Exception' 230–231; Monod, *Penser l'ennemi, affronter l'exception*, 75–76; Oren Gross, 'Extra-Legality and the Ethic of Political Responsibility' in Victor Ramraj (ed), *Emergencies and the Limits of Legality* (CUP 2008) 60–75.

53 François Saint-Bonnet noticed the paradoxical relation of agency that necessity has towards the law: at the same time 'nécessité fait loi' and 'nécessité n'a point de loi'. Saint-Bonnet, *L'état d'exception*, 2. At the same time necessity can be used in order to differentiate between the state of exception from emergency: '[t]he state of exception in a specific sense presupposes a constitutional order, while the state of emergency is a general category without specific reference to an existing order, because *necessitas non habet legem*'. George Schwab, *The Challenge of the Exception. An Introduction to the Political Ideas of Carl Schmitt between 1921 and 1936* (Greenwood Press 1989) 7. On the role of necessity in the state of exception, see also Böckenförde, 'Der verdrängte Ausnahmezustand', 1885.

54 For a brief overview of exceptional devices, see Gross, 'Providing for the Unexpected' 22–28; Ferejohn and Pasquino, 'The Law of Exception', 215–217.

system—but a permanent struggle to constitute itself as normal by repelling the non-legal and managing its traces through compartmentalisation of exceptionality.

The internal ideologies of the law are, therefore, an almost natural counterpart to the process of normalisation through which the modern legal system comes into being. This system creates—during normalisation—its own past and future, distributing the otherness of exceptionality into a temporal frame. Just as in Benjaminian perspective, history is written by victors,[55] so within the legal ideology, history is written from the position of the normalised law. In this account, the law has a history, whereas the exception appears as Freud's unconscious,[56] that is, in itself non-temporal and ahistorical, always present. This is a patent myth of legal ideology: the 'non-normal' of the law has its own tale but reconstructable only from the perspective of exceptionality. In a nutshell, exceptionality is a means to grasp *the internal historicity of what is exceptional but was relegated to a special zone of posited atemporality*.

If so, the general theory of exception needs to offer a crafted account of how exceptionality relates to temporality. Such a task, contrary to what may appear at first sight, does not boil down to mere archivisation. The division between the exception and normality is not neutral in relation to history:[57] as we mentioned previously, history takes the side of normality by the very force of its construction. As a consequence, the exception does not have a temporality in the proper meaning of the term, as it is obfuscated by the normative history that clarifies its position and role. In order to search for its temporal dimension, we need to reach the level of exceptionality, from which not only the history proper to normality appears in its construction but also particular instances of exceptional acts and measures are preserved and recorded as *traces*.

The exception haunts the history of legal normality. And just as it is proper to spectres, it does not have a daylight story. The official narrative that it possesses is an apparent eternity which it receives from the compartmentalisation within legal institutions—such as the state of exception. If we read the exception through the lens of such institutions, we never reach its proper temporality; what we receive is an artificial atemporal phantasmatic structure produced by legal ideology.[58] The temporality of the exception can

55 Walter Benjamin, 'On the Concept of History' in *Illuminations. Essays and Reflections* Hannah Zohn transl. (Schocken Books, 1969) 256.

56 'In the unconscious nothing can be brought to an end, nothing is past or forgotten'. Sigmund Freud, *The Interpretation of Dreams* James Strachey transl. (Basic Books 2010) 576.

57 On the more conventional problems with writing history of exceptional measures, see Saint-Bonnet, *L'état d'exception*, 4.

58 As Ninon Grangé noticed (but with a reference to the state of exception, not exceptionality): 'L'état d'exception est un état traduit, fruit d'un recodage, marqué par le passage rhétorique par la guerre, assuré par le paradigme de l'état de siège. Il transforme un ou des événements

be rather reconstructed from *marks* that it leaves on the legal system—marks seen as irruptions of the exceptional and the political into the field protected and supported by the permanent process of normalisation.[59] Most importantly, only the perspective of exceptionality allows for reconstructing the exceptional mark in acts or measures that were first adopted as exceptions but later have been normalised. Seen in this light, *the legal system is a palimpsest of exceptionalisations and normalisations, engaged in a complex historical interplay in which the current position of the exception/distinction reflects the current goals of the system but obfuscates its past.*

Exceptionality has its own temporality, but it is reconstructable only genealogically (in the Foucauldian sense):[60] as a discontinuous and cracked form of temporality, mystified by all-too-neat proper stories of normality with which it intersects. It can be identified from the acts of proclaiming exceptional states, acts of terminating them, as well as from all procedures of normalisation that happen afterwards. Still, it seems that there is a certain ontological memory of exceptionality, a form of spectral recurrence of exceptional measures and acts. And again, as in the case of Freud's unconscious, it works its way through an obscure gravitational pull on the normal, bending it towards extraordinary measures. This gravitational influence is—to tap into Foucault's reworking of Clausewitz's concept—a war with other means:[61] a trace of how, in the long run, the distinction between normality and the exception preserves and retraces an old struggle that has its roots in the origins of modernity.

In this light, exceptionality can be seen as a *fil rouge* of the historical forms of the legal systems, one that allows us to see how *different horizontal stories of legal normality are threaded onto one string* that cannot be seen without taking into account the exceptional dimension. Exceptionality is thus a discontinuous counterpart to a stream of ideologically continuous histories that obfuscate their origins.

Consequently, it is not possible to identify what measures are 'truly' exceptional or normal. Instead, we can have two strategies. The first one, quite typical in legal scholarship, keeps to the normative level of the exception: we can determine how given acts and measures are labelled in a current legal system, taking into account the interplay between the normative qualification

en une réalité hors du commun, il ouvre le temps et un espace politiques différents de ceux que l'on mesure et délimite par une linéarité historique régulière'. Grangé, *L'urgence et l'effroi*, 284.

59 It is in this light that we can read Ninon Grangé's claim that the temporality of the exception is not historical, but political. Grangé, *L'urgence et l'effroi*, 18–19, 286.

60 Michel Foucault, 'Nietzsche, Genealogy, History' in *Language, Counter-Memory, Practice. Selected Essays and Interviews* Donald F. Bouchard and Sherry Simon transl. (Cornell University Press 1977) 140.

61 Michel Foucault, *"Society Must Be Defended". Lectures at the Collège de France 1975–1976* David Macey transl. (Picador 2003) 15.

and the effective actions and consequences. In other words, in this approach, we can analyse to which extent a given act or measure deviates from the general normative framework (e.g., constitution or international law), whether it was adopted lawfully or not, as well as confront it with social reality through the lens of sociology of law.

The second strategy is properly genealogical: it attempts to retrieve the obfuscated archive of exceptions and normalisations, grasping them from the perspective of exceptionality. Its intrinsic value consists of the ability to functionalise the normative distinctions between the exception and normality and relativise them to their political purposes. Moreover, only within this perspective, we can identify how exceptional traces mark allegedly normal acts and measures. In other words, we can decipher *the work of normalisation as a crucial tool of legal ideology.*

Ultimately, there are no measures which are 'essentially' exceptional; they can be identified in four dimensions: (1) defined as such by a given legal system and thus relative to its normative labelling, (2) in a comparative perspective, with identification of what kind of measures are typically exceptional in given types of systems or in a historical perspective, (3) read as such in genealogical perspective of a given legal system, in the palimpsest of exceptionalisations and normalisations or (4) through the tension between the official classification of an act or measure and the normalising/exceptionalising effect that it *actually* has on a certain stratum of the society (including the cognitive dissonance for the lower class that experience a subdued war against itself amongst illusions of societal tranquility). Finally, the genealogical strategy offers a possibility of reconstructing the *longue durée* of exceptional acts and measures, their iterability and the undead recurrence that permeates reaction patterns of legal systems.[62] It is thus focused on the trans-historical dimension, by which we can understand the unnarrated continuity and recurrence beyond—and through—official histories constructed by legal ideologies.

Every functioning legal system will attempt to maintain its internal congruence through a historical narrative whose function is normalisation. Hence, periods of emergency and exception will be declared finished by normalising procedures, such as declaring the end of the 'special time' and suspension or termination of institutions like the state of emergency.[63] At the same time, the practico-normative legacy of a special period will be absorbed into the system; some of the exceptional acts and measures will be normalised. It is quite typical to end the state of exception solemnly by adopting a new law which uptakes procedures and measures developed in the special period and,

62 On this strategy, see more in Przemyslaw Tacik, 'Exceptionality as the Gravitational Point of the Legal: The Example of the Polish Covid-19 Legislation in the Exceptional *Longue Durée*' (2021) 12:2 *Romanian J Comp L* 309.

63 Gross, 'Providing for the Unexpected' 33–34.

under the guise of 'needs of new normality', introduces them into the legal system as 'normal' provisions. Historicisation proper to every legal system—and its ideology—will describe this process as natural re-establishment of the standard everydayness.

Against this ideological vision of the legal system, which always returns to its 'normality' after periods of challenge, we should—in the general theory of exception—oppose the vision of exceptionality as the beating heart of legality. *Contractions and expansions of exceptionality produce marks that constitute the real genealogy of a legal system.* Legality emerges through a primordial normalisation and distribution of exceptionality through an act of contraction. Conversely, the expansion of exceptionality eats away at the effects of normalisation.

To sum up, the general theory of exception needs to pierce through the shroud of mystification that enfolds the relationship between the exception and normality. *Legality does not exist without its procedures of normalisation of exceptionality*, part of which is the permanent struggle to isolate, fix and manage its excess into legal institutions. Normalisation of exceptionality is—as we will see—the cornerstone of the myth of the law, which works, esp. without its political foundation. Agamben rightly noticed that wherever we pose the question of the exception, we touch upon the law's very ability to be applied. In other words, *the key to the myth of applicability lies in the obfuscating normalisation of exceptionality.*

Exceptionality remains a hidden component within the application of the law, with which the law plays itself. In a nutshell, the more the law tries to caulk the relation between a norm and its act of application, the more it needs to seal off exceptionality within special legal institutions such as the state of exception. Nonetheless, exceptionality remains a form of non-normative excessive energy that traverses the legal system. The law cannot function without it; at the same time, defects in its flux may disturb the effectiveness of law application.

With all these introductory foundations, we can now progress to building the general theory of exception.

2.3 Elements of the General Theory of Exception

2.3.1 The Axes of the Exception

The exception within modern law gains attention due to its being a focal point for three separate, though interrelated problems. First, the exception does not refer to a cluster of marginal institutions occasionally used in the law; the relative rarity of their use—especially in relation to normal measures—does not reflect its true role. The exception cannot be accounted for in terms of the statistical prevalence of normal situations over exceptional ones. *Its role can be grasped when the exception is seen in relation to the entire legal system* as its special point and—to a certain extent—a symptom.

In other words, the exception—no matter how practically insignificant it would be, how rarely it would be used or what normative role it would don in a particular legal order—remains part of the machinery that makes the law applicable. Therefore, the exception belongs to the domain of *possibility*: it does not need to be used (and, in fact, formally, it is not often used in liberal democracies)[64] in order to remain a permanent eventuality which, precisely in this suspended state, shapes the solid *actuality* of the legal order. Schmitt recognised this feature of the exception with great acuity by noticing that it corresponds to the sovereign. Meanwhile, as I argued elsewhere,[65] modern sovereignty also belongs to the domain of ultimate possibility rather than actuality. In more colloquial terms, both the exception and the sovereign belong to the bottom line of every legal order; its *nec plus ultra*, the final support, the one which intervenes when everything else is lost. For this reason, the exception, no matter how it is buried in a given legal institution, exudes a peculiar glow, as if revealing its extra-legal nature at the heart of the legal.

Secondly, the exception is also a key to the crucial problem of modern sovereignty: its split. The sovereign identified in the Schmittean way—the one who will decide on the exception and defend the politico-legal order—does not correspond to the sovereigns nominally identified by most constitutions, that is, nations. The former will say that it acts in the name of the latter for the latter's survival, but, of course, the nation as the nominal sovereign will not 'itself' trigger an exceptional state or adopt an exceptional measure. In other words, we can say that modern polities are based on the split of the sovereign between two incarnations: the designated (the ultimate defender) and the imaginary (the nation). The situation is even more complicated if we take into account that the designated sovereign itself splits into two: the one envisaged in the constitution and the one that will have actually exercised this function. History of coups following exceptional proclamations demonstrates that the latter two do not necessarily need to overlap. Constitutions predict the designated sovereign to be ready to act, although that might not happen.[66]

The split between the nation as the imaginary sovereign and the one designated by the constitution interacts, albeit does not overlap, with the split between *pouvoir constitué* and *pouvoir constituant*.[67] The nation exercising

64 Ferejohn and Pasquino, 'The Law of Exception', 215.

65 Przemysław Tacik, *A New Philosophy of Modernity and Sovereignty. Towards Radical Historicisation* (Bloomsbury 2021) 29–31, 115–130.

66 See Hofmann, 'Souveran ist, wer über den Ausnahmezustand entscheidet', 174–175.

67 Emmanuel Joseph Sieyès, 'What is the Third Estate?' in *Political Writings* Michael Sonenscher transl. (Hackett 2003) 135–136; Claude Klein, *Théorie et pratique du pouvoir constituant* (Presses Universitaires de France 1996); Joel Colón-Rios, 'Five Conceptions of

pouvoir constituant will accept (or reject) a draft constitution rather than pen it by itself (whatever this should mean). It requires an 'operator' who will act as its speaker. It is the designated sovereign that not only stands for the imaginary one—governing it, representing it, saving it from calamities—but also creates it as a symbolic agent through its discourse. Once a nation 'has' a state, this state produces it retroactively, defining and managing it. But if an exceptional period features a dissolution within the designated sovereign between the nominal and the effective ones (for example, a military coup makes a certain functionary claim exceptional powers instead of the head of state or the government, whichever holds it according to the constitution), then exceptionality performs a reshuffle within *pouvoir constituant*.

But it would be a mistake to believe that only the designated sovereign exists, whereas the imaginary one acts as a mere legitimising prop. As Foucault demonstrated in his biopolitical analyses,[68] modern politics revolves around the question of the survival of the people (not accidentally, Hobbes makes it a crucial condition of establishing the body politic).[69] In critical moments, the effective sovereign is embarked on the task of guaranteeing survival, although the practical aspects of this survival itself may be variously understood. Moreover, as demonstrated by the right of peoples to self-determination, the destruction of the effective sovereign (collapse of the state) does not annihilate the possibility of restoring state sovereignty with the forces of the people.[70] In this sense, *the people act both as a tacit object and agent of survival, calling for and restoring, if need be, the effective sovereign*. The exception is the focal point in which this link comes into light. Precisely for this reason, wherever the exception is invoked, survival appears as a category and a goal. Therefore, the exception brings into question the crucial modern myth of the sovereign people 'governing itself', but through an intermediary who runs the distinction between the exception and the normal.

Thirdly and finally, the exception is also a *place* through which the axis between the political and the legal passes. As we noticed in the previous subchapter, an exceptional institution is an excrescence on the corpus of the law, through which it aims to contain and fix the intrusion of the political

Constituent Power' (2014) 13:2 *LQR* 306; Martin Loughlin, 'The Concept of Constituent Power' (2014) 13:2 *Eur J Pol Theory* 218; Yaniv Roznai, *Unconstitutional Constitutional Amendments. The Limits of Amendment Powers* (OUP 2017) 105–110; Mark Tushnet, *Advanced Introduction to Comparative Constitutional Law* (Edward Elgar 2014) 13–18; Yaniv Roznai, '"We the People", "Oui, the People" and the Collective Body: Perceptions of Constituent Power' in Gary Jacobsohn and Michael Schor (eds), *Comparative Constitutional Theory* (Edward Elgar 2014) 295–315.

68 Foucault, "*Society Must Be Defended*", 239–240.

69 Thomas Hobbes, *Leviathan* J. C. A. Gaskin transl. (OUP 1996) 86–88.

70 Jörg Fisch, *The Right of Self-Determination of Peoples. The Domestication of an Illusion* Anita Mage transl. (CUP 2015) 221; Elena Konnova, 'The Right to Self-Determination and Time' in Sebastian Wuschka (ed), *Zeit und Internationales Recht* (Mohr Siebeck 2019) 292–298.

acting in relation to the whole legal order (as opposed to the political curbed in 'normal' institutions). Consequently, the exception is not just a containment of the political by the legal—or, in a converse manner, the emissary of the political within the legal. Numerous norms, especially of public law, are the containment of the political by the legal, most notably almost entire constitutions. But, the exception is the ultimate remainder of the process of exceptionalisation, the final thread by which all contained incarnations of the political are held within the legal system. For this reason, the exception brings to the fore what is concealed in every norm: the political component of the legal, which gives the latter the power to apply its norms.

The fascinating power of the exception lies precisely in the fact that it becomes the focal point of all these three relations. Addressing the exception in such complexity must become the task of a general theory of exception.

2.3.2 *Philosophical Engines of Thinking the Exception*

The question is, however, what kind of philosophical engine should be employed in order to build it. As I mentioned in the previous subchapter, the example of Schmitt's conceptualisation clearly proves that the dialectical paradigm, inspired by Hegel, is a gateway into giving the exception the proper revealing role within legal systems. Indeed, if the exception is to be grasped as a local point corresponding to the entire totality of the legal order and revealing its inner machinery, dialectics seems most adapted to capture the interplay between the local and the total. Psychoanalytically informed versions of dialectics, such as Žižek's theory (especially from the periods marked by books such as *The Parallax View*,[71] *Less Than Nothing*[72] and *Absolute Recoil*[73]), are perfectly crafted to grasp the exception as the symptom of the totality to which it refers despite its apparent empirical marginality.

Nonetheless, it remains an open question of what incarnation of dialectics—or post-dialectics—should be used. In *Political Theology*, Schmitt mentions Hegel marginally and in reference to his theory of the state and of history rather than dialectical thinking.[74] Still, it is clear that since the beginning of this work, when he claims that the problem of sovereignty is to be sought in the 'borderline case and not with routine',[75] he engages in his own form of open Hegelian dialectics, which does not seek reconciliation between the norm and the exception, but inquisitively analyses their mutual relations.

71 Slavoj Žižek, *The Parallax View* (MIT Press 2009).
72 Slavoj Žižek, *Less Than Nothing. Hegel and the Shadow of Dialectical Materialism* (Verso 2012).
73 Slavoj Žižek, *Absolute Recoil. Towards a New Foundation of Dialectical Materialism* (Verso 2014).
74 Schmitt, *Political Theology* 29, 44, 50, 54. See also Gross, 'The Normless and Exceptionless Exception', 1840–1842.
75 Schmitt, *Political Theology*, 5. See also Monod, *Penser l'ennemi, affronter l'exception*, 103.

Moreover, Schmitt employs the classically dialectical 'thinking in three dimensions': the exception and the norm are linked not only on the surface of the legal system, within its own logic and narrative, but more importantly, there is a whole concealed machinery underneath that crises bring to light.[76] Naturally, for those clinging to legal ideology, this appears at best a hermeneutics of suspicion, to use Paul Ricœur's concept.

Once we accept the dialectical starting point, the real dilemmas reveal themselves. The legacy of dialectics in the 20th and 21st centuries, from Adorno and Lacan up to Derrida and Žižek—to name just a few thinkers—is a twisted path of searching subtlety and shunning decisive totalisations. If so, what line of dialectics should we use? Schmitt's version of it contrasts with Agamben's thought primarily as to the philosophical procedures that are performed on the exception as a dialectical starting point. Given that there is no place here to develop a self-standing study of differences between these two thinkers, suffice it to say that Agamben engages in a form of post-dialectics that brings the analysis of the relationship between the exception and the totality to a programmatic suspension. Agamben's keyword here is 'indistinction'. In one of the early passages of *Homo sacer*, he notices:

> The situation created in the exception has the peculiar characteristic that it cannot be defined either as a situation of fact or as a situation of right, but instead *institutes a paradoxical threshold of indistinction between the two* [emphasis added]. It is not a fact, since it is only created through the suspension of the rule. But for the same reason, it is not even a juridical case in point, even if it opens the possibility. of the force of law. . . . In this sense, the sovereign exception is the fundamental localization (*Ortung*), which does not limit itself to distinguishing what is inside from what is outside but instead *traces a threshold (the state of exception) between the two, on the basis of which outside and inside, the normal situation and chaos, enter into those complex topological relations that make the validity of the juridical order possible* [emphasis added].[77]

'Indistinction' as a philosophical term[78] found a way of thinking which can be seen as a particular solution to the problem of post-dialectics: how to navigate the legacy of Hegel. This problem has haunted 20th-century philosophy,

76 On the role of the exception in circumscribing the boundaries of the law, see Finke, 'Funktion und Wirkung der Ausnahme im Recht', 524, 540.

77 Schmitt, *Political Theology*, 18–19.

78 As noticed by William Watkin, 'Agamben habitually places the reader in what he calls a zone or threshold of indistinction, inoperativity, indiscernibility, suspension or indifference. He uses various terms to name the zone and various other terms to designate its specific quality, but the structure is always the same'. William Watkin, *Agamben and Indifference. A Critical Overview* (Rowman & Littlefield 2014) xi.

at least since Lukács. Agamben's proposal is not far from deconstruction; similarly to Derrida, he opts for *immobilisation* of dialectical difference, although the roots of this practice are more openly late-Heideggerian than in the case of Derrida. Agamben's version of immobilisation identifies a certain *site* in which the entanglement is *located* precisely in order to hold the problematic excess in one area and apparently free the rest of the legal system from it. In other words, his thinking about indistinction corresponds to how the exception effectively manages it. This peculiar correspondence between thought and reality is naturally also a dialectical gesture. Analogously, Agamben performs another significant dialectical overlap: he uses the term 'state of exception' both for a legal institution of this name and *an actual state of indistinction* that becomes produced—deliberately or accidentally from the perspective of the legal system—in a given site.

Derrida's approaches, in turn, would be more complex. One strategy would be to perform a thorough deconstruction of a certain entanglement of concepts and institutions, which will result in identifying problematic excesses in them that correspond to aporias. A general example from *Force de loi*—focused on the status of the law—gives a telling illustration:

> Since the origin of authority, the foundation or ground, the position of the law can't by definition rest on anything but themselves, they are themselves a violence without ground. Which is not to say that they are in themselves unjust, in the sense of 'illegal.' They are neither legal nor illegal in their founding moment. They exceed the opposition between founded and unfounded, or between any foundationalism or anti-foundationalism. Even if the success of performatives that found law or right (for example, and this is more than an example, of a state as guarantor of a right) presupposes earlier conditions and conventions (for example in the national or international arena), the same 'mystical' limit will reappear at the supposed origin of said conditions, rules or conventions, and at the origin of their dominant interpretation.[79]

The primordial recognition of this incarnation of deconstruction concerns untameable and unfixable excess that haunts concepts and devices. They participate in a game that they cannot control, being subjected to dissemination and aporeticality dynamically organised around a third non-term.[80] But, another dimension that Derrida's deconstruction brings to law concerns the

79 Jacques Derrida, 'Force of Law: The "Mystical Foundation of Authority"' in Drucilla Cornell, Michel Rosenfeld and David Gray Carlson (eds), *Deconstruction and the Possibility of Justice* (Routledge 1992) 14.
80 Jacques Derrida, *La dissémination* (Seuil 1993) 35–36.

relation between two fundamental categories: the present and the trace. In *Of Grammatology*, he notices that

> [t]he reassuring evidence within which Western tradition had to organize itself and must continue to live would therefore be as follows: the order of the signified is never contemporary, is at best the subtly discrepant inverse or parallel—discrepant by the time of a breath—from the order of the signifier. And the sign must be the unity of a heterogeneity, since the signified (sense or thing, noeme or reality) is not in itself a signifier, *a trace:* in any case is not constituted in its sense by its relationship with a possible trace. The formal essence of the signified is *presence*, and the privilege of its proximity to the logos as *phonè* is the privilege of presence. This is the inevitable response as soon as one asks: 'what is the sign?,' that is to say, when one submits the sign to the question of essence, to the 'ti esti.' The 'formal essence' of the sign can only be determined in terms of presence.[81]

This theme of deconstruction, one of the oldest, allows of dismantling structures of legal ideology that can be dubbed *metaphysics of applicability*. The law exists mainly in writing. Accordingly, just as—according to Derrida—the dimension of writing is covered up by the idea of a perfect sign referring to a present referent, a guarantor of stability, so is the law stabilised by the belief that it is *structurally applicable*. Its dimension of writing is ultimately held in place by the conviction that its norms will retain its *possibility of application*. This allows for abstracting from the law's actual effectivity, which is relegated to the domain of factuality. The normative order is, in a sense, always self-referential: it assumes that it needs to be applied and can be applied, only to be satisfied with the result. In other words, the law stabilises itself and, by itself, re-presenting itself with its own myth.

What would Derrida's deconstruction offer as a paradigm for interpreting the exception? Aporeticality of oppositions and their inherent excess is one ingredient. In particular, the distinction between the exception and normality should not be seen as stiff, even within the constructionist paradigm. Although relative to a given politico-legal constellation, it never fully manages to present a solid picture of actual normality supported by trapping exceptionality in institutions. *Exceptionality is a dimension ruled by inertia*: to paraphrase Nietzsche, exceptions cast long shadows and die slowly.[82] The second ingredient borrowed from deconstruction proves valuable here: despite the obfuscating need of legal institutions to present themselves—incarnate the apparent eternity of applicability—they are ravaged by traces. As we mentioned earlier, the concept of trace—or even more radically, of *an exceptional*

81 Derrida, *Of Grammatology*, 18.
82 Friedrich Nietzsche, *The Gay Science* Josephine Nauckhoff transl. (CUP 2001) 109.

scar on the corpus of the law—allows for grasping the proper history of exceptionality.[83] The law does not return to its former shape after the use of exceptional measures: such an assumption would be, above all, a fallacy of presentism that the law itself aims to produce. Effective functioning of the law can be grasped only with reference to the effects of exceptional scarification and the inner *longue durée* of exceptionality.[84]

Finally, we can identify a Protean paradigm of thinking, the exception that—although in a loose relation to Foucault's philosophy—can be dubbed Foucauldian. Just as Foucault dropped analyses of 'big concepts', especially sovereignty, focusing instead on practices, discontinuous patterns of thinking, genealogy of institutions, etc.[85]—so does this paradigm move beyond the realm of acting concepts, the exception and normality, to grasp the whole plurality of practices that happen around the exception: in parliaments, governments, courts, law enforcement, institutions and the society. Karin Loevy appears as a key proponent of this approach; she presented her paradigm in the following words:

> This book frames the field of emergency powers beyond the dichotomy. It methodologically assumes that to frame a field implies, first and foremost, to define the space within which the practices of the field occur. The practices of emergency management do not respond to the dichotomy between the normal and exceptional but to theoretical and practical problems, questions, and tensions . . . . [T]he book distinguishes emergencies not by legal limits and political decision but by dynamic engagement, norm productivity, and contestations over the terms of response to threatening events.[86]

This paradigm makes visible the practical consequences of the exception, its spread throughout the society and the inevitable counter-reaction and contestation. By doing so, it effectively demonstrates how legal fiction—the state of exception, the exception, normality—disfigure the changes in social reality

83 Tristan Barczak also noticed the process that we can call here 'exceptional scarification'. It consists of the formal repeal of a previously proclaimed state of exception (state of emergency, etc.) and transfer of exceptional measures to legal instruments now dubbed normal. As Barczak claims, this results in 'einer erheblichen sicherheitsrechtlichen Verschärfung des Normalzustands bei einigen Abschwächungen von Geringer praktischer Reichweite'. Nonetheless, he also recognises 'resilience of the law': its ability to recompose itself after the intrusion of the exceptional. See Barczak, *Der nervöse Staat*, 345, 606–617, 682.

84 On the awareness of the traces that the use of exceptional measures can leave in the legal system, see Fionnuala Ni Aolain and Oren Gross, 'A Sceptical View of Deference to the Executive in Times of Crisis' (2008) 41:3 *Israel L R* 545, 546.

85 Foucault, "*Society Must be Defended*", 1–64; see also Eli B. Lichtenstein, 'Foucault's Analytics of Sovereignty' (2021) *J Phil Soc Theory* 22, 287.

86 Loevy, *Emergencies in Public Law*, 5.

provoked by exceptional measures. In this light, exceptional measures are read as sociological facts whose formal legal status is seen more in its practical consequences rather than normative labels.

All the preceding considerations bring us to resuming the initial question: what kind of philosophical engine can be used in order to build the general theory of exception? It definitely needs to be rooted in dialectics but also aptly use the post-dialectical legacy described previously. The exception that we investigate is not just a simple internal limitation of a rule, which has accompanied legality since its beginnings.[87] The exception is explicable only in dialectical terms of how it relates to the totality of the legal order: how it sets it in motion, how it preserves exceptionality and conceals it as potentialities within legal institutions. This kind of exception—as we will see—emerges with the onset of modern law based on the sovereign. Another useful source of inspiration will be psychoanalysis, not necessarily in terms of concepts, but structures of thinking. If we conceive of exceptionality as excess energy that haunts the legal system, we can easily adapt the Freudian concept of *Besetzung* (maladroitly translated into English as 'cathexis'[88]) in order to explain how legality attempts to capture it in institutions.

All these traditions should allow us to conceive *the exception as an effectively fleeting configuration of exceptionality, fixed in a given boundary between the exception and normality as a result of the process of normalisation performed by the law in order to gain applicability and stability.* The exception cannot be understood without referring it dialectically to a broader framework of exceptionality—both synchronically, in all the functions that it and diachronically, that is, including the map of traces (normalisations and exceptionalisations) that scar the legal system in its historical dimension. The very concept of exceptionality allows us to *build a general theory of the field*, one that does not only dialectically relativise its elements (the exception to normality, the exception to the state of exception, etc.), but provides an overarching framework that mediates between all of them. Most importantly, the general theory of exception does not aim to relate it to the legal system; on the contrary, both the exception and the legal system need to be explained as entangled but separate entities. For this reason, the main concept of this theory is *exceptionality in its effective activity within legal systems.*

87 Therefore, I believe that purely linguistic and temporally universalist attempts to define the exception—as a necessary by-product of a general rule—obfuscate the role of exceptionality in modern law. On exception from the linguistic point of view, see Barbara Cassin, 'Exclure ou inclure l'exception?' in Spyros Théodorou (ed), *L'exception dans tous ses états* (Parenthèses 2007) 13–19.

88 Jean Laplanche and Jean-Bertrand Pontalis, *The Language of Psychoanalysis* Donald Nicholson-Smith transl. (London: The Hogarth Press 1973) 61–64.

In sum, the general theory of exception is able to give solid foundations to identify and functionalise four aspects of exceptionality-related matters. First, the role of the distinction between the exception and normality in a given legal order can be investigated by mapping their serrated line of division and relating it to their politico-legal functionalities. Second, it allows for identifying the ways in which a given legal order fixes and compartmentalises exceptionality within legal institutions. Third, as we will see in the two following chapters, the general theory of exception expounds the biopolitical role of exceptionality as a corollary of the modern idea of survival of the body politic. Finally, what opens up is the historical dimension of the legal order as an interplay of normalisations and exceptionalisations. As I will argue in Chapter 4, they can be seen as contractions of the legal around its exceptional core.

2.3.3 *Temporality of the Exception and Sovereign Control of the Future*

In the final part of his first chapter on sovereignty, Schmitt makes the following famous statement:

> The exception is more interesting than the rule. The rule proves nothing; the exception proves everything. It confirms not only the rule but also its existence, which derives only from the exception. In the exception the power of real life breaks through the crust of a mechanism that has become torpid by repetition.[89]

Schmitt's use of the category of life—symbolising energy, potency and creativity—is rooted deeply in the rightist imagery. It frequently returns in *The Concept of the Political*,[90] upholding the vision of 'real', irremovable competition between human beings as the natural part of their existence.[91] The previously cited fragment is meant to present the exception as a mechanism that stands on the side of the time itself. The norm appears as dysfunctional in the long run, repeating the old, often obsolete patterns, whereas the exception connotes an infusion of fresh, 'real' life, present-day circumstances. Together with a declaration of a clear primacy of the exception over the norm, Schmitt identifies the former with

89 Schmitt, *Political Theology*, 15.
90 Carl Schmitt, *The Concept of the Political* Georg Schwab transl. (The University of Chicago Press 2007).
91 'Just as the term enemy, the word combat, too, is to be understood in its original existential sense. It does not mean competition, nor does it mean pure intellectual controversy nor symbolic wrestlings in which, after all, every human being is somehow always involved, for it is a fact that the entire life of a human being is a struggle and every human being symbolically a combatant'. Schmitt, *The Concept of the Political*, 33.

interesting one-offs and the latter with the 'torpid' due to 'repetition'.[92] Given that repetition is the obvious condition of normativity—norms are laid down precisely to be applied repeatedly, creating patterns of action—this fragment is, in fact, a judgement passed on the law itself.

Before we scrutinise this vision in more theoretical depth, let us notice that Schmitt suggests how the relation between the exception and the norm corresponds to the way in which a given legal system—together with its politico-legal infrastructure—manages temporality. *Legislation can be seen as a foray of the past into the future, mediated by the present as the artificial time mark on an adopted norm.* No legal act arises in a given moment of the present, although it bears a daily date; it always carries both memory and accumulated traces of the past. But more importantly, the adoption of a legal norm is meant to preserve a certain type of resolution—for example, a way of deciding interests between individuals in civil law—in the moments to come. Hence, the natural conservatism of the law which always drags with itself the burden of past determinations. As a consequence, the application of the law constitutes a frontier conquerable through the forceful act of both interpretation and moving the law forward.

The areas of the legal order which are marked by exceptionality display a peculiar relation to temporality. They contain unusual openness to the future mixed with the traditional approach of normativity, that is, taming the future with the past. The less a given legal system attempts to regulate exceptionality—for example, the fewer norms control the proclamation and exercise of the state of exception—the more the future takes over the past. Günter Frankenberg noticed that proclamations of state of exceptions are focused on *transitions* (*Übergänge*);[93] these should also be understood as temporal marking points that strive to keep the balance between the future and the past. Regulating exceptional institutions is a permanent shifting front between the political and the legal, but not exclusively. As we said, it can be seen as part of the immunological fight of the legal system against non-legal intrusions. But this front represents the management of temporality as well. Measures marked by exceptionality represent intrusions of the future into the past out of which the legal system is carved.[94] In this sense, we can understand Schmitt's claim in the following way: the existence of exceptional measures may have a refreshing effect on the legal system by updating it to

92 On Schmitt's idea of 'torpidity' of law see Leonard C. Feldman, 'The Banality of Emergency: On the Time and Space of "Political Necessity"' in Austin Sarat (ed), *Sovereignty, Emergency, Legality* (CUP 2010) 141.

93 Günter Frankenberg, 'Im Ausnahmezustand' (2017) 50:1 *KritJ* 3, 4.

94 This thought develops the traditional claim that exceptional measures are the law's safety valves for situations that cannot be predicted. See Saint-Bonnet, *L'état d'exception*, 9; Grangé, *L'urgence et l'effroi*, 19. Böckenförde points out the structural imperfection of such safety valves, as the law cannot entirely predict the unpredictable. Böckenförde, 'Der verdrängte Ausnahmezustand', 1885.

present-day conditions. The crucial problem is, naturally, that this 'refreshment' takes place within a perturbed order of decision-making institutions, giving a strong preference to the executive over the legislative (which Schmitt theorised alongside the exception).[95]

This means, however, that the modern legal order would be permanently suspended between its normalised past—standing for the law, the legislative and the normal—and the pending future, for whose intervention exceptional measures and special prerogatives of the executive are preserved. The future is always-already embedded in the structure of the law: the exception acts as a guarantee that it remains open to what will happen. If we assume—anticipating Chapter 4—that modern law emerges historically in the process of normalisation of the power whose remnants we now recognise in the executive, then exceptionality would be both the remainder of the normalisation process and the paradoxical *trace of the future*. It thus resembles Ernst Bloch's paradoxical category of *Eingedenken*, remembrance of the future.[96] To strike a more philosophical tone, we could follow Bloch in his musings on the future concealed in the present:

> [t]here is much that contrasts with a mere Beginning, a simple Has-been. First of all there is the darkness of the present Moment, always impinging but never grasped, never in possession of itself. The darkness which means that every real beginning is a future thing, alive in the past as a fore-shadowing of the future. Or, to put in other words, the veiled presence of the future here-and-now is the open-ended darkness of each present Moment, is the pregnant state of all that it contains.[97]

From the perspective of exceptionality, the very existence of a modern legal order based on normalisation excludes its proper self-recognition. Consequently, it locates in exceptional areas the projection of its future, making it both an expectation and self-defence. In this dependence on exceptionality, modern law reveals its structural foundation in modern sovereignty. In a sense, modern law is tantamount to *the zone created by the contraction*

95 Carl Schmitt, *The Crisis of Parliamentary Democracy* Ellen Kennedy transl. (The MIT Press) 3–15. See also Gross, 'Providing for the Unexpected', 34.

96 'Wenn Erinnerung voraussetzt, daß etwas vergessen worden ist, so ist Vergessen insgesamt die Unterlassung, woran und wogegen Erinnern und Hoffen als Besinnung sich letzthin begegnen. Vom Ausfall Vergessen her erscheint Erinnerung als Mahnung, Hoffnung als Eingedenken . . . Vergessen ist ein Modus der Erinnerung wie des Eingedenkens, ist jenes Defiziens, das im Gedächtnis Verlassen, im Eingedenken Verrat heißt. Vergessen ist so Mangel an Treue und wieder nicht einer Treue gegen Erloschenes, sondern gegen Unabgegoltenes'. Ernst Bloch, *Werkausgabe, Band 13. Tübinger Einleitung in die Philosophie* (Suhrkamp 1985) 282.

97 Ernst Bloch, *Atheism in Christianity. The Religion of the Exodus and the Kingdom* (Verso 2006) 206.

of sovereignty. As we will see in Chapter 4, within this zone, exceptionality subsists like cosmic background radiation after the Big Bang.

The modern temporal relations between the norm and the exception are not just consequences of the most simple trait of normativity, namely the fact that every norm must somehow address unpredictable circumstances to come. It seems that the temporal dynamics revealed by exceptionality touches upon the very genealogy of modern legality in its dependence on sovereignty. The norm is positioned as the normalised past; the exception—is the irremovable intrusion of the future.[98] Exceptionality would thus reveal the legal order as a *corpus produced by normalisation—a corpus carved out of the past, whose structure rests on fundamental misrecognition of itself that calls for a supplement in the form of exceptional zones opening into the future.*

The link between the normative past and the exceptional future is also present in the very applicability of the law. For each norm, even the ones which fit factual circumstances almost without any doubt, the act of application entails a certain admixture of uncertainty as to its consequences. The act of applying the law—as perspicaciously noticed by Agamben[99]—is a leap, also in the temporal sense. Possible obsoleteness or inadequateness of a norm, which requires creative interpretation or simply an application of *praeter legem*, is one dimension, but it is independent of another one, in which *no norm can fit the 'facts' on its own*. The act of mediation between the norm and the facts, enquired by Schmitt and Agamben, is, therefore, a privileged site where exceptionality may intrude into the normative. Given the circumstances, exceptionality may diffuse throughout the legal system, with its resistance or not, with symbolic registration of exceptional measures or just tacit presence. But, from the side of legal exceptionality, it carries the norm into the future. Within 'normal' legality, exceptionality performs minor acts entirely obfuscated by legal ideology. In 'special' legality, however, it appears as a force that leaves its compartmentalisation within particular norms and condenses into one potency, related not to singular rules but to the entire legal system: this one potency is a *force that carries the entire legal system into its future, its own survival*. In other words, exceptionality can perform the day-to-day work of shifting every norm into its own small future, but in emergencies, it becomes one powerful lever that lifts the entire legal system into its generalised future. Quite importantly, the scope of compartmentalisation of exceptionality can easily be made operational in concrete analyses.

At the same time, exceptionality displays a concealed relation to the fundamental uncertainty that haunts every legality: the scepticism about

98 Karin Loevy proposes different models of reaction of legal systems to the future in relation to the exception. See Loevy, *Emergencies in Public Law*, 271–280.

99 Agamben, *Homo sacer*, 20–21.

rule-following. As Saul Kripke demonstrated[100] in relation to Wittgenstein's remarks from *Philosophical Investigations*,[101] there is a fundamental paradox of normativity: no finite set of past applications of a rule can determine its future applicability. In other words, although normativity seems to conquer the future with some past matrix of decision-making, *in itself* it can never determine it exhaustively. Setting aside the purely philosophical analyses of this paradox,[102] let us notice here that it concurs in many respects with Agamben's thought. *Normativity requires an external intervention so that it can leave its own realm.* What Wittgenstein names an impossible 'private language'—equivalent to thinking that one follows a rule[103]—can then be viewed as pure legality ensconced in its own way of functioning and ideology. From this realm, there is no internal step forward towards reality or the future; it can be done only in the dimension of which exceptionality is another part. The general name for this dimension is sovereignty.

From the legal perspective, sovereignty appears within the logic of supplement. It adds to the normative the strategic push so that it may touch the social reality through a decision. This also means that sovereignty seals the normative by adding to it the real dimension of the future. What we thus recognise in exceptionality is the shock wave that surrounds every legality: through this shock wave, the legal order meets its temporal outside. In other words, time flows into the legal order through a lock of channelled exceptionality. It is a boundary in which temporality planned by the law confronts the temporality of reality itself—that is, the temporality of unpredictable happening.

2.4 Conclusions

This chapter was meant to lay down the foundations for the general theory of exception, which aims to develop, generalise and reframe concepts familiar to studies of exceptional measures. First of all, the philosophical engine of thinking the exception needs to be updated, taking into account the legacy of post-dialectics and deconstruction. Its pivotal concept is exceptionality, conceived of as a *field of energy* rather than a stable locus. Exceptionality

100 Saul A. Kripke, *Wittgenstein on Rules and Private Language. An Elementary Exposition* (Harvard University Press 1982) 7–54.

101 Ludwig Wittgenstein, *Philosophical Investigations* G. E. M. Anscombe transl. (Blackwell 1958) 81.

102 G. P. Baker and P. M. S. Hacker, *Scepticism, Rules and Language* (Basil Blackwell 1984); Colin McGinn, *Wittgenstein on Meaning: An Interpretation and Evaluation* (Basil Blackwell 1984).

103 'And hence also "obeying a rule" is a practice. And to *think* one is obeying a rule is not to obey a rule. Hence it is not possible to obey a rule "privately": otherwise thinking one was obeying a rule would be the same thing as obeying it'. Wittgenstein, *Philosophical Investigations*, 81.

as energy is an inherent, proto-legal part of the legal system. It corresponds to particular *cathexes*—such as exceptional legal devices, e.g., the state of exception, *état de siege*[104] or state of emergency—through which the legal order aims to curb and channel it, although always leaving an ungovernable remainder of exceptionality. This theoretical move allows for grasping not only the historically changing and dialectical relation between exceptionality and its cathexes but also the irremovable excess of exceptionality vis-à-vis them.[105] Moreover, it paves the way for making the normality/exception distinction *a functional feature* of each legal system—corresponding to a variable and often incoherent map of its needs, both official and unavowed. This distinction is autonomous vis-à-vis exceptionality as such: parts of the 'normal' legal system may be actually exceptional, sparking off tensions, contradictions and socio-legal taboos. The exception as a sum of cathexes of exceptionality is thus just a lens through which we can see ongoing transformations, migrations and spillovers that happen around the designated exceptional places.

In the perspective of the general theory of exception, each legal system is a palimpsest of normalisations and exceptionalisations. It thus gives a proper foothold for a genealogical analysis, in which the normality/exception distinction gains its own sense abstracted from concrete forms of the legal system and its legal ideology. This distinction assures distribution of exceptionality—most importantly, by separating its work in relation to the entire legal order from its role in day-to-day law application.

Exceptionality remains thus an indispensable part of every legality: compartmentalised, resisted, immunised against, but also prone to destabilisation, migration and stray travels. What we now need to analyse is how it can put a legal system in a genealogical perspective through the lens of the concept of exceptionalisation.

104 For a brief overview of the *état de siège*, see Gross and Ní Aoláin, *Law in Times of Crisis*, 26–30.

105 A good example of such an excess is the French administrative institution of 'circonstances exceptionnelles', which adds additional exceptional possibilities when *état de siège* is not declared, but the administration needs to address very unique situations by disregarding procedural and competence norms. See Karine Roudier, Albane Geslin and David-André Camous, *L'état d'urgence* (Dalloz 2016) 8–26. Analogical excess can be visible in the German distinction between *Ausnahmezustand* (state of exception as part of written law) and *Notrecht* (form of exceptionality based just on invoking self-preservation of the state). See Belling, 'The State of Exception and Limits of the Rule of Law', 53. In a nutshell, no method of exhausting exceptionality in established devices can tame such excess. See also Lukáš Kollert, 'To Regulate, Or Not to Regulate? A Study on the State of Exception and Its Regulation' in Jakub Jinek and Lukáš Kollert (eds), *Emergency Powers. Rule of Law and the State of Exception* (Nomos 2020) 86–92.

Chapter 3

Exceptionalisation

Distributing Exceptionality

Przemysław Tacik

3.1 Introduction

Present-day legality is afflicted by the general increase in the number, types and qualities of broadly understood exceptional measures. Quite clearly, the rebound from the quite brief period of liberal hegemony, in which the doctrine of the rule of law strove to cement the domination of the legal over the political—and to isolate exceptionality in limited areas—has modified the way in which exceptionality functions nowadays. In a nutshell, it seems that the intra-legal distinction between the normal and the exceptional—which we identified in the previous chapter as the key attempt of the legal to distribute exceptionality and stabilise law application—has entered into a period of confusion, both in many domestic jurisdictions and international law (although in the latter it has always been more problematic). Yet more and more measures have an exceptional genealogy are treated as normal.[1] The ideological centre of the legal system no longer seems potent enough to demarcate the distinction between the normal and the exceptional with adequate precision. Agamben's concept of the threshold of indifferentiation is a clear response to this transformation.

Naturally, our epoch, in many aspects liminal, is symbolised by what Clifford Geertz identified, in reference to social sciences, as 'genre mixing' and 'blurring of kinds'.[2] It is no wonder that the legal began to use the distinction between normality and exception in a much more fluid and unclear way. Nonetheless, if, according to Chapter 2, we see the politico-legal system as a palimpsest of processes of normalising and exceptionalising, then the current developments will not be a surprise from a theoretical point of view. In many respects, we will be able to notice how the general 'return of sovereignty' is a transformation that used to happen in the past. Our surprise stems from the

1 Karin Loevy, *Emergencies in Public Law. The Legal Politics of Containment* (CUP 2016) 4.
2 Clifford Geertz, 'Blurred Genres: The Refiguration of Social Thought' (1980) 49:2 *The American Scholar* 165.

DOI: 10.4324/9781003490449-4

typical ensconcement in the horizons of our own epoch, particularly presentist and the strength of the crumbling liberal hegemony.

What we need in order to enquire into this transformation are new conceptual tools. In the previous chapter, I focused mainly on static elements of the general theory of exception. Now, however, it needs to be enriched in order to grasp how a legal system evolves in time. I will focus on the concept of exceptionalisation, by which I will aim to understand how patterns of distribution of exceptionality change in time and how it relates to shifts in the intra-normative distinction between the normal and the exception. 'Exceptionalisation' is meant to allow for not only describing the current transformations but also seeking its reasons and effects.

This chapter will be structured in the following way. First, I will focus on the existing theoretical attempts to grasp the ongoing process of normalising the exceptional. Then, I will propose an in-depth enquiry into the concept of exceptionalisation, followed by an analysis of its relations with the axis of legal/political. Finally, I will ask what the concept of exceptionalisation can bring to the general theory of exception.

3.2 Repressed Exceptionality

A growing trend in legal scholarship identifies *structural blurriness* that begins to afflict the distinction between normality and exception.[3] It is something more than just an increase in the number of exceptional measures adopted and used—which, in fact, is nothing really surprising from the theoretical point of view. But it seems that the solidness and precision with which legal orders draw the line between what they qualify as normal or exceptional has been on the wane. The operative role of this distinction appears to change its role, as if legal systems profited more and more from the vague qualification of measures that they use. Whereas one of the principal goals of exceptional legal devices has always been to render them more visible (and, assumingly, more delimitable, controlable and restrained), exceptionalisation blurs their visibility. In other words, *exceptionalisation connotes moving exceptionality from the zone of visibility to structural obfuscation.*

Tristan Barczak, in his recent monumental work diagnosed this transformation with the concept of the 'nervous state' (*der nervöse Staat*).[4] What this term connotes is a situation in which the state of exception is not a remedy to the malaise but rather a source of the latter or its symptom.[5] The

3 Oren Gross, 'The Normless and Exceptionless Exception: Carl Schmitt's Theory of Emergency Powers and the Norm-Exception Dichotomy' (2000) 21 *Cardozo L R* 1825, 1858.

4 Tristan Barczak, *Der nervöse Staat. Ausnahmezustand und Resilienz des Rechts in der Sicherheitsgesellchaft* (Mohr Siebeck 2021).

5 Barczak, *Der nervöse Staat*, 1.

state of exception displays a tendency to be prolonged (as in the case of the British fight with terrorism since the 70s or the French long aftermath of the 2015 attacks), and even when it is terminated, new laws tend to be adopted which overtake some exceptional measures into 'normal' law.[6] This proneness corresponds to a condition of the 'nervous state' which becomes more and more preoccupied with possible threats.[7] Bursting with readiness to deflect an attack, it corresponds to the society in 'permanent alarm' and in 'permanent excitement'.[8] The state of exception displays a global tendency to normalisation and prolongation.[9] Terrorism becomes a new model of threat: potentially ubiquitous, unpredictable and essentially chaotic. As a response, some states build a permanent counter-terrorist defence, analogously ubiquitous and acting within the self-propelling securitisation logic.[10]

The rule of law—or rather *Rechtstaatlichkeit* in the German tradition, to which Barczak refers—is crumbling, subjected to the erosive force of the permanent and diffused state of exception,[11] 'normalised' and 'banalised'.[12] As a result of this process, it is difficult to still operate with the notion of the state of exception. It sinks into the legal order, being gradually replaced with the preventive state: one that in advance reacts to threats.[13] Anticipating constatations from Chapter 4, it can be noticed that with the general increase of unpredictability, the temporal logic of law application becomes disturbed: more and more instruments of the executive are legitimised with the need for prompt reaction to suddenly appearing menaces. The past inscribed in the legal system is being gradually replaced with the future pertaining to sovereign power and, hence, the need to loosen up legal constraints imposed on the latter. Barczak identifies this process as 'deconstitutionalisation of the state of exception' (*Entkonstitutionaliesierung des Ausnahmezustands*), which not only transfers its regulations to the level of ordinary statutes but generally augurs 'dejuridification' (*Entrechtlichung*) of it.[14] The normal becomes exceptionalised and the exception—normalised.[15] Nonetheless, Barczak's observations suggest a more general question: why is this dejuridification of exceptionality happening in a covert, repressed form? Why does it not develop through a constitutional reform, in which the executive would

6 Barczak, *Der nervöse Staat*, 87–92, 336–345.
7 Barczak, *Der nervöse Staat*, 673.
8 Barczak, *Der nervöse Staat*, 2–3. See also Clement Fatovic, *Outside the Law. Emergency and Executive Power* (The Johns Hopkins University Press 2009) 262.
9 Barczak, *Der nervöse Staat*, 379–380.
10 On the securitisation logic, see Thierry Balzacq, *Securitization Theory: How Security Problems Emerge and Dissolve* (Routledge 2011).
11 Barczak, *Der nervöse Staat*, 65.
12 Barczak, *Der nervöse Staat*, 346–347.
13 Barczak, *Der nervöse Staat*, 70.
14 Barczak, *Der nervöse Staat*. See also Id. 291–292.
15 Barczak, *Der nervöse Staat*, 444.

openly receive more power, but rather as a creeping *de facto* process that saps legality of its ability to control exceptionality? In short: Why do the legal systems seem more and more to refrain from operating the normality/exception distinction? Why do they aim to reduce the visibility of exceptionality assured by exceptional devices?

Before I try to answer this question, it needs to be mentioned that Barczak rightly recognises the role of the sovereign in this process. The sovereign alone remains untouched when the law loses its grip on exceptionality, towering above the chaos in very Hegelian imagery:

> Der Hüter der Verfassung, ein letzter Fels in der Brandung, ragt wie ein Monolith aus der See, der so mächtig wirkt, als ob ihm Wasser und Winde auch in den nächsten hundert Jahren nichts anhaben könnten, und doch dem beständigen Andrängen der See wenig entgegenzusetzen hat.[16]

In other words, the sovereign (understood in well-recognisable tradition as '*der Hüter der Verfassung*') is the ultimate—and perhaps sole—winner of these tendencies. It is able to model, Barczak claims, normality after exceptional measures.[17] Meanwhile, the state of exception, despite all the disputes and controversies that surround its content, role and practical functioning, has one particular advantage: it allows of *recording* what is exceptional within the legal system and in the symbolic tissue that underpins public opinion. Naturally, such a recording has concrete functions both within a legal order and outside of it. It allows for mobilising a greater quantum of sovereign power through the promise of its temporary—and temporally determined—use. The recording can take place even outside legality, that is, in the public sphere—when regular legal measures are mobilised to achieve a special goal that is publicly avowed and recognised. Legal and social recording of exceptionality plays a vital role in shaping the map of mobilisations of the society and its accompanying forms of temporality.

But what we seem to witness nowadays is the waning role of official recording and visibility that it entails: exceptional measures proliferate beyond the distinction of normality/exception. In Barczak's account, the nervous state—or, according to his other classification, the preventive state—no longer needs the state of exception because it makes its legal system rife with safety valves through which sovereign power can operate promptly and with minimalised legal constraint:

> Er entpuppt sich bei heuristischer Betrachtung als potentiell dauerhaftes Merkmal innerhalb der Rechtsordnung und folgt dabei dem

16 Barczak, *Der nervöse Staat*, 4–5.
17 Barczak, *Der nervöse Staat*, 441.

Handlungsimperativ des präventiv-orientierten Staates, indem er zukünftige Gefahren bereits heute zu bekämpfen sucht. Diese Wandlung zeigte sich bereits im Verlaufe des Ersten Weltkriegs.[18]

Thus, the ongoing exceptionalisation perturbs the hitherto existing temporality of exception and makes the future—intertwined with sovereign power—present here and now in the legal system.[19] The logic of prevention, instead of reaction, is a sign of a changing balance between the legal and sovereign power present within it under the form of exceptionality. Exceptionality seems to move from its isolated posts held by the legal towards a greater unconstrained dispersion.

Moreover, Barczak introduces the notion of an 'anticipated state of exception' (*der antizipierte Ausnahmezustand*). It consists of an array of essentially police measures focused on prevention, whose aim is to prevent triggering an actual—typically constitutional—state of exception.[20] We could thus say that the constitutional state of exception thus turns into a kind of fetish, a proverbial 'nuclear option' whose main sense is that it is never actually used but works as a potential that exerts influence on here and now. The fetishist logic of the anticipated state of exception consists in the fact that the legal system does everything in order to avoid a menace, which actually fully materialises, but without its official and formal recording in the system[21]—and, naturally, without the checks and balances that a constitutional state of exception would require (abstracting from their efficiency). Thus, the visibility of exceptionality becomes muddled and relegated to social perception only without its proper recording in the law. To this fetishism, I will return as the key explanation of why the contemporary process of exceptionalisation has a creeping and unrecorded character. Barczak notices that the anticipated state of exception is able to join two features that, for the constitutional state of exception, would be contradictory

18 Barczak, *Der nervöse Staat*, 125.

19 As noticed by Pauline Gervier in relation to the French exceptional measures from the 2010s, the prolonged state of exception perturbs the temporal logic of reaction/prevention in the legal system: 'Une telle appréhension de l'état d'urgence modifie, dès lors, sa fonction. Défini comme un *état de réaction* rendant applicables des mesures exorbitantes du droit commun prises à la suite d'atteintes graves à l'ordre public, envisagé ensuite comme un *état d'anticipation*, compte tenu d'évènements futurs laissant présager des atteintes graves à l'ordre public, l'état d'urgence est désormais pensé comme un *état de transition*'. Pauline Gervier, 'Quels obstacles à une sortie de l'état d'urgence en France? Une analyse des débats parlementaires (2015–2017)' in Pauline Gervier (ed), *La sortie de l'état d'urgence* (IFJD 2020) 50.

20 Barczak, *Der nervöse Staat*, 349.

21 As Barczak writes, '[d]er antizipierte Ausnahmezustand bezweckt mit anderen Worten die Verhinderung des Ausnahmezustands mit den Mitteln des Ausnahmezustands'. Barczak, *Der nervöse Staat*, 383.

and unachievable: permanence and temporariness.[22] As we will see, fetishist logic is precisely what allows for the upholding of such a construct.

Ninon Grangé, in quite a similar vein, noticed the proliferation of different statute-regulated 'states', such as the French *état d'urgence*, in lieu of constitutionally anchored states of exception.[23] Such states 'introduce a new form of relation between the governed',[24] but do so while anchored in normal legality, unlike the state of exception.[25] Meanwhile, Karin Loevy identified the exception as a useful tool for testing out measures that the public opinion is first exposed to in a special situation, only to experience them as part of normality later.[26] As a consequence, the normality/exception distinction becomes more and more blurred and no longer properly useful.[27] In her paradigm, Loevy tries to see the exception as just a small, formal part of political and social practices, adopting a bottom-up perspective and grasping plurality as well as the complexity of every actual exceptional 'event'. In this view, an emergency is a complex field of actions and reactions that correspond to what we call here 'exceptionalisation' and 'normalisation'.

According to Loevy, emergency is a regular method of governance.[28] In particular, it offers a special context of law-making:[29] what we call normalisation is a typical way of adopting norms that would be too unpalatable to society in order to be adopted under normal circumstances.[30] Yet the practical work of emergency is multi-dimensional. It can consist not only in the creation of new norms or more typical suspension of valid norms but also in acting *contra legem*.[31]

The American tradition began to identify the creeping exceptionalisation, a sign of our times, much earlier: in the aftermath of the 9/11 attacks. Although the current process is much more deeply anchored in the transformation of the public sphere and the general weakening of constitutional law, it was over 20 years ago that the first forebodings of the current trend appeared. This is not only under the guise of exceptional laws adopted especially in the US,

22 Barczak, *Der nervöse Staat*, 381.
23 Ninon Grangé, *L'urgence et l'effroi. L'état d'exception, la guerre et les temps politiques* (ENS 2018) 66.
24 Grangé, *L'urgence et l'effroi*, 65.
25 Grangé, *L'urgence et l'effroi*, 66.
26 Karin Loevy, *Emergencies in Public Law. The Legal Politics of Containment* (CUP 2016) 1–3.
27 Loevy, *Emergencies in Public Law*, 4.
28 Loevy, *Emergencies in Public Law*, 282.
29 Loevy, *Emergencies in Public Law*, 281.
30 For historical examples, see Oren Gross and Fionnuala Ní Aoláin, *Law in Times of Crisis. Emergency Powers in Theory and Practice* (CUP 2006) 174–179.
31 Loevy, *Emergencies in Public Law*, 312.

but, even more tellingly, in the well-known *exceptional practices undertaken in legal loopholes*. As David Dyzenhaus claimed,

> [e]ven more dramatic are the legal black holes created by the government of the United States. Notorious here is the situation of aliens detained offshore at Guantanamo Bay, which the government claimed to be beyond the jurisdiction of the federal courts. These individuals are not detained because the US government refuses to deport them to face torture. Indeed, the government of the United States has deported people in order that they will be tortured in countries in which torture is condoned. Moreover, its own treatment of detainees has raised questions about whether it practises torture, spurred by signals from the highest reaches of the Bush administration that torture is acceptable, given the severity of the emergency.[32]

Terrorism, in itself based on the structure of exception (an intentionally contingent event exerts a general effect by fear of its ubiquitous possibility), mandates an exceptional response that displays the tendency to prolong itself.[33] Apart from the fact that Guantanamo and other similar places, for example, US-run detention facilities in CEE countries,[34] confirmed the astounding far-sightedness of Giorgio Agamben, they demonstrate well how exceptionalisation connotes reshuffling of exceptionality in its distribution around the legal system. The case of the US is specific insofar as exceptionality is largely channelled through the general regulation of the executive with scant exceptional devices in the constitution, which makes such distributions easier and less visible.[35] Shifting effective spheres of competence between state powers is also part of this process, with the executive typically arrogating to itself excessive exceptionality. The result, according to Dyzenhaus is nonetheless familiar in comparison with other countries: 'emergency government has become the norm'.[36] The US not only changed laws managing exceptionality but, even more importantly, transferred it to the existing legal black holes, such as the territory of Guantanamo. Parenthetically, this process shows that for the purposes of analysing exceptionality, the legal system needs to be taken

32 David Dyzenhaus, *The Constitution of Law. Legality in a Time of Emergency* (CUP 2006) 2.

33 Otto Depenheuer, 'The Exceptional Case in Situations of Normalcy' in Jakub Jinek and Lukáš Kollert (eds), *Emergency Powers. Rule of Law and the State of Exception* (Nomos 2020) 38–40.

34 See ECtHR's rulings in: *Al Nashiri v Poland* App no 28761/11 (ECHR, 24 Jul 2014) and *Husayn (Abu Zubaydah) v Poland* App no 7511/13 (ECHR, 24 Jul 2014).

35 Clinton Rossiter, *Constitutional Dictatorship. Crisis Government in the Modern Democracies* (Routledge 2017) 211–216, 232; Fatovic, *Outside the Law*, 33.

36 Fatovic, *Outside the Law*, 51.

comprehensively, both in its domestic and international branches: exceptionality can migrate to a tectonic rift between them.[37]

Finally, this overview of exceptionalisation literature should be ended with earlier but stunningly prophetic observations by Ernst-Wolfgang Böckenförde.[38] His theory of 'the repressed state of exception' (*der verdrängte Ausnahmezustand*) assumes that it is the law that holds the crucial role of dividing between the normal and the exceptional.[39] Referring to the constitutional specificity of the FRG, Böckenförde aims to demonstrate that if what we call here exceptionality is not properly regulated by the law, it will return in reality.[40] The psychoanalytical concept of repression (*Verdrängung*) provides a proper context for an unwanted return here. A repressed state of exception consists of diminishing the force of the law to keep the exceptional to the *Notstand*, which turns into a day-to-day way of bureaucracy of how to deal with affairs.[41] At the same time, the state of exception is a hole in between the constitution and sub-constitutional statutes, through which the logic between these acts can be perturbed.[42]

In order to avoid normalisation of the exception, Böckenförde postulates that each exceptional legal device should have a clearly determined goal of restoring normality.[43] In other words, the normality/exception distinction should remain as the overarching framework within which exceptional measures operate. In particular, the moments of proclamation and repeal of an exceptional device should be clearly determined in order to avoid any kind of slippage.[44] But ultimately, despite this optimist rule of law postulates, Böckenförde admits law's defeat vis-à-vis exceptionality: 'Die *rechtliche Begrenzung* der Ausnahmebefugnisse ist nicht durch eine inhaltliche Normierung erreichbar'.[45] Quite clearly, the law struggles here with a more potent adversary, as the norms are part of the framework in which exceptionality functions, not its external bulwarks. Ultimately, the control over the exceptional can only be political.

All the preceding considerations substantiate the claim that we witness nowadays a process of exceptionalisation, in which exceptionality

37 See also Gross and Ní Aoláin, *Law in Times of Crisis*, 282–283.

38 Ernst-Wolfgang Böckenförde, 'Der verdrängte Ausnahmezustand. Zum Handeln der Staatsgewalt in außergewöhnlichen Lagen' (1978) 38 *NJW* 1881.

39 Böckenförde, 'Der verdrängte Ausnahmezustand', 1881.

40 Böckenförde, 'Der verdrängte Ausnahmezustand', 1884. See also Hasso Hofmann, 'Souverän ist, wer über den Ausnahmezustand entscheidet' (2005) 44:2 *Der Staat* 171, 179–180.

41 Böckenförde, 'Der verdrängte Ausnahmezustand', 1883.

42 Exceptional states thus practically illustrate Schmitt's observation that constitutions and laws cannot protect themselves mutually. Carl Schmitt, *Der Hüter der Verfassung* (Mohr Siebeck 1931) 40.

43 Böckenförde, 'Der verdrängte Ausnahmezustand', 1887.

44 Böckenförde, 'Der verdrängte Ausnahmezustand', 1888–1889.

45 Böckenförde, 'Der verdrängte Ausnahmezustand', 1890.

becomes re-distributed within the legal system and outside of it. This re-distribution is peculiar in at least three respects. First, exceptionality not only becomes built into areas of legality in which it was largely absent—through the multiplication of concrete entitlements of the executive, for example[46]—but it also appears in various cracks and rifts within the legal system. As a result, exceptionalisation does not appear as a process over which the executive would have an overarching control exercised from the position of supreme surveillance. On the contrary, the executive, pace its agency, remains enmeshed in the process as one of pawns on the chessboard. Second, the normality/exception distinction loses its centring and holding power, making the normal and the exceptional blend. As Agamben noticed in *Homo sacer*, '[o]ne of the theses of the present inquiry is that in our age, the state of exception comes more and more to the foreground as the fundamental political structure and ultimately begins to become the rule'.[47] The same applies to how we see reality through the lens of the law. Michel Rosenfeld claimed that we no longer live in normal times or in conditions of emergency, but rather in a state that combines the two that he names 'conditions of stress'.[48] In other words, not only is the law itself permeated with exceptionality, it also projects this blurring on reality itself, forming with it a special entanglement. Third, this exceptionalisation is a process that, in many aspects, remains unrecorded constitutionally as long as it concerns chiefly sub-constitutional acts and *de facto* forms of exceptionality. In this sense, it is entangled in the ongoing deep transformation that destabilises legality—constitutional law in particular—in relation to the political.

Consequently, the creeping state of exception obviously erodes the already weak division between *pouvoir constituant* and *pouvoir constitué*, with the effective sovereign using emergency situations as a pretext for a *de facto* constitutional change—which should be, in Schmitt's language, an autonomous assumption of sovereign dictatorship by a commissarial dictatorship.[49] Naturally, many constitutions prohibit amending them under exceptional regimes.[50] Still, this is an intra-legal ban which does not take into account

46 David Dyzenhaus, 'The Compulsion of Legality' in Victor Ramraj (ed), *Emergencies and the Limits of Legality* (CUP 2008) 55.

47 Giorgio Agamben, *Homo Sacer* Daniel Heller-Roazen transl. (Stanford University Press 1998) 20.

48 Michel Rosenfeld, 'Should Constitutional Democracies Redefine Emergencies and the Legal Regimes Suitable for Them?' in Austin Sarat (ed), *Sovereignty, Emergency, Legality* (CUP 2010) 242.

49 Giacomo Delledonne, 'Crises, Emergencies and Constitutional Change' in Xenophon Contiades and Alkmene Fotiadou (eds), *Routledge Handbook of Comparative Constitutional Change* (Routledge 2021) 245, 249–253.

50 Oren Gross, 'Providing for the Unexpected: Constitutional Emergency Provisions' (2003) 33 *Isr YB Hum Rts* 1336.

how effectively exceptionality pushes away legal bulwarks and diminishes their relevance. The distinction between *pouvoir constituant* and *constitué* crumbles together with the separation between normality and the exception.[51] Just as the difference between these two powers is meant to create a field in which usurpation of constitution-making authority by constitutional organs is not only prohibited but also visible when it happens, so does the visibility of exceptionality wane. The legal devices of recording and making visible *the outside of legality* become porous and overdetermined.

Contemporary exceptionalisation is tacit and assumes a fetishist structure because it aims to undertake a major overhaul of the legal system while preserving the semblance that liberal legality, based on the rule of law, has been preserved. Consequently, it avoids the symbolic recording of its actions. Usually, they do not take place as major constitutional reforms—also because constitutional law lost its position as the main place where key political changes were recorded. Current exceptionalisation is thus coupled with *fetishist constitutionalism*, which preserves the formal structure and main guarantees of former legality while effectively hollowing them out. The rule of law in many countries has never been formally repealed, but its semblances have been retained as fetishes that no longer influence the means practically adopted and used. In other words, exceptionality is not only escaping its previous channels of distribution, but the very functionality of these channels no longer seems effective. With fetishist constitutionalism, exceptionality becomes akin to Marx's mole digging under the edifice of the liberal order.

3.3 The Concept of Exceptionalisation: Towards a Meta-Description of the Exception

The previously described transformations can be grasped with the concept of exceptionalisation on which we now need to focus. Let us begin with an illustrative comparison: exceptionalisation is to exceptionality what is, in mathematics, a derivative is to a value of a function at a given argument. Speaking more descriptively, the concept of exceptionality corresponds to a map of exceptional measures effective or latent in a legal system at a particular moment. Meanwhile, exceptionalisation describes the vector of changes in the map of how legality distributes exceptionality. It allows for grasping the system in its transformation and reading exceptionality in its tendencies.

51 Ferejohn and Pasquino notice that when emergency powers slip into arrogating *pouvoir constituant*, they perform 'an abrogation or transformation of the constitution' and no longer function 'to preserve it'. John Ferejohn and Pasquale Pasquino, 'The Law of Exception: A Typology of Emergency Powers' (2004) 2:2 *ICON* 210, 223. Yet although this slip can be banned by the law, it happens in a space where the law does not have control over it, but is rather subjected to its work.

When a legal system undergoes exceptionalisation, the overall quantum of exceptionality may increase. It also withdraws from the hitherto existing channels of distribution, including capillary ones, and either finds new, broader and more general outlets or disperses throughout the whole system as loose energy. Under exceptionalisation, the remainder that exceptionality always preserves—beyond any legal institutions that strive to curb it—begins to prevail and the normality/exception distinction becomes alienated from how the law effectively functions.

Dispersion of exceptionality as loose energy in the legal system is a particularly significant situation. Thus accumulated in the system, exceptionality corresponds to a decay in the ability of the legal to separate itself from the political. When that occurs, decision-making seems less and less bound by legal norms. Such a process can be independent from any use of institutional forms of exceptionality, such as the state of exception. Dispersed exceptionality means that effective decisions are being taken in a looser relation to the legal system, no matter if any norms have been formally suspended. The state of exception, as we mentioned in Chapter 2, is precisely the means to bind exceptionality by fixing its activity to given circumstances and temporal limits. Meanwhile, dispersed exceptionality, so well visible in the legal response to the COVID-19 pandemic,[52] means that decision-makers do not seem entirely bound by legal norms, esp. constitutional ones, and practice power parallel to what these norms stipulate.

In a more analytical sense, exceptionalisation finds its counterpart in the process of normalisation, through which exceptionality becomes bound again in the legal system through particular norms and institutions. As we remarked in Chapter 2, the legal system can thus be seen—from a genealogical perspective—as a palimpsest of exceptionalisations and normalisations. This means that the process of exceptionalisation cannot abstract from the genealogy of the legal system; it has no meaning outside of a framework which was established in previous normalisations. Moreover, exceptionalisation and exceptionality are two analytical concepts that grasp different aspects of transformations between the legal and the political. No map of exceptionality can be meaningfully established and interpreted without the context of the direction towards its transformation. Nonetheless, we should avoid a simplifying view that exceptionalisation and normalisation are necessary subsequent movements in which a legal system develops; they can overlap and interplay, or, contrariwise, a legal system can be involved in one

52 See Angelo Jr. Golia, Laura Hering, Carolyn Moser and Tom Sparks, 'Constitutions and Contagion. European Constitutional Systems and the COVID-19 Pandemic' (2020) 42 *MPIL Research Paper Series* 1; Pavel Ondřejek, *Threshold of Justification of Emergency Regulations: On Coherentism Requirement for the Justification of Measures Adopted in the Czech Republic During the COVID-19 Pandemic* (2021) 2 *Archiwum Filozofii Prawa i Filozofii Społecznej* 48.

of these processes for a longer time. Pure exceptionalisation cannot, however, be permanent because it would reach the plenitude of dictatorial power and thus lose its sense. There needs to be a counterweight in normalisation which restores the difference vis-à-vis which exceptionalisation can be seen.[53] Moreover, exceptionalisation itself normalises previous exceptional measures, thereby containing a nucleus of normalisation already within itself.[54]

Another crucial issue that the concept of exceptionalisation allows us to grasp is the special dynamics between *using exceptionality* contained in particular exceptional legal measures and the nature of legal bulwarks in which it is contained. Here, we encounter a particularly rich Agambenian nest of problems. The two most important ones are: (1) how does the legal fix and contain exceptionality? and (2) how is exceptionality used or 'applied' within exceptional legal devices?

In order to address both questions, let us begin by noticing that by containing exceptionality, the legal enters into a peculiar mode of functioning, in which it imposes its own logic of 'application' on what repels it. The law, as we noticed in Chapter 2, conveys the vision of a general rule that—through the process of interpretation and application—determines an act in a particular case. In its generic structure, this is a process of movement from the general to the individual and from the past to the future. In every law application, there is an admixture of exceptionality which constitutes a future supplement to the past which cannot, by itself, leave its domain. In other words, a modicum of exceptionality awaits every legal norm and allows its application. At the same time, the law obfuscates its role by producing the illusion of *iterable applicability*.

This observation allows us to address the first question. Fixing exceptionality within the legal can occur through various means, but the most crucial is isolating it through *explicitly exceptional measures*, such as states of exception, martial laws, etc. What they have in common are three features, usually

53 Steffen Augsberg grasped part of the interaction between the normal and the exceptional in this regard: 'Die Ausnahme darf nicht zu Regel werden, kann dies auch gar nicht, weil sie im selben Moment ihren Ausnahmecharakter verlöre und gleichzeitig die bisherige Normallage in nicht vorhersehbarer Weise beinflusste'. Steffen Augsberg, 'Denken vom Ausnahmezustand her. Über die Unzulässigkeit der anormalen Konstruktion und Destruktion des Normativen' in *Freiheit—Sicherheit—Öffentlichkeit. 48. Assistententagung Öffentliches Recht* (Nomos 2009) 30–31. See also Markus Kotzur, 'Die Weltgemeinschaft im Ausnahmezustand?' (2004) 42:4 *AVR* 353, 358.

54 Gross and Ní Aoláin perspicaciously grasped this process in the following way: '[m]uch like the need gradually to increase the dosage of a heavily used medication in order to experience the same level of relief, so too with respect to emergency powers: the perception may be that new, more radical powers are needed to fight impending crises. In turn, new extraordinary emergency measures confer an added degree of ex post legitimacy and respectability, as well as a sense of normality, to previously used, less drastic emergency measures'. Gross and Ní Aoláin, *Law in Times of Crisis*, 228.

adduced in emergency studies:[55] (1) the potency to suspend other selected norms (for example, freedom of movement), (2) the determination of special circumstances in which such a device can be triggered and (3) temporal limitations.[56] Not entering into the age-old debate on whether the law is structurally able to contain exceptionality (as the general theory of exception aims to reframe this very question), let us notice that what these special exceptional devices do is transposing the idea of exceptionality onto the law. This is a truly particular process. *The law takes its foreign supplement and recreates its logic within itself*, creating two illusions: that it can control it and that exceptionality has its separate place within the law.

Paradoxical as it may look, at first sight, the law mimics—with legal means—the work of exceptionality on the legal. Exceptional measures that allow certain legal norms to suspend other legal norms give the illusion that it is the law, solely and entirely, deciding on exceptionality. *Suspension of the law through the law* in exceptional devices thus remains an intra-legal projection of how exceptionality is truly situated vis-à-vis the law. *Whereas exceptionality fills in the abyss of suspension that the law encounters in relation to reality, exceptional institutions perform an explicit suspension within the law.* In this sense, exceptional devices within the law can be seen as colonisation of exceptionality by the law. But using psychoanalytical language, we can go further and claim that an exceptional device is akin to a symbolic replay of an extra-symbolic trauma experienced by the subject. Just as a psychoanalytic patient replicates what happened to them, trying to incorporate otherness into their own history and personal narrative, so is the legal system prone to *repeating* its structural deficiency with exceptional devices created on its own terms and within its own logic. Through them, the legal system aims to reconstruct—and thus absorb—the structural foreignness of exceptionality.

With this recognition, we approach the detailed explanation of Agamben's intuition: the state of exception as a legal institution corresponds somehow to the state of exception as a fact, a factual status of the law. But, in fact, it is not law application that replicates the structure of the state of exception. It is the other way around: *the state of exception as a legal device aims to repeat within the legal framework what happens between the law and reality*. It seems that exceptional devices, based on the concept of suspension of the law through the law, strive to advance an illusory replication of

55 Gross, 'Providing for the Unexpected', 22–33; Ferejohn and Pasquino, 'The Law of Exception', 213–219; Rossiter, *Constitutional Dictatorship*, 298–310; Linda F. Bishai, 'The Inertia of the Exception' in Linda F. Bishai (ed), *Law, Security and the State of Perpetual Emergency* (Palgrave Macmillan 2020) 13–14; Vojtěch Belling, 'The State of Exception and Limits of the Rule of Law' in Jakub Jinek and Lukáš Kollert (eds), *Emergency Powers. Rule of Law and the State of Exception* (Nomos 2020) 58–62.

56 On possibilities of binding the exception temporarily, see Nomi Claire Lazar, *States of Emergency in Liberal Democracies* (CUP 2009) 22.

exceptionality within the boundaries of the law. The effect corresponds to the psychoanalytical compulsion to repeat:[57] as the law cannot by itself reach reality and requires a modicum of exceptionality to this purpose, it plays its command over reality by mimicking exceptionality within itself. In this aspect, law application would be to a legal norm what a state of exception pretends to be vis-à-vis the legal system.

Hence also the structural juxtaposition between exceptional devices and the *necessitas non cognoscet legem*[58] doctrines—which is based on the proper categorial error, namely confusion between normativity and reality. What is an error in a neutral analysis, however, turns out to reveal the real role of exceptional devices: replaying exceptionality within the law in an immunological reaction of the legal system to tame it. Through this act, the legal system helplessly aims to build itself around exceptionality as the channel that links it to reality. In this sense, establishing the state of exception is a futile attempt by the law attempt to autonomise itself against its own foundation, proto-legal political power.

Establishing exceptional institutions effectively brings into the law a necessarily fetishist component: norms are suspended by a norm whose validity seems to uphold the whole legal order. By suspension, the law does what exceptionality would do at any rate but assumes that it does so on its own decision and consent. Consequently, it definitely *records* the use of exceptionality but then only pushes the problem further down: once an exceptional device has been triggered, it needs to be recorded whether exceptionality within it does not exceed the imposed limits. Through the fetishism of suspension, the law appears to have a grip on exceptionality, but in fact, it cannot properly record the slow multi-layer transformations that happen when an exceptional institution is triggered. It just lives off the fiction that once normality is restored—through a normative determination, naturally—exceptionality will become contained again and the status quo ante returns. This is nothing less but a fetishist cover-up of the process of exceptionalisation that has effectively taken place when the exceptional device was in use.

Such a recognition brings us to the second of the questions posed previously: What does it mean to 'use' an exceptional device and how does that relate to exceptionalisation? Fixing exceptionality within legal devices aims at imposing on it the legal idea of iterability: producing a pattern of actions in which a general rule produces a frame of standardised 'cases'. With iterability comes a particular vision of temporality. Once the law lays down a general rule, it fixes the time to come as marked by the pre-formed rhythm

57 See Sigmund Freud, *Beyond the Pleasure Principle* James Strachey transl. (Norton & Co. 1961) 28–58.

58 See Gross and Ní Aoláin, *Law in Times of Crisis*, 47.

of its application. Naturally, the use of the law changes the law—through interpretation and productive jurisprudence of courts, for example—but the overarching temporal frame seems to belong to the law itself.

Meanwhile, 'using' exceptional devices does not take place without influence on the legal system. My working hypothesis is that *spending exceptionality—that is, 'using' exceptionality accumulated in devices such as the state of exception—causes exceptionalisation*. Exceptional devices are not tools of the legal system, although they appear as such. Their 'use' reshuffles the very distribution of exceptionality within the legal system. Aspects of this process have been recognised in the literature. It is quite typical to worry about the perpetuation of emergency measures and the authoritarian drift that their use may entail.[59] François Saint-Bonnet notices that the application of exceptional devices can modify two types of delimitations ('*limitations*')—horizontal (between state powers) and vertical (between the state and individuals).[60] Use of the state of exception, martial law or analogical devices exerts an eroding influence on how state power is curbed within the law. '[E]mergency powers across jurisdictions have had pervasive and insidious effects on law and legal institutions',[61] claim Gross and Ní Aoláin. *Exceptionality can hardly be safely spent within devices that contain it; on the contrary, they produce a necessary excess through which their own legal anchoring is displaced.*

But exceptionalisation is a more complicated process that takes place on two additional levels: (1) 'use' of legally contained exceptionality changes the dynamic between the law and the exceptional as its supplement: exceptionality is allowed to operate more broadly and openly in areas of the legal system in which its previous presence was limited and (2) the law loses the ability to maintain its function of *recording* what actions are undertaken when exceptionality travels across the legal system. It is this level that we recognised in the previous subchapter as dismantling of the normality/exception distinction. Crucially, however, both levels of this process are concurrent and interconnected. Maintenance of the normality/exception distinction is correlative to the ability of the legal system to fix and distribute exceptionality. Meanwhile, the very structure on which exceptional devices rely—suspension of some norms by other norms—allows exceptionality to spread within the legal system, with only a general level of registration.

Lacan's psychoanalytic thinking offers significant theoretical advancement. Lacan claims that there is no Big Other of the Big Other (*l'Autre de l'Autre*)[62]—which means, in adaptation to our theoretical development here,

59 Ferejohn and Pasquino, 'The Law of Exception', 219.
60 François Saint-Bonnet, *L'état d'exception* (PUF 2001) 28.
61 Gross and Ní Aoláin, *Law in Times of Crisis*, 3.
62 Jacques Lacan, *Le Séminaire. Livre XXIII—Le Sinthome* (Seuil 2005) 56.

that there is no symbolic anchoring of the symbolic system. *L'Autre de l'Autre* is a place to which the Big Other seems to refer, seeking its foundation, '*sa propre loi*',[63] Lacan says, where the speech of the Big Other seems to be produced.[64] Such a place is assumed but does not exist. Analogically, *within the legal system, there is no proper recording of the normality/exception distinction outside of what the law currently poses as such.* This recording can happen in other layers of the public symbolic—including individual perception of tensions between nominal normality and effective abnormality—but the law does not include it. Its peculiar feature is to both act on reality and render it visible. The legal registration never has a neutral status: if it picks up a trace to make it recorded, the trace is retroactively posited as regulating reality. Therefore, the intra-legal history of exceptionalisation is obviously not only selective but also in itself absorbed into the current normality/exception distinction.[65]

This recognition gives an insight into exceptionalisation. It is a process that changes both the way in which exceptionality functions within the legal and the way in which the law can record it. In other words, the symbolic layer that allows for registering what shifts are happening is in itself bound to the process of transformation. For this reason, the normality/exception distinction is not a stable anchoring that permanently delineates the normal from the exceptional, but rather a moving cap on exceptionality traversing the legal system. In other words, it is impossible to separate the normative and the recording functions of the law vis-à-vis exceptionality.[66] For this reason, the process of exceptionalisation is not formally graspable within the legal system only. The very framework which would allow to register it is the one that takes place in the law's struggle for containing exceptionality and is subjected to transformations as well. Therefore, it can be theoretically true that when exceptional measures go too far, they produce a regime change: such 'emergency is not a conservative form of temporary government, but the starting point of a new political order',[67] as Ferejohn and Pasquino notice. The trouble is that exceptionalisation performs this 'regime change' without

63 Lacan, *Le Séminaire. Livre XXIII*, 192.

64 Lacan, *Le Séminaire. Livre XXIII*, 475.

65 In this sense, there is no 'continuity' between the exceptional and the normal *as such*. Nomi Claire Lazar may be right in stating that '[n]ormal and emergency values are continuous. Normal and exceptional institutions have important elements of continuity also', but this is precisely what cannot be said, as there is no Big Other of registering exceptional dis/continuities. Lazar, *States of Emergency*, 5.

66 Gross's and Ní Aoláin's model of extra-legal measures, which can be debated and assessed in terms of individual responsibility for the acts adopted in their duration, assumes the possibility of distinguishing the two aspects of law vis-à-vis exceptionality: defining the normal and operating on the normal. But, in fact, this is precisely the short circuit through which exceptionalisation operates, blurring the distinction. See Gross and Ní Aoláin, *Law in Times of Crisis*, 112–113.

67 Ferejohn and Pasquino, 'The Law of Exception', 233.

registering it, and thus opens a question of what the exceptionalised regime really is.

From an epistemological point of view, this conclusion corresponds to what we saw in Chapter 2: exceptionalisation can be read only through traces and scars on the corpus of the law. The legal system does not have its own Big Other capable of registering it; therefore, only genealogical and comparative studies can point to exceptionalisation in operating on the law. In a nutshell, when exceptionalisation creates grey zones within the legal system, they are not only normative but also epistemological. It undermines not only the ways in which the law operates but also the ways in which we can describe it. Unsurprisingly, legal scholarship is rife with declarations of being baffled by the rise of grey zones. As David Dyzenhaus wrote,

> grey holes cause more harm to the rule of law than black holes. . . . I want simply to establish that minimalism is too close to the black hole end of the continuum for comfort. A little bit of legality can be more lethal to the rule of law than none.[68]

What Dyzenhaus fears is not political power unbridled by law, but rather this peculiar blend of legality and the political, in which both are inseparable, yet it cannot be said that the law guides the execution of power. Much as the vision of 'the executive doing what it needs to do', without donning a pseudo-legal garb, may appeal to one's craving for clarity and order, it is a misunderstanding of how the legal and the political are intertwined in (post-)liberal states.[69] Exceptionalisation is not just the liberation of the political from the constraints of the legal; it is releasing exceptionality, which, for its life, always requires both. Hence the obscurity of the current transformations.

Exceptionalisation can take many directions, but the one we identify nowadays—described in the previous subchapter—releases exceptionality from its capillary constraints, builds for it new, broad outlets, but, most

68 Dyzenhaus, *The Constitution of Law*, 50.

69 Oren Gross expresses a similar craving, claiming that the law should not impose constraints where they are going to be fictitious, since it only exposes itself to ridicule: '[i]ndeed, a constitutional suspension clause is both unnecessary and undesirable. It is unnecessary because if government is to go outside the constitutional boundary it would do so regardless of whether the constitution itself allows such actions. If one strives to maintain as complete a separation between normality and emergency as possible, including a suspension clause in the constitution is also undesirable. It makes constitutional that which is otherwise unconstitutional and ought to remain so. Emergency measures may, under certain circumstances, go beyond positive law and sometimes even against it, but when they do they must be openly acknowledged for what they are. Allowing the constitution to prescribe its own suspension confers a false sense of legality and legitimacy on these exceptional measures and facilitates the breaking down of the demarcation lines between normality and emergency'. Gross, 'Providing for the Unexpected', 39.

importantly, allows it to spill over the entire legal system.[70] The registration of this process from within the law is impossible, as the foothold for registration is part of the changing 'object' it aims to grasp. It is precisely these shifting sands—caused by the double role of the law, regulating reality and recording exceptionality—that in the past fuelled the demands for 'clear' exceptional devices which would separate laws from facts and the use of exceptionality from the effective transformation it produces. But interestingly, nowadays, calls for exceptional legal devices to tame exceptionalisation are less resonant. It seems that exceptionalisation has become a trend for contemporary legal systems and no state of exception is even believed to be able to cope with it.

In its current incarnation, exceptionalisation connotes the gradual weakening of the normality/exception distinction and the ability to record how exceptionality travels across the legal system, appearing in more and more previously contained areas.

3.4 Exceptionalisation and the Two States within One

Exceptionalisation unbinds exceptionality from its cathexes. This process has a few aspects. As soon as exceptional devices lose hold, the political begins to infuse the legal. What appears is a growing zone of indifferentiation between the two, in which legal norms lose the power of determination vis-à-vis law application. The temporal boundaries for exceptional measures lose sense: the end of exceptional measures enters into permanent deferral. The boundary between normality and exception is no longer solid and resembles an oscillation traversing the legal order.

A classic case study of exceptionalisation was given by Ernst Fraenkel in his theory of the dual state.[71] Although this work is not focused on exceptional measures per se, its great value consists in demonstrating how exceptionality becomes released from its cathexes and begins to operate beyond formal legal devices and constraints. 'The Dual State', consisting of the Normative State and Prerogative State,[72] is a conceptual framework for analysing a thoroughly exceptionalised regime of Nazi Germany, in which '[m]artial law provides the constitution'.[73] Its key feature is that these two states

70 See Ferejohn and Pasquino, 'The Law of Exception', 235.

71 Ernst Fraenkel, *The Dual State. A Contribution to the Theory of Dictatorship* E. A. Shils, Edith Lowenstein and Klaus Knorr transl. (The Lawbook Exchange 2010).

72 Fraenkel defines the Normative State as 'an administrative body endowed with elaborate powers for safeguarding the legal order as expressed in statutes, decisions of the courts, and activities of the administrative agencies' and the Prerogative State as a 'governmental system which exercises unlimited arbitrariness and violence unchecked by any legal guarantees'. Fraenkel, *The Dual State*, xiii.

73 Fraenkel, *The Dual State*, 3.

co-exist, intertwined, in a common volatile structure. In other words, in Fraenkel's view, the Third Reich should not be seen as defined solely by unbridled authoritarian power, but rather as an interaction of a preserved and curbed Normative State, on which the Prerogative State operates and parasites. 'The Prerogative State cannot be a direct and positively controlling power, but rather a limiting and indirectly supporting power'.[74] In other words, the Prerogative State is a negative force that cannot exist on its own, requiring its legal counterpart to operate on what it perceives as not related to 'political issues'. Such a structure corresponds to the fetishist regime based on martial law, nominally aimed at restoring normality,[75] but, in fact, using an exceptional device to spread exceptionality all over the legal system.

Fraenkel notices that long before Hitler, the doctrine of necessity and expediency of martial law pushed German courts to open a crack in legality, which was taken out of judicial review.[76] Nonetheless, with the advent of the Nazi regime, prompt exceptionalisation began, as a result of which the boundaries between the Normative State and the Prerogative State became defined flexibly and dynamically. Released exceptionality meant that no area of the Normative State could rely on its freedom from interventions by the Prerogative State, which Fraenkel perceived as born out of martial law and being tantamount to 'a continuous siege'.[77] Potentially, every issue can become 'political' as soon as the Prerogative State claims it.[78] *The boundaries of exceptionality are thus defined from the side of exceptionality, not normality*: 'the presumption of jurisdiction rests with the Normative State. The jurisdiction over jurisdiction rests with the Prerogative State'.[79] On a more theoretical note, this observation can be read as evidence that exceptionalisation renders visible the operative priority of exceptionality vis-à-vis the legal.

Consequently, Fraenkel argues, a seemingly most innocent civil dispute belonging to the domain of the Normative State could be intercepted by the Prerogative State if reasons of 'public defence' are invoked by appropriate organs (the Gestapo, the NSDAP, etc.).[80] Exceptional temporality is visible in the fact that a distinction between the Normative and the Prerogative States could not be drawn in advance; it changed according to the conjunctural demands of Nazi politics.[81] The domain of the Prerogative State cut through the entire legal order. It applied in advance to people labelled as enemies by the Nazis (Jews, gay persons), in whose cases the Normative State was

74 Fraenkel, *The Dual State*, 186.
75 Fraenkel, *The Dual State*, 10.
76 Fraenkel, *The Dual State*, 3.
77 Fraenkel, *The Dual State*, 24.
78 Fraenkel, *The Dual State*, 30–40.
79 Fraenkel, *The Dual State*, 57.
80 Fraenkel, *The Dual State*, 40–42.
81 Fraenkel, *The Dual State*, 42.

blocked from normal operation.[82] But, in other cases, the Prerogative State could easily snatch an area from the jurisdiction of the Normative State.

Fraenkel grasps here a crucial paradox. The Prerogative State seems to come later in relation to the Normative State as its 'parasite'. But in fact, it was produced by the expansion of an exceptional core already present at the heart of the Normative State. For this reason, the Prerogative State 'legally' has 'unlimited jurisdiction',[83] whereas the Normative State appears as its self-limitation. In other words, even the exceptionalised legal system demonstrates the logic of contractions and expansions of exceptionality in relation to the legal. The Normative State is, of course, not rule of law, just a counterpart to the Prerogative State,[84] but it remains within the same dialectical relation with exceptionality.

To sum up, Fraenkel's theory epitomises how exceptionalisation makes exceptionality—previously contained in an exceptional device, martial law—dispersed throughout the legal system. The Nazi Dual State was not entirely lawless. Reality was more complex: it preserved the binding between the political and the legal but made their quilting point extend over the entire system with privileged organs, such as the Gestapo or the NSDAP, deciding on the boundaries for legality.

3.5 Conclusions

Exceptionalisation, which—as we saw at the beginning of this chapter—many contemporary authors diagnose to be a malady of our times, is inscribed in the modern structure of relations between sovereignty, the law and exceptionality. Historically speaking, the binding of exceptionality within the law has been notoriously difficult and unstable.[85] Already, Schmitt noticed how volatile the legal anchoring of exceptional powers becomes while these are used more than occasionally.[86] In fact, exceptional devices serve as fetishists and formal re-identification of the continuity of the legal system, which abstracts from what material changes effectively happen during the exceptional time. Accordingly, it is also quite typical to criticise the state of exception precisely by this formalistic obfuscation. As Ninon Grangé noticed, '[l]e recours à l'état d'exception est contesté par la dénonciation de la forme de l'alibi *ante* et de la justification *ex post*'.[87] The normality/exception distinction is a method not only of binding exceptionality but also of reconfirming

82 Fraenkel, *The Dual State*, 89–93, 42.
83 Fraenkel, *The Dual State*, 58.
84 Fraenkel, *The Dual State*, 71.
85 Ferejohn and Pasquino, 'The Law of Exception', 228.
86 Carl Schmitt, *Die Lage der europäischen Rechtswissenschaft* (Internationaler Universitäts-Verlag 1950) 18.
87 Grangé, *L'urgence et l'effroi*, 93.

the identity of the legal system as a formal feature, symbolically separated from its transformations happening effectively.

Exceptionalisation, therefore, takes place as a spiral movement that not only modifies the material content of the law—unbinding exceptionality and shifting its positions within the legal order—but also modifies the ability of the law to record such transformations formally. It thus eats away at the capacity of the law to reaffirm its identity through the normality/exception distinction. In exceptionalisation, not only the field of exceptionality within the law changes in itself, but also the goalposts through which this field is marked and recorded are being shifted.

It is commonly recognised that triggering exceptional devices may have as its result a constitutional, if not revolutionary, change.[88] It opens, as Monod claims, 'political creativity in absolute indetermination of its power to decide', equivalent to a revolutionary gesture.[89] But, in fact, little blocks this change from becoming tacit and unregistered. Exceptional devices can be easily abused precisely to create a crisis situation and mask coups retroactively.[90] As Giacomo Delledonne argues, 'commissarial dictatorships should not transform into sovereign dictatorships: in more familiar terms, states of emergency should not be exploited in order to modify and possibly radically alter the constitutional order'.[91] That statement is postulatively correct, but it is built on the humble 'should'. Meanwhile, exceptionalisation proves that such a process often happens in practice, modifying politico-legal regimes without formal registration, a constitutional or revolutionary moment. Olivier Beaud and Cécile Guérin-Bargues rightly noticed that '[d]ans le cas de l'état d'urgence, *le juge arrive toujours trop tard*'.[92] This observation, however, should be extended: in case of exceptionalisation, the whole formal registration by the legal system comes too late.

In our times, exceptionalisation tends to produce what Barczak calls a 'preventive state' (*Vorsorgestaat*), the legal system which reorganises its temporality in order to focus on future possibilities through the legislative establishment of flexible and general exceptional measures.[93] The result is that the normality/exception distinction becomes muddled. Exceptional states are

88 Saint-Bonnet, *L'état d'exception*, 314.

89 Jean-Claude Monod, *Penser l'ennemi, affronter l'exception. Réflexions critiques sur l'actualité de Carl Schmitt* (Editions de la découverte 2006) 97.

90 Günter Frankenberg, 'Im Ausnahmezustand' (2017) 50:1 *KritJ* 3–6.

91 Delledonne, 'Crises, Emergencies and Constitutional Change', 245.

92 Olivier Beaud and Cécile Guérin-Bargues, *L'état d'urgence. Une étude constitutionnelle, historique et critique* (LGDJ 2016) 215. See also a practical example from the British legal system: Keith Ewing, 'The Political Constitution of Emergency Powers: A Comment' (2007) 3 *Int J L Context* 313–315 and international judiciary: Gross and Ní Aoláin, *Law in Times of Crisis*, 249–316.

93 Barczak, *Der nervöse Staat*, 676.

more and more difficult to distinguish from normality,[94] which Frankenberg called 'cannibalism of the exception'.[95] At the same time, the logic of the division of powers as well as the distinction between *pouvoir constituant* and *constitué* are blurred. Modern exceptionality, unlike its counterpart in ancient Rome, is typically not based on the strict division between the organs triggering the exceptional device and the ones acting in it. Therefore, exceptionalisation reshuffles the institutional logic to the same degree as the logic of powers and normality/exception distinction.

This process, which we observe nowadays in numerous jurisdictions, is not anyhow unprecedented, let alone inexplicable. Exceptionality is an energy that always needs to be somehow bound by the legal system, although it contracts and expands depending on the political conjecture. What we witness now are two concurrent and intertwined processes: (1) the unbinding of exceptionality and its general dispersion throughout legal systems, as well as (2) a decrease in functionality of the normality/exception distinction. As a corollary, our legal systems undergo tacit de-/re-constitutionalisations, 'revolutions without revolutions'.[96] In the meantime, constitutional fetishism becomes more and more observable: regimes defined as liberal democracies formally no longer meet the material criteria of such a qualification, but they purposefully retain the hiatus of hybridity between liberalism and non-liberalism. The obvious counterpart of this process is the fact that the role played by exceptional devices in reaffirming the identity of legal systems is on the wane. The identity of the legal system is no longer something that needs to be declared, let alone affirmed: that would only spoil illiberal hybridisation.

In this way, exceptionalisation not only nowadays unbinds exceptionality from legal constraints but advances the transformations of today's constitutionalism towards fetishist indistinction.

94 'Die Folge dieser Vergesetzlichungsstrategie ist eine Normallage, die den Ausnahmezustand dauerhaft und in einer Weise absorbiert, dass Ausnahmezustand und Normalzustand ununterscheidbar zu werden drohen'. Barczak, *Der nervöse Staat*.

95 Frankenberg, 'Im Ausnahmezustand', 18.

96 Przemysław Tacik, 'Polish Constitutionalism Under Populist Rule: A Revolution without a Revolution' in Martin Belov (ed), *Populist Constitutionalism and Illiberal Democracies Between Constitutional Imagination, Normative Entrenchment and Political Reality* (Intersentia 2021) 275–300.

Chapter 4

Exceptionality, Exceptionalisation and Sovereignty

Przemysław Tacik

4.1 Introduction

In the previous two chapters, I developed key concepts for the general theory of exception, which can offer the field a diachronic and aspiringly universalist perspective. Exceptionality, as we saw, had two aspects: (1) it connoted all forms of acts, measures, practices and discourses that preserved a pre-legal quality of non-normality—a shortcut to direct action of political power—regardless of however they would be classified in a given legal system and (2) it constituted an energy that traverses the normative and assures its welding with reality. In this sense, exceptionality remained an indispensable companion of legality, being responsible for its applicability but requiring proper management through legal channels, such as the state of exception. Exceptionalisation, the second crucial term, describes how reshuffling in the distribution of exceptionality through these channels takes place. In particular, it offered a description of the process in which exceptionality can spill over the entire legal system, muddling the normality/exception distinction and infusing the legal with the political.

Both of these concepts call into question the notion of sovereignty. Naturally, we stumbled upon it already a few times, but in this chapter, it needs to be given a proper analysis in the context of the general theory of the exception. In this chapter, I will attempt to link the two concepts analysed previously in a link with sovereignty. For this purpose, I will present the modern idea of sovereignty as connoting survival and taking the upper hand. In relation to it, modern law emerges from a truce inaugurated by the sovereign. Based on this recognition, I will proceed to analysing the exception and exceptionalisation as correlated to the relation between the political and the legal. Finally, I will present modern law as suspension welded to the work of sovereignty.

DOI: 10.4324/9781003490449-5

4.2 Sovereign as the One Who Lasts: Survival and the Upper Hand

If the general theory of the exception is meant to see its object not as just part of the legal—even if as an excess and borderline category—it needs to theorise the relation between the law, the exception and the sovereign. This link, established by the famous first sentence of Schmitt's *Political Theology*,[1] requires thorough reconsideration. In particular, we need to refrain from perceiving the sovereign as a person holding a position or an office, which Schmitt suggested.[2] As we saw in Chapter 2, there are at least three sovereign positions: (1) nominal-imaginary (e.g., the nation as the assumed ultimate holder of sovereignty), (2) nominal-designated (position or positions in the state apparatus to which the law delegates biggest chunks of exceptionality) and (3) effective (the one who *has already used and exercised* exceptionality). Both three types of positions are, naturally, not inherent in the qualities of any individual; even if a popular leader stages a coup using her charisma, her sovereign powers appear retroactively when they have been successfully exercised, so within a larger legal-symbolic framework.

Sovereignty as a concept precedes these positions. Just as exceptionality was previously understood as a general field corresponding to its particular cathexes, sovereignty can be seen as a field that precedes, upholds and leaves its own *loci*: the sovereign positions. In other words, sovereignty appears as a primordial category vis-à-vis its cathexes (and any 'sovereigns'), whose structure needs to be investigated in the obscure links it has with the construction of modernity.[3] If we invoke a 'sovereign', this one cannot be identified with any actual person holding any office: it is a point of stabilisation of sovereignty, whose personal occupation remains secondary. If so, we need to establish *how sovereignty maintains its role within the legal through exceptionality—that is, through what remains after its contraction due to normalisation.*[4]

1 'Sovereign is he who decides on the exception'. Carl Schmitt, *Political Theology. Four Chapters on the Concept of Sovereignty* George Schwab transl. (MIT Press 1985) 5.

2 Michael Hoelzl and Graham Ward (eds), 'Introduction' in Carl Schmitt (ed), *Political Theology II. The Myth of the Closure of any Political Theology*, Michael Hoelzl and Graham Ward transl. (Polity 2008) 13.

3 Przemysław Tacik, *A New Philosophy of Modernity and Sovereignty. Towards Radical Historicisation* (Bloomsbury 2021).

4 This claim denaturalises Austin Sarat's idea (backed up by a reading of Hobbes) of the jurisgenerative role of emergency, according to which emergency 'is the ever-present threat of chaos that creates the need for law—and the very antithesis or negation of law'. Austin Sarat, 'Introduction: Toward New Conceptions of the Relationship of Law and Sovereignty under Conditions of Emergency' in Austin Sarat (ed), *Sovereignty, Emergency, Legality* (CUP 2010) 4. In my view, the dialectics between unpredictable emergency and the law that tries to contain it obfuscate the role of exceptionality and sovereignty, which mediate between the law and reality and are politically active *within* the law (unlike the naturalised emergency).

Let us begin with a Lacanian observation. The law, as every part of the Symbolic, can be seen as a stream of signifiers, referring to each other in an endless one-dimensional chain. But in this condition, it cannot establish a proper meaning—and therefore an application[5]—otherwise than through what Lacan names '*point de capiton*': a quilting point that stops the chain to stabilise a *signifié*. In his late thought Lacan identified *point de capiton* with *signifiant-maître*, master signifier.[6] What this gesture means is that the temporal fixation of the stream of signification happens through a self-sustained instance.[7] This relation can be easily transposed onto the relation between the law and the sovereign—which, in many respects, corresponds to Lacan's vision of *signifiant maître*. *The sovereign's power intervenes into the signifying chain of the law, not only establishing a momentary signified but allowing this signified to discharge the law-informed decision into social reality.*

By doing so, the act of sovereign power becomes a key to Kripkenstein's paradox that we discussed in Chapter 2. The paradox remains as long as we stick to the dimension of normativity. But the sovereign's power adds to it precisely the missing push which turns the norm into practice. Metaphorically speaking, it provides a third dimension to the otherwise two-dimensional realm of the law. The sovereign's act not only quilts the signifying chain of the law and makes it applicable, but even more importantly, it decides *on itself* that the law has been applied.

This sovereign's power, exercised primordially by the executive (directly) and the judiciary (often in an obfuscated form, as law 'applying itself' through the allegedly neutral mouth of the judge[8]), is thus indispensable in the operation of the law. As Agamben lucidly demonstrated, the day-to-day application of the law is somehow related to exceptional situations.[9] Developing this recognition, we can say that the sovereign

5 On the role of *point de capiton* in the functioning of the law and legal ideology, see Peter Čuroš, 'Who Stands in the Mirror and Who Stares Back. Traditions of Populism in Slovakia' in Rafał Mańko, Adam Sulikowski, Cosmin Cercel and Przemysław Tacik (eds), *Law, Populism and the Political in CEE* (Routledge 2023) 188–192.

6 Jacques Lacan, *Le Séminaire. Livre XVII—L'envers de la psychanalyse* (Seuil 1991) 219.

7 This role of the sovereign also explains the old problem embodied in the adage *quis custodiet ipsos custodies?* that Schmitt applied to the relations between the sovereign and the constitution. Carl Schmitt, *Der Hüter der Verfassung* (Mohr Siebeck 1931) 7. Just as in Lacan's theory, there is no Big Other of the Big Other, the sovereign, as the quilting point, ends the process of interpreting constitution and blocks a metaquestion on its controllability. Naturally, such a conclusion, interpreted in a decisionist spirit, ultimately drove Schmitt to affirm Hitler's role as the 'protector' of the law. Carl Schmitt, 'Der Führer schützt das Recht' in *Gesammelte Schriften 1933–1936* (Duncker & Humblot 2021) 200–201.

8 For an Agambenian interpretation of judicial decisions see Stephen Humphreys, 'Legalizing Lawlessness: On Giorgio Agamben's State of Exception' (2006) 17:3 *EJIL* 677, 682.

9 Giorgio Agamben, *Homo Sacer* Daniel Heller-Roazen transl. (Stanford University Press 1998) 17–18.

appears in two incarnations: the day one, in which its powers—restrained and concealed—are used at the service of the law, and the night one, in which the sovereign reveals its full potency in exceptional situations, revealing itself at the *Ursprung* of previously divided powers. The key observation for the general theory of exception is that these two roles are connected—that the manifest return of the sovereign partakes in the day-to-day tacit execution of the law. In other words, *exceptionality is the price to be paid for the fact that the law is at all practically applicable*. The law without exceptionality could be only a non-operative legal corpus, which is not applied (Agamben's vision of messianic law that is studied but not applied[10] offers a model of the law without exceptionality and, thus, without sovereignty). At the same time, this link is usually dissimulated by legal systems because they aim to compartmentalise exceptionality in particular institutions in order to draw attention to how it remains indispensable. In his famous opening of *Political Theology*, Schmitt grasped much more than he had originally intended: exceptionality remains within the legal as an active shadow of sovereignty.

But how should the general theory of exception understand sovereignty? Naturally, there are not many concepts of political philosophy that would have more definitions and understandings. There would be no place—and sense—here to develop an overview of theories of sovereignty. It rather seems that we should develop a vision of the sovereign that explains how exceptionality represents its power within the legal.

First and foremost, modern sovereignty connotes survival.[11] The sovereign is the one who is certain that they will survive; to occupy the post of sovereignty means to always get an upper hand vis-à-vis the subordinated field, because one is certain of its survival. In this sense, the sovereign embodies the future. It does not know what is going to happen or what powers are going to come, but it knows one thing: it will not let go. A sovereign who lets go ceases to be a sovereign. Thus, as Saint-Bonnet rightly claims, the principal goal of the modern exception is the survival of the state.[12] In this sense, *the theorem of indivisibility of sovereignty is not descriptive, but practically postulative*: sovereignty is *assumed* to be held by the one who survives and offers a foothold for the state's survival. The sovereign thus acquires a peculiar kind of most basic and ultimate reality, as if it were an anchor of the symbolic order.

10 Giorgio Agamben, *State of Exception (Homo Sacer II, 1)* Kevin Attell transl. (The University of Chicago Press 2005) 64.

11 Thomas Hobbes, *Leviathan* (J. C. A. Gaskin tr, OUP 1998) 79–88; John Locke, *Second Treatise of Government* (Hackett 1980) 9–12; Jean-Jacques Rousseau, *The Social Contract in The Social Contract and Discourses* (Dent and Dutton 1920) 30–32. See also Marie-Laure Basilien-Gainche, *État de droit et états d'exception. Une conception de l'État* (PUF 2013) 27.

12 François Saint-Bonnet, *L'état d'exception* (PUF 2001) 39–42, 192, 225.

Hobbes, Schmitt's arch-patron, posed survival as a key philosophical concept. First, it founds the right of nature, that is, 'the liberty each man hath, to use his own power, as he will himself, for the preservation of his own nature; that is to say, of his own life'.[13] Natural law is, therefore, for Hobbes, based on the rule 'by which a man is forbidden to do, that, which is destructive of his life, or taketh away the means of preserving the same; and to omit, that, by which he thinketh it may be best preserved'.[14] *Preservation becomes a living absolute, almost a divine force.* Hobbes notices that when the death of a human being is at stake, the sovereign loses its power and cannot expect obedience.[15] '[N]o law can oblige a man to abandon his own preservation'.[16] But—and here Hobbes makes the crucial move—this conclusion applies to the sovereign itself as well:

> no man that hath sovereign power can justly be put to death, or otherwise in any manner by his subjects punished. For seeing every subject is author of the actions of his sovereign; he punisheth another, for the actions committed by himself.[17]

In Hobbes' vision, the sovereign is properly untouchable not by any divine grace or protection but because it partially overlaps with the subject of sovereignty. In this regard, the biopolitical function of the sovereign corresponds to it representing not only its own survival, its eternity, but the eternity of the people as the totality of its subjects.[18] The survival of the sovereignty is almost tautological: the sovereign cannot be properly attacked because, by doing so, the attacker assaults herself. And unlike a human individual with suicide, human totalities cannot choose their own mass death.

The sovereign represents mere existence as its basic level, an existence which is stubborn and meaningless—hence the special relation between the sovereign and bare life which Agamben theorised[19]—but invincible in its conviction that it is eternal and no future can make it surrender. Naturally, *a certain* sovereign can be put to death by decapitation, for example, as it has often been preferred, but the structure of sovereignty remains and soon another puppet individual begins to function at the heart of it. Hegel—in his dialectics of the master and the slave[20]—demonstrated clearly that the sov-

13 Hobbes, *Leviathan*, 86.
14 Hobbes, *Leviathan*.
15 Hobbes, *Leviathan*, 93.
16 Hobbes, *Leviathan*, 199–200.
17 Hobbes, *Leviathan*, 118.
18 See Basilien-Gainche, *État de droit et états d'exception*, 200.
19 Agamben, *State of Exception*, 71–103.
20 G. W. F. Hegel, *Phenomenology of Spirit* (A. V. Miller tr, OUP 1977) 111–119.

ereign is ultimately this capacity of survival, resisting death, by confronting it directly and resisting it with a simple negative decision that coincides with one's pure existence. The sovereign could use Luther's famous words: *ich kann nicht anders*. In a more adapted transposition, it should be read as follows: 'I exist, by virtue of being who I am, and I cannot disappear'. Once Bodin articulates sovereignty in its absolute cut from any higher earthly power,[21] it appears as a force of pure negativity self-sustained over an abyss.

Legality, in contrast, can disappear very easily, either by repealing or, more interestingly, by non-application. If, as we said previously, the law depends on exceptionality in its applicability, then the relation between the law and the sovereign can be couched in terms of survival. *The law risks its end with every act of application*. Therefore, through exceptionality, the sovereign assures continuous survival of the law. It does so both in the day-to-day application of concrete norms and in times of emergency when the sovereign emerges as the saviour of the legal.

The law, which—as we saw previously—belongs essentially to the past, can always be suspended by the sovereign who embodies the reiterated present and the future under the guise of the certainty of survival. On its own, the law has nothing that would guarantee its continued applicability. Naturally, the law has its own version of eternity: a norm that was not repealed but repeatedly non-applied or violated still holds a claim for normative validity that, on its own grounds, cannot be denied by facts.[22] But even Kelsen admitted that ultimately, the law needs to be applied and, without application, can lose its status even as the law: 'a legal order as a whole, and a single legal norm, can no longer be regarded as valid when they cease to be effective'.[23] The eternity of the law is imaginary; it requires applicability and, thus, the sovereign. As Franz Neumann noticed, sovereignty is an essentially polemic notion—negatively vectored against its enemies—which relies on effectiveness.[24] To the positive and normatively idealist idea of the law, sovereignty adds a power of changing reality, which at the same time maintains a bulwark around the legal system. Sovereign is the mediator—and the invisible wall—that shields the legal from its outsides, both external and internal. Whenever the need to defend the law becomes conspicuous, the sovereign intervenes in the form of exceptionality. In this sense, sovereignty is an empty, negative principle of resilience. Its certainty of continued presence is based on a lack of an alternative—imagined as stubborn self-continuation of life as such.

21 Jean Bodin, *Les six livres de la république* (Fayard 1985) 191–228, 297–299.

22 See Przemysław Tacik, 'Melancholy of the Law' (2022) 33:1 *L & Crit* 32.

23 Hans Kelsen, *Pure Theory of Law* (Max Knight tr, The Lawbook Exchange 2005) 212.

24 Franz Neumann, *Behemoth. The Structure and Practice of National Socialism, 1933–1944* (Dee 2009) 167.

This last claim requires a closer enquiry. As we recall, the exception is the axis of three types of the sovereign: the nominal-imaginary, the nominal-designated and the effective one. Amongst these, the first one plays a crucial role of a stabilising assumption. Nationalism, as a discursive practice,[25] obsessively returns to the idea of the nation as an eternal entity, the one which will always be alive. Such claims are obviously ideological constructs; sociologically and ethnologically speaking, ethnicities, tribes and peoples have always been in perpetual flux, and only the modern idea of the nation, propped by state power, aimed to transform them into eternal, stable and homogenised communities.[26] The surprisingly late discovery that the nation is a product of modern sovereignty and nationalism—the discovery which we owe to Ernest Gellner,[27] Benedict Anderson,[28] Michel Foucault[29] and Eric Hobsbawm[30]—demonstrates the particular link between sovereignty and survival.

As I claimed elsewhere, sovereignty replaces pre-modern transcendence in the modern world.[31] It thus transposes the pre-modern idea of eternity, which in modernity becomes a *perpetual survival.* Where pre-modern symbolic forms were based on the idea of tranquil (o use Hegel's term) eternity rooted in the metaphysical position of divinity, modernity no longer practically believes in anything otherworldly. Nonetheless, it has sovereignty as its proper form of divinity: this one, however, is exposed to the corruptive force of time. It is not outside temporality but within it. Therefore, its specific form of eternity is survival: being in time, experiencing its attacks, but maintaining itself in existence. *There is no (modern) sovereign without battles to fight: if they do not happen in reality, the sovereign always prepares its subjects for them and manage fear in order to create its appearance as the ultimate guarantor of survival.*

The role of the nation in modern political imagery is precisely assuming survival as the feature of sovereignty—through the operation of the effective sovereign who runs the modern state. Naturally, the nation as a mere gathering of individuals has nothing eternal in itself. But as a biopolitical product, it appears like a pre-modern God: someone who has always been here and

25 Benedict Anderson, *Imagined Communities. Reflections on the Origin and Spread of Nationalism* (Verso 2006) 11–12.
26 See Przemysław Tacik, *Deconstructing Self-Determination in International Law. Sovereignty, Exception, Biopolitics* (Brill 2023) 245–271.
27 Ernest Gellner, *Nations and Nationalism* (Cornell University Press 1983).
28 Anderson, *Imagined Communities.*
29 Michel Foucault, *Security, Territory, Population. Lectures at the Collège de France 1977–78* Graham Burchell transl. (Palgrave Macmillan 2009).
30 Eric Hobsbawm, *Nations and Nationalism Since 1780: Programme, Myth, Reality* (CUP 1991).
31 Przemyslaw Tacik, *A New Philosophy of Modernity and Sovereignty. Towards Radical Historicisation* (Bloomsbury 2021) 9–68.

will always be there. Sieyès's identification of the nation with *pouvoir constituant*[32]—the one who will always remain as the ultimate source of political power and any future constitutional determinations—demonstrates precisely this binding between always-surviving communal life and power. Through such a naturalisation a 'life' of the whole community is imagined.[33] As an agent of perpetual survival, it provides an imaginary foothold for political institutions and, through them, the law. Such equivocation is well-discernible in Schmitt's *Verfassungslehre*, in which one of the senses of the term 'constitution' is a political form that a nation takes at a given moment.[34]

Consequently, the imaginary sovereign is the one who lasts and the one who can afford survival. As such, it builds the matrix of the communal 'we'. 'We', the political community, are those who need to survive and will survive. Where sovereignty triggers this dimension, all richness of individual, interpersonal and communal life fades; what begins to matter is *just* 'our' continued existence. 'We are who we are, we need to simply live' is the most basic rhyme that the sovereign wants its subjects to sing together. Fear for survival throws us into the throes of a biopolitical structure of a sovereign community. The structure of sovereignty corresponds to the question of who will eventually make it through. But, in fact, it is only the permanency of sovereignty projected onto the community that produces all this imagery of continued life. Sovereignty holds us captives by making its own continued existence the issue of 'our own' survival. Whoever lives, whoever dies, it is the sovereign that throws the dice. The Shoah as a mass crime committed by a polity built on the obsession of its own survival and threats thereto—perpetrated against a people that was positioned as a threat—demonstrates in an ultimate way the upper hand of sovereignty and its permanent obsession of deciding on survival or death.

From this perspective, projects that strove to found the law on some kind of presumed naturality—such as the liberal idea of deducing the law from natural human freedom—ultimately clash with the vision of the law as the concession of the sovereign. Much as both visions can compete, the sovereign has—as it is its wont—the upper hand: assuring survival. Once the tones of protection and defence are struck, the sovereign prevails and begins to appear as the source of power, whose emanation the law becomes. Therefore, the great modern invention of popular sovereignty—of the presumed rule of us over us—is, in fact, a trick of sovereign structures that construct a certain

32 'The nation exists prior to everything; it is the origin of everything. Its will is always legal. It is the law itself. Prior to the nation and above the nation there is only natural law'. Emmanuel Joseph Sieyès, 'What is the Third Estate?' in *Political Writings* (Michael Sonenscher tr, Hackett 2003) 136.

33 Michel Foucault, *"Society Must Be Defended". Lectures at the Collège de France 1975–1976* David Macey transl. (Picador 2003) 239–263.

34 Carl Schmitt, *Constitutional Theory* Jeffrey Seitzer transl. (Duke University Press 2008) 59.

'us' from which they subsequently draw legitimacy. The effective sovereign interpellates—to use Althusser's term[35]—the nominal sovereign in order to create it as its own prop. What is more self-evident than the question of whether we want to be ourselves and—as ourselves—survive? But once it is answered approvingly, the nominal sovereign 'recognises' itself as a subject. Meanwhile, the effective sovereign already imposes itself as the mediator of identity, operator of power and guarantor of survival.

Thus, modern law is in the throes of the sovereign who imposes itself as its *Hüter*, to quote Schmitt's famous formula.[36] It becomes enmeshed in the biopolitical machine, in which the effective sovereign interacts with the nominal-imaginary one, posing itself as its protector. The sovereign will not exist without being assigned the role of the cyclical organisation of a spectacle, in which the promise of survival ('we will overcome') fully overlaps with proclaiming the identity of the subject who is to survive. But whenever *salus populi* or *salut public* are invoked, exceptionality present within the legal system acts like a lightning rod through which the impulse of sovereign power is discharged. The legal field contracts in order to allow the sovereign to act.

For this reason, modern states are, to a certain extent, thanatocracies. In his dialectics of master and slave, Hegel rightly noticed that the power of the master—whom we can identify with the sovereign—establishes itself through an ability to confront death.[37] In Hegel's narrative, this confrontation does not necessarily seem one-off: just like the visions of the social contract in the 17th- and 18th-century philosophy, it is rather a permanent source of the present state of affairs. The peculiar essence of the modern sovereign is its relationship to death: assuring survival means a constant confrontation with it. As a consequence, the sovereign reasserts itself in the situation of war. The typical (and usually legally asserted) link between the state army and the head of state as commander-in-chief demonstrates this affinity. The army is the ultimate force of the state, able to confront the Schmittean enemy—the one with whom the final political rift established itself.[38] The army is the borderline force of the state, as it aims at the annihilation of the enemy; in this fight, it represents precisely the Hegelian position of the sovereign as hovering above the abyss of death, founded ultimately on nothing but pure resilience.

35 Louis Althusser, *Sur la reproduction* (PUF 1995) 226.

36 'Der Ruf nach einem Hüter und Wahrer der Verfassung ist meistens ein Zeichen kritischer Verfassungszustände'. Schmitt, *Der Hüter der Verfassung*, 1.

37 Hegel, *Phenomenology of Spirit*, 117.

38 Carl Schmitt, *The Concept of the Political: Expanded Edition* George Schwab transl. (The University of Chicago Press 2007) 26. See also Arthur F. Utz, 'Die politische Theologie von Carl Schmitt' (1999) 85 *ARSP* 398, 401; Oren Gross, 'The Normless and Exceptionless Exception: Carl Schmitt's Theory of Emergency Powers and the Norm-Exception Dichotomy' (2000) 21 *Cardozo L Rev* 1825, 1831.

No wonder, therefore, that the threat of the use of armed forces is inextricably intertwined with some forms of exceptionality, martial law in particular.[39] By establishing martial law, the sovereign quickly contracts the scope of the legal in order to replace it with the threat—or the actual use—of bare force, naturally with the aim of assuring survival. In this context, the link between, on the one hand, the norm/exception distinction and, on the other hand, the distinction between friend and enemy—that Karin Loevy retraces after Schmitt,[40] joining his two fundamental theorems—is particularly telling. The sovereign retains normality for those who are 'friends', so that enemies may experience pure exception as a bare violent force.

Exceptionality is based on the immunological logic of thanatocracy.[41] This is why entering the exceptional mode often replaces the modern sense of penal law, based on individual accountability for concrete actions, with the logic of protecting against particular threats.[42] Ernst Fraenkel demonstrated convincingly how, in the Third Reich, the Prerogative State involved precisely this discourse of *possible threat*, which rendered it unpredictable when it will act to suspend the Normative State.[43] As I remarked earlier, the sovereign represents the future and the possibility; as such, it is mandated to reverse the temporal logic of penal law so that it is no longer focused on what has been done but on what *may be done*.

Consequently, exceptionality modifies the status of the legal subject as created by the legal ideology of the modern state. Various Marxist theorists sought to demonstrate that the fiction of the modern legal subject produces it as a rational executioner of inherent entitlements entangled in the normatively backed chain of exchange.[44] But this is the 'daylight subject' of the law. The presence of exceptionality within the legal adds another layer to it. From the perspective of exceptionality, the legal subject is split as both a member

39 On the war-like component in the state of exception, see Ninon Grangé, *L'urgence et l'effroi. L'état d'exception, la guerre et les temps politiques* (ENS 2018) 126.

40 Karin Loevy, *Emergencies in Public Law. The Legal Politics of Containment* (CUP 2016) 18.

41 Cf. Achille Mbembe, *Necropolitics* (Duke University Press 2019) 66–92. International relations today can be seen as a result of the absorption of exceptionality into international law: as soon as war was generally prohibited, the enemy lost the legal protection and the fight against them turned into a domain of fact. Hence, as noticed by Schmitt, penalisation of war paradoxically accompanies growing tendencies to annihilate the enemy. See Carl Schmitt, *Nomos der Erde. Im Völkerrecht des Ius Publicum Europaeum* (Greven 1950) 298.

42 François Saint-Bonnet, 'De l'urgence à la résilience: la reconquête du temps long' in Pauline Gervier (ed), *La sortie de l'état d'urgence* (IFJD 2020) 81–82.

43 Ernst Fraenkel, *The Dual State. A Contribution to the Theory of Dictatorship* E. A. Shils, Edith Lowenstein & Klaus Knorr transl. (The Lawbook Exchange 2010) 40–42.

44 Slavoj Žižek, *Surplus Enjoyment. A Guide For The Non-Perplexed* (Bloomsbury 2022) 33; Isaac D. Balbus, 'Commodity Form and Legal Form: An Essay on the "Relative Autonomy" of the Law' (1977) 11 *Law & Soc* 215, 220; Richard Kinsey, 'Marxism and the Law: Preliminary Analyses' (1978) 5 *Brit JL & Soc'y* 202, 210; Oskar Negt, 'Thesen zur marxistischen Rechtstheorie' (1973) 6 *Krit Just* 1, 6.

of the biopolitical community whose survival the sovereign assures and, at the same time, a potential bearer of the threat. All the intricate cobwebs of entitlements that build up a stable legal subject who enjoys human rights, concludes contracts and makes claims are thus always at risk of potential suspension invoked by the sovereign. The exception protects the biopolitical welding of the state and the population.

The stability of the legal subject—and, naturally, of the legal framework that upholds it—can thus be seen as a result of a *truce* between the law and the sovereign, the normal and the exceptional. In exploration of this truce, we need to enter the genealogy of relations between the legal and the sovereign.

4.3 The Truce: The Emergence of the Law from the Modern Tsimtsum of Sovereignty

After writing *Se questo è un uomo . . .*,[45] his famous first book on Auschwitz, Primo Levi published a volume of memoirs and considerations of the time that ensued immediately after his liberation from the camp. The volume is—tellingly—entitled *The Truce* (*La tregua*).[46] The title is sobering: in Levi's account, the war is not properly 'over' in the sense of being definitively ended. It is rather a truce that was reached, a new period of peace of inherently limited duration. No messianic hopes for the end of the conflict should be harboured. One side 'won' (although Jewish survival is a victory marred by unspeakable tragedy), but the other did not lose, as it could not lose—it would keep re-establishing itself permanently.

Levi poignantly describes how the war against the Jews was not over. After leaving the camp, he passed through a small Polish town near Auschwitz, where some local inhabitants questioned him at the train station. A Polish lawyer acted as interpreter. While introducing Levi to the crowd, he presented him as a former camp internee who was detained as a member of the Italian Resistance, not as a Jew. Appalled, Levi asked him for an explanation, to which the lawyer answered, embarrassed: 'C'est mieux pour vous. La guerre n'est pas finie'.[47] The war was indeed not finished, although nominally ended; it cast its long shadow on everything. Upon returning to Italy, it seemed to Levi a temporal respite which necessitated the regrouping of forces, but at a moment of great exhaustion:

> We felt in our veins the poison of Auschwitz, flowing together with our thin blood; where should we find the strength to begin our lives again, to

45 Primo Levi, *Se questo è un uomo* (Einaudi 2014).

46 Primo Levi, *La tregua* (Einaudi 2017).

47 Levi, *La Tregua*, 60–61; Primo Levi, *If This is a Man and The Truce* Stuart Woolf transl. (Abacus 1987) 227.

> break down the barriers, the brushwood which grows up spontaneously in all absences, around every deserted house, every empty refuge? Soon, tomorrow, we should have to give battle, against enemies still unknown, outside ourselves and inside; with what weapons, what energies, what willpower? We felt the weight of centuries on our shoulders, we felt oppressed by a year of ferocious memories; we felt emptied and defenceless. The months just past, although hard, of wandering on the margins of civilization now seemed to us like a truce, a parenthesis of unlimited availability, a providential but unrepeatable gift of fate.[48]

The Shoah was over, but the permanent conflict of which it was the most drastic stage continues. Nothing is permanently decided or ended; the conflict will surely be rekindled. At the same time, the world celebrated the end of the war, oblivious to those for whom it was not ended but rather suspended.

Levi's concept of the truce can be read as a stunningly fruitful inspiration for modern political thought—and, in particular, our considerations on exceptionality. To start with a boldly general claim: *between the law and sovereignty in modernity, there is a fleeting truce*. The concrete content of this truce is subject to permanent change. As we noticed previously, the concept of exceptionality is able to grasp how the boundaries keep shifting. Yet the war behind the truce is not over; as long as the eon which shapes our political horizons stays with us, we live in times of truce interspersed with rekindled sprees of war.

The presence of exceptionality within the legal is a token of this truce. A legal system that would be able to evacuate exceptionality totally and establish itself without a reference to sovereign power could be imagined as clusters of norms, especially of civil law, before the solidification of modern legality in its dependence on sovereignty. But such a vision is a *contradictio in adiecto*: escaping the truce by an anachronistic withdrawal. The truce (and exceptionality as its permanent remainder) inscribes modern legal systems into the lineage of struggles and tensions between the legal and the sovereign. Schmitt's nihilist enemy-friend theorem is not universal; it should rather be properly read as an interpretation of the truce, which delineates the very border conditions of modern legality in its relation to sovereignty.

This remark corresponds to the perspective in which modern legality can be seen as a product of the process of normalisation in which sovereign power contracts to make space for the law.[49] As Saint-Bonnet notices,

48 Levi, *If This is a Man and The Truce*, 378.

49 This process corresponds to the creation of what Schmitt called 'the neutral state', an authoritarian arbiter in worldview and religious conflicts that tore Europe apart in the 17th century. Carl Schmitt, *The Leviathan in the State Theory of Thomas Hobbes. Meaning and Failure of a Political Symbol* George Schwab and Erna Hilfstein transl. (Greenwood Press 1996) 56–66.

'la pratique de l'autolimitation ouvre un espace pour l'exception'.[50] Locke's concept of the prerogative, which founded the role of the exception in liberalism born out of the English compromise between the king and the parliament in the 17th century, corresponded to the moment of this contraction.[51] In reference to the also early modern theologico-metaphysical concept of the *tsimtsum*—connoting Isaac Luria's vision of the primordial contraction of God, who makes space for the creation of the world[52]—we can imagine the establishment of the modern legal order as the creation of positive normativity out of the negative self-limitation of sovereign power. This process can be seen either as a contraction (from the side of the sovereign, often obfuscated by the idea of *octroi*—self-limitation through the establishment of the law[53]) or normalisation (from the side of the legal, in whose ideology the sovereign has been conquered and limited by the law). Yet, quite importantly, there is no neutral description of it that could abstract from deciding between either of these labels. Contraction and normalisation are both valid descriptions, with both parties of this relationship being active in the struggle.

Naturally, sovereign power holds no obvious historical primacy vis-à-vis the law. Yet, in the lineage of modern European politics, the cut-off point happens around the 19th century, when almost all legal norms began to draw their legitimacy from sovereign state power.[54] This process seems almost like a trade-off: in the developing rule of law/*Rechtstaat* the sovereign allows the law to curb its power and, in return, obtaining the position of the ultimate source of the law.[55] Yet, as perspicaciously noticed by Marie-Laure Basilien-Gainche, the rule of law is based on exceptional regimes which are like a 'preface' to it and their 'vecteurs de fondation'[56]—both historically and as a continuous back-up. Exceptionality can thus be seen precisely as the product of this process: the sovereign leaves a huge space for the law

50 Saint-Bonnet, *L'état d'exception*, 31.
51 John Locke, *Second Treatise of Government* (Hackett 1980) 82–84. See also Loevy, *Emergencies in Public Law*, 27–28, 262; Gross, 'The Normless and Exceptionless Exception', 1842–1843; Clement Fatovic, *Outside the Law. Emergency and Executive Power*(The Johns Hopkins University Press 2009) 4–5, 47–53; Nomi Claire Lazar, *States of Emergency in Liberal Democracies* (CUP 2009) 73; Oren Gross and Fionnuala Ní Aoláin, *Law in Times of Crisis. Emergency Powers in Theory and Practice* (CUP 2006) 120–123.
52 Christoph Schulte, *Zimzum. Gott und Weltursprung* (Jüdischer Verlag im Suhrkamp 2014); Lawrence Fine, *Physician of the Soul, Dealer of the Cosmos. Isaac Luria and His Kabbalistic Fellowship* (Stanford University Press 2003) 126–144.
53 See Basilien-Gainche, *État de droit et états d'exception*, 21.
54 Murray Raff and Anna Taitslin, 'Private Law in the Shadow of Public Law: A Legacy of 20th Century Marxism and the Soviet Legal Model' in Thomas Bustamante and Oche Onazi (eds), *Human Rights, Language and Law* (Franz Steiner Verlag 2012) 157.
55 Cf. Heiner Bielefeldt, 'Deconstruction of the "Rule of Law": Carl Schmitt's Philosophy of the Political' (1996) 82 *ARSP* 379, 382–386.
56 Basilien-Gainche, *État de droit et états d'exception*, 10.

to manage, but it controls entry locks to the system, acting as its ultimate protector. At the same time, the truce has a distinctly class character. Just as noticed by Benjamin, the lower classes experience the truce as war with non-military but police means.

For the rule of law, this seems an *almost* perfect victory. The legal system begins to manage and control the exercise of political power, yet the price to be paid is that it starts to depend on the sovereign centre. The law as a command of the sovereign—barred from the kind of legitimacy that natural law disposed of—may form itself as a system with its own principles and internal hierarchies, but the sting of sovereignty remains within it under the guise of exceptionality (and thus maintains a special position of the executive, even if obfuscated by constitutional narratives).[57] In other words, *exceptionality is both a remainder of the original contraction/normalisation process and a guarantee that the sovereign will hold the ultimate say over the legal.* It entails a suspended temporality whose heart is in the sovereign decision on invoking exceptionality.

Exceptionality is, therefore, a counterpart of the general liberal movement of ruling by abstracting the state from economy and society. Foucault's analyses of liberalism as active but negative management of society correspond to exceptionality as remaining rein over what was apparently let loose.[58] Still, the rule of sovereignty remains, and it operates as a membrane between the inside and the outside, peace and order. The creation of this order, which in some respects is connoted by the concept of the rule of law, necessitates the remainder of sovereign power which upholds it, and this remainder is precisely exceptionality. First states of exception in the modern sense of the word occur in post-revolutionary France[59] both as a token that an order had been established and as an exemplification of how exceptionality binds the internal and external in one totality of threat, against which normality is being constituted through abstraction, suspension and 'protection'.

A very particular field of these tensions is human rights. Usually, there are legal limitations to the extent of their suspension; *de facto* suspendability, as demonstrated during the COVID-19 pandemic, can go much further. Is not this suspendability, *de iure* or *de facto*, a token of the fact that human rights—precisely against their inner ideology—were octroyed by sovereign power and thus subjected to the sovereign's exception? The irremovable character of human rights

57 See Fatovic, *Outside the Law*, 35; Christian Bjornskov and Stefan Voigt, 'The Architecture of Emergency Constitutions' (2018) 16 *ICON* 109.

58 Michel Foucault, *Naissance de la biopolitique, Cours au Collège de France, 1978–1979* (Gallimard, Seuil 2004) 22, 120–125. See also Agamben's historico-theological commentary on the split of divine power between *regno* and *gloria*, which corresponds to the structure of this modern divided sovereignty: Giorgio Agamben, *Il regno e la gloria. Per una genealogia teologica dell'economia e del governo* (Bollati Boringhieri 2009) 124–131.

59 Saint-Bonnet, *L'état d'exception*, 291–314.

in modernity corresponds to the most profound biopolitical binding between sovereignty and 'its' populations: they were octroyed with the same movement that created modern sovereigns, entangling the strings with which the truce has been woven. But the widespread factual ignorability of human rights—if the sovereign finds it necessary—demonstrates that no law can withstand the power of sovereignty manifested in exceptionality.

Modern law is thus positioned in a structurally transient position between an original event and the possibility of future revocation of its autonomy. From the legal point of view, this dependence of the law on the sovereign is expressed in the distinction between *pouvoir constituant* and *pouvoir constitué*: the nominal-imaginary sovereign retains the right to amend a constitution or to adopt a new one.[60] Consequently, it is this kind of sovereign that is expected—and *assumed*—to survive no matter what happens to the law. Meanwhile, the nominal designated and effective sovereigns position themselves as counterparts to the nominal one and its protectors who operate on the legal system in liminal moments.

Moments when exceptionality is mobilised are performative acts, in which the effective sovereign (either the nominal-designated or the one which emerges through a *de facto* coup) invokes—that is, assumes, presences and refers to—the effective sovereign as the object and subject of survival. The particularity of this performance is that it embodies the biopolitical crack: protection of the nation as the sovereign takes place on an apparent mandate that the effective sovereign finds in need of assuring its master/object's survival (even if with reference to the law, as Lincoln did evoking his presidential oath).[61] With the same act, the effective sovereign reconfirms its position.[62] As Franz Neumann once noticed, sovereignty finds limitations not 'in the law, but in the bases on which sovereignty rests, in the area in which it is effective, and in the people from whom the state can command obedience'.[63] It is precisely in the exceptional moments that the effective sovereign asserts itself, retroactively, in a staged unity with the subject of survival.

Exceptional measures—through their performed radicality and the crisis context which they evoke—make an impression that they revive some primordial forms of power. They often aim at creating an acute sense of existence, in which individual tremors would biopolitically overlap with the

60 On this point, see Saint-Bonnet's critique of Schmitt's binding between the sovereign and the exception, with the apparent omission of constitutional powers—Saint-Bonnet, *L'état d'exception*, 314.

61 Clinton Rossiter, *Constitutional Dictatorship. Crisis Government in the Modern Democracies* (Routledge 2017) 224–229; Michael Stokes Paulsen, 'The Constitution of Necessity' (2004) 79 *Notre Dame L Rev* 1257–1277; Gross and Ní Aoláin, *Law in Times of Crisis*, 50.

62 As Günter Frankenberg noticed, these moments exude a force of 'raw masculinity' and 'border experience' that make them attractive spectacles for many. Günter Frankenberg, 'Im Ausnahmezustand' (2017) 50:1 *KritJ* 3.

63 Neumann, *Behemoth*, 167.

anxiety of the whole population whose survival is at stake. But there is, in fact, nothing essentially primordial or ancient in the brutality of biopolitical power. Exceptional measures cause their own distortion of history in two dimensions: (1) by creating artificial continuity of the subject who is to survive and (2) by assuming that suspension of the truce—withdrawal from the sovereign's *tsimstsum*—is somehow natural and historically justified. But there is no historical point that would hold this kind of validity: exceptional measures produce their own artificial past to gain legitimacy.

Exceptionality remains a tool of the effective sovereign through which it can invoke the totality of the body politic that it aims to protect. It seems, therefore, that *the presence of exceptionality within the legal corresponds to the permanent production of the biopolitical community (presented as nominal sovereign) through the invocation of the potential risk to its survival.* This recognition solves a classical problem of legal theory—namely, the question: How can the law be ultimately created by the nation and, at the same time, decide on what this nation is? In international law, this paradox has a peculiar form related to the right to self-determination: How can a people exercise self-determination if somebody needs to determine this people first?[64] The obvious answer is that the nominal-imaginary sovereign (the nation or the people) has, as its counterpart, the effective sovereign who manages it and, through the idea of assuring survival, determines its boundaries. The Kelsenian ideal of the state as just a pure legal order[65]—in other words, the ideals of the law that triumphed over sovereignty—misrecognises the role of the secret intermediary without which the connection between the nation as law-giver and the subject of the law would be impossible. Therefore, the presence of exceptionality within the law remains proof that modern law needs an instance that will weld it with the population.

The biopolitical component of modern exceptionality marks a clear cut with pre-modern forms of emergency. Naturally, it is quite common to begin narratives on emergency measures with usual references to Roman dictatorship[66] or by claiming, like François Saint-Bonnet, that '[l]'exception est de tous les temps'.[67] Much as this historical background can be informative, we should not forget that modern exceptionality functions: (1) against the backdrop of the idea of the rule of law, that is, the idea of the normalisation of politics, (2) in a legal order that is theorised as dependent on the sovereign's command, (3) in the historical context of contraction of sovereign power

64 Ivor Jennings, *The Approach to Self-Government* (CUP 1956) 55–56.

65 Kelsen, *Pure Theory of Law*, 286–319.

66 John Ferejohn and Pasquale Pasquino, 'The Law of Exception: A Typology of Emergency Powers' (2004) 2:2 *ICON* 210, 213; Jean-Claude Monod, *Penser l'ennemi, affronter l'exception. Réflexions critiques sur l'actualité de Carl Schmitt* (Editions de la découverte 2006) 81–83; Gross and Ní Aoláin, *Law in Times of Crisis*, 18–26.

67 Saint-Bonnet, *L'état d'exception*, 1; Rossiter (n 61) 20–28.

and, finally, (4) in the biopolitical field between the community as the subject/object of survival and the effective sovereign.

Therefore, modern exceptionality is structurally different from its pre-modern forms. This is best visible in the fact that Roman dictatorships were directed outwards and used strictly military means to repel an external threat.[68] But, modern exceptionalities are predominantly directed inwards and use police means in order to govern the population through emergency measures.[69] They are activated in response to an existentially threatening impulse,[70] in which the internal and external are often entangled. As Hannah Arendt rightly noticed, the peculiarity of Nazi totalitarianism was that it blurred the distinction between the inside and the outside: in fact, from the point of view of Nazi racism, the whole relationship to the outside world was theorised as a matter for the police.[71] This feature of Nazism, however, represents a broader specificity: modern exceptionality has a biopolitical component displayed in its focus on managing the population through police methods. It is in this sense that we can understand Ninon Grangé's claim that 'la guerre civile se dit et se vit sous le régime de l'exception':[72] exceptionality and civil war display an affinity which is based on their biopolitical relation to sovereignty.

If sovereignty is necessarily split and distributed throughout the legal system, can exceptionality be linked with any particular position within the state? Famously, Schmitt identified the sovereign through the ability to decide on the exception.[73] But if exceptionality is a concept that goes beyond the scope of such a stable pairing, can we say that exceptionality has a particular locus or loci?

If exceptionality is seen as a palimpsest of fleeting constellations of exception/normality distinctions, then it does not correspond to *the* sovereign imagined as a stable and determined post. In the general theory of the exception,

68 Saint-Bonnet, *L'état d'exception*, 46–54. See also Grangé, *L'urgence et l'effroi*, 139–149.

69 As Barczak writes, 'Ein charakterisches Merkmal des Ausnahmezustands ist seit jeher die Aufhebung der Trennung zwischen den Rechtsbereichen *domi* („zu Hause") und *militiae* („im Kriegsgebiet") und damit der Einsatz der „bewaffneten Macht" zur Gefahrenabwehr bzw. der umfassende Übergang der Exekutivgewalt von der Zivil-auf die Militärverwaltung auch ohne Anforderung durch erstere'. Tristan Barczak, *Der nervöse Staat. Ausnahmezustand und Resilienz des Rechts in der Sicherheitsgesellchaft* (Mohr Siebeck 2021) 594.

70 Wolfgang Fach, 'Souveränität und Terror' (1978) 6:3 *Leviathan* 333, 350.

71 'Totalitarianism in power uses the state administration for its long-range goal of world conquest and for the direction of the branches of the movement; it establishes the secret police as the executors and guardians of its domestic experiment in constantly transforming reality into fiction; and it finally erects concentration camps as special laboratories to carry through its experiment in total domination'. Hannah Arendt, *The Origins of Totalitarianism* (A Harvest Book 1976) 392.

72 Grangé, *L'urgence et l'effroi*, 12.

73 Schmitt, *Political Theology*, 5.

the proper correlate of exceptionality is sovereignty—understood not as a general concept of political philosophy but as a map of posts associated with sovereign power in a concrete order. Depending on a particular politico-legal system, it can be distributed variously throughout its space. Naturally, the simplest form is the one in which sovereignty would be contained within one particular locus, the sovereign. Nonetheless, as we already saw, sovereignty works through split and assumptive reference, thereby not offering containability within one point. The legal fiction of channelling sovereignty corresponds strictly to legal channelling of exceptionality. They both haunt the law which strives to fix them in institutions.

In this way, we can develop and generalise Schmitt's postulate about the relation between the sovereign and the exception: *sovereignty involves agency vis-à-vis exceptionality*. In concrete situations, this may mean indeed that the sovereign decides on the exception.[74] But it is not a universal rule. First, even in most organised politico-legal systems, there is a quantum of exceptionality apart from the exception (states of exception, martial laws, emergency measures, etc.)—just as there is a quantum of sovereignty beyond the formal post of the sovereign. They should rather be imagined as energies that can be concentrated in certain institutional frameworks, but not without remainders and stray currents that travel across the systems. It is for this reason that no designated sovereign can be sure of her position, as stray sovereignty always travels around it (hence the sovereign paranoia).[75]

Second, maps of exceptionality and sovereignty evolve over time; quite often, sovereignty vacates the nominal designated post of the sovereign and is claimed elsewhere. Good examples of such situations are usually given in prolonged conditions of war when sovereign power migrates from the sovereign (the head of state, the executive, etc.) to military commanders or general staff. The role of the duumvirate Paul von Hindenburg and Erich von Ludendorff at the end of WWI in the German Empire, who effectively took over a significant chunk of sovereign power from the Kaiser in the exercise of their military command, is a perfect illustration. Moreover, sudden crises may reposition the cathexis of exceptionality and sovereignty: even without a proper constitutional act, the relation between *pouvoir constituant* and

74 As Hasso Hofmann notices, 'Wer die Möglichkeit des Ausnahmezustands einräumt und für diesen Fall an der Wiederherstellung der bisherigen Rechtsordnung interessiert ist, muß einen handlungsfähigen Souverän postulieren'. Hasso Hofmann, 'Souverän ist, wer über den Ausnahmezustand entscheidet (Carl Schmitt)' in Ulrike Müßig (Hrsg), *Konstitutionalismus und Verfassungskonflikt. Symposion für Dietmar Willoweit* (Mohr Siebeck 2006) 273.

75 Gross and Ní Aoláin link sovereignty, paranoia and exception in the following way: '[t]he existence of an exception, or a possibility thereof, means that the sovereign must always be vigilant and, in fact, paranoid. The result is that the sovereign is not only the one who decides on the exception, but also the one who definitely decides whether the normal situation actually exists'. Gross and Ní Aoláin, *Law in Times of Crisis*, 165.

pouvoir constitué may change and a new organ or person can claim effective sovereignty.

Third, especially in liminal moments, different institutions of the state may compete to claim sovereignty. A situation of dual power can occur, in which the legal system breaks down into two: one being a constitutional order maintained by courts and the other being a *de facto* order built by the executive. In such situations, there is no longer one effective sovereign. Ultimately, if sovereignty is understood as having *the potential to enforce its ultimate say*, quite often, there cannot be one sovereign until this final say is enforced in a confrontation. *Sovereignty should be imagined as an expectation of victory in the final clash*, but this clash rarely happens in reality and remains a vision that acts upon the present. In this sense, sovereignty is like state debt in a late capitalist economy. The debt is like the future acting here and now, permanently maintained in this condition. It is very rarely requested and, if so, mainly for political goals. Consequently, sovereignty is the expectation of victory in a battle that will probably never come but influences the present without actually happening.

Therefore, sovereignty should be imagined more like energy travelling around the system, fixable in institutions but subject to evaporations, migrations and sudden transfers. Naturally, there are two privileged sites of sovereignty: the head of state and the executive (sometimes fused, as in the US Constitution). Many constitutional systems aim to include parliaments in deciding on exceptional measures, thus trying to ascribe to them part of sovereign power. Still, it is important to notice that concrete maps of sovereignty and exceptionality can be deduced from constitutional determinations, but retain an indelible factual component. Beyond any constitutional provisions, heads of state and the executive remain privileged loci of sovereignty as those who are supposed to assure the polity's survival in times of emergency ultimately. Additionally, there is a marked link between sovereignty, exceptionality and administrative discretion.[76] The executive (including administration) and the heads of state can thus be seen as posts on which the shadow of the pre-normalised sovereign power is cast—as places where the historical axis of normalisation pierces the present. But sovereignty can easily migrate out of these privileged loci and be found elsewhere, especially in moments of crisis.

In sum, modern law should be perceived as structurally inscribed into a logico-chronological order that can be seen in its entirety only from the perspective of genealogy of exceptionality. Modern legal orders *appear as* born out of the process in which sovereign power was contracted (from its own

76 Günter Frankenberg, *Authoritarianism: Constitutional Perspectives* (Edward Elgar 2020) 98–100; Saint-Bonnet, *L'état d'exception*, 8; Karine Roudier, Albane Geslin and David-André Camous, *L'état d'urgence* (Dalloz 2016) 17–19.

side) and normalised (from the side of the law). Exceptionality remains both a trace of this process and a foothold for sovereign power through which it brings the future into the legal. All this politico-legal system is based on a permanently shifting equilibrium, with the struggle between the law on the one side and sovereignty/exceptionality doublet ending in a truce, but not the final peace.

Sovereignty and exceptionality are two bound concepts that, in particular systems, ossify into the pair the sovereign—the exception. But, from the point of view of the general theory of exception, *sovereignty and exceptionality are two modalities describing the same field*. They both connote a singular intervention into the general. Sovereignty entails the expectation of a victory, the imagined final battle and, consequently, survival of concrete life. Interestingly, sovereignty ultimately relates to some particular here and now, *a surviving life*. What it brings into the legal is precisely this factual concreteness, without which the law would not have a foothold in the world of *Sein*. Meanwhile, exceptionality connotes patterns of reaction through which general law confronts factual particularity that the future inevitably holds. But, what ultimately unites them is the position of *singularity*, which offers a foothold to the circumscribed generality of a legal order. What this singularity entails is radical solitude of liminality and non-generalisable existence.

Schmitt's theorem can thus be correct in particular orders, but within the general theory of the exception, it needs to be seen as a concrete incarnation of the general binding between sovereignty and exceptionality.

4.4 Exception as an Intersection of Axes: The Political v. The Legal and The Rule v. The Case

In the previous section, we built the general concepts of sovereignty and exceptionality, taking them for intertwined types of energy that penetrate the legal. When fixed, they give rise to the interconnected pair: the sovereign and the exception. As we saw, the general link between sovereignty and exceptionality—*the agency* that binds them—turns then into its reduced form: Schmitt's theorem on the sovereign deciding on the exception. The last thing that remains to be enquired about here is how exceptionality relates to the axis 'general rule—individual case' and, consequently, the relationship between the political and the legal.

As we mentioned previously, it was Agamben who established—albeit somewhat cryptically—the link between the exception (understood in the context of the state of exception) and the typical application of the law.[77] At

77 On Schmittean antecedents of this claim, see Regan Burles, 'Exception and Governmentality in the Critique of Sovereignty' (2016) 47:3 *Security Dialogue* 239, 249.

first sight, linking these two contexts seems unusual: the exception connotes special situations, emergencies, martial laws, etc., whereas the application of the law is the most normal of the normal. How can the general theory of exception react to his postulate? First, let us recapitulate Agamben's proposal:

> The exception is a kind of exclusion. What is excluded from the general rule is an individual case. But the most proper characteristic of the exception is that what is excluded in it is not, on account of being excluded, absolutely without relation to the rule. On the contrary, what is excluded in the exception maintains itself in relation to the rule in the form of the rule's suspension. The rule applies to the exception in no longer applying, in withdrawing from it. The state of exception is thus not the chaos that precedes order but rather the situation that results from its suspension. In this sense, the exception is truly, according to its etymological root, taken outside (*ex-capere*), and not simply excluded.[78]

In Agamben's thought, the exception remains a *device* through which the law captures the zone from which it withdraws. But, this device concerns not only a situation in which the whole legal order aims to control its outside (as the state of exception) but *every situation in which the normative struggles to control the case*. In other words, Agamben's 'exception' stands for the general relationship between, on the one hand, the general and the normative and, on the other hand, the particular and the real. Consequently, it is *a frontier of the normative vis-à-vis reality and the future*.

Here, I come back to the previously mentioned postulate: a quantum of sovereignty (and, accordingly, exceptionality) is necessary as a mediation between the law and reality. If so, the structure of the truce analysed in the previous subchapter occurs not only in the 'grand axis' between the whole legal order and general suspension (in the state of exception, for example) but *in every capillary of law-controlled execution of power*. Sovereignty is thus indispensable as the structure for the link between the rule and the case, even in the most detailed and particular areas of the legal order.[79] At the same time, it necessarily brings with itself a quantum of exceptionality. Even if this power can be limited and very local, it is of the same nature as the 'grand' exceptionality of emergency measures.

78 Agamben, *State of Exception*, 17–18.

79 Although international law remains outside of the scope of these considerations, it needs to be noticed that as an area which is a backstage to state sovereignty—thus reigned by a mix of both plurality and absence of sovereign power—international law exhibits a particular perturbation between rules and cases, making exceptions a permanent component of its applicability. See Inger Osterdahl, 'The Exception as the Rule: Lawmaking on Force and Human Rights by the UN Security Council' (2005) 10 *J Conflict & Sec L* 1–10.

Consequently, the modern truce should not be seen as a replacement of some area of political power by the law. A better picture is the one that portrays the law as a *system of distribution of power which operates through complex ramifications*. Each detailed legal norm is a capillary through which power is discharged. Therefore, modern law would not necessarily limit this power in total but rather trailed the paths of its execution.

If, as we noticed previously, exceptionality and sovereignty offer the necessary future supplement to the legal rule, then we can say that the process of normalisation corresponds to the management of exceptionality. Agamben's postulate quoted earlier would mean that a modicum of exceptionality accompanies every rule. But this observation can be just the beginning of further theorisation. The legal system aims to manage exceptionality by establishing the distinction between normality and exception. By doing so, it attempts to evacuate exceptionality from a certain area of the legal order—creating there an illusion of almost automatic self-applicability of the law—and concentrate it in another designated area, normatively dubbed as the exception. Therefore, the distinction between normality and the exception—as an intra-normative device—is a necessary step in normalisation and management of exceptionality.[80]

The most crucial bulwark erected by normalisation separates exceptionality at every end of capillary norms from exceptionality at the foundations of the legal order. In other words, normalisation aims at the possibly greatest separation between day-to-day norm application and the state of exception, even though both are built with exceptionality. Still, as it was established previously, exceptionality spills over these bulwarks and can migrate between them. In the process of exceptionalisation, analysed in Chapter 3, these two areas of exceptionality can melt together, rendering a legal system inoperative. Agamben's postulate can be thus read at two levels: (1) theoretically—as the recognition that exceptionality operates both in 'normal' application of the law and in exceptional measures and (2) factually—as a constatation that legal bulwarks for exceptionality can crumble and make both its 'normal' and 'exceptional' normative incarnations conflate.

Exceptionality at the outlet of each 'normal' legal norm involves the fundamental uncertainty of law application, typically obfuscated by interpretation techniques. As this theme was well explored by legal realism and critical legal theory,[81] let us proceed here to analysing exceptionality as the locus of interaction between the political and the legal. In the incarnation

80 See also Rebecca Gould, 'Laws, Exceptions, Norms: Kierkegaard, Schmitt, and Benjamin on the Exception' (2013) 162 *Telos* 1, 17.

81 See Peter Goodrich, *Reading the Law. A Critical Introduction to Legal Method and Techniques* (Basil Blackwell 1986); Duncan Kennedy, *A Critique of Adjudication [fin de siècle]* (Harvard University Press 1998); David Kennedy, *International Legal Structures* (Nomos 1987).

of a concrete legal system, where it appears as the exception intertwined with the sovereign, it appears to make law application precisely an axis in which the political and the legal interact. *The relationship between the legal and the political can be presented as part of a cross-entanglement with another axis, rule/case, with both the sovereign and the exception serving for the quilting point of both axes.* The sovereign (and the exception) are in the black zone that dissociates the rule and the case—and, at the same time, the political and the legal. In this zone, there is no rule and no case but pure *krinein*; simultaneously, the political and the legal become indifferentiable.

The sovereign would thus be the crucial point of binding in which the political is interlaced with the legal, becoming its essential part. Retroactively, the political is entangled in the play of the legal: it thus cannot be *entirely* primary in relation to it since it is already absorbed in the legal as a part of its apparatus. The sovereign—born from the truce that dissociates between the legal and the political—occupies the point of their intersection. This is precisely the point that corresponds to the link between the rule and the case maintained by the exception.

Seen in this perspective, the relationship between the sovereign and the exception is not necessarily based on causality denoted by the term 'decision'. In Schmitt's thinking, the decision is a level-zero term for the irreducible: it accounts for what is decided but in itself cannot be further accounted for.[82] But if we are to go further, perhaps it should be rather grasped through the lens of Kafka's last sentence in *The Trial*: K., the victim of a pseudo-judicial murder, watches—face to face with his executioners—the decision (*Entscheidung*) that has taken place.[83] Its singularity takes precedence, creating and binding the sovereign, its act and its subjects/victims forever.

If so, the relationship between the sovereign and the exception can be more generally seen as taking place within the third dimension that mediates between the legal and the political. From the perspective of the legal, they occupy one and the same place: in its two-dimensional perspective, the sovereign *would be* the exception proper. Yet only if we take into account that the legal and the political are two separate, though entangled, orders, quilted precisely by the dialectical relationship between the sovereign and the exception, can we take into account that the sovereign and the exception do not overlap fully. *The sovereign would be the position within the political which corresponds to a puncture within the legal known as the exception.*

82 In this sense, the exception is a 'metaphysical matter', as Andrew Norris noticed. Andrew Norris, 'Sovereignty, Exception, and Norm' (2007) 34 *JL & Soc* 31, 38.

83 'Aber an K.s Gurgel legten sich die Hände des einen Herrn, während der andere das Messer ihm tief ins Herz stieß und zweimal dort drehte. Mit brechenden Augen sah noch K., wie die Herren, nahe vor seinem Gesicht, Wange an Wange aneinandergelehnt, die Entscheidung beobachteten'. Franz Kafka, *Das Prozeß in Das Werk* (Dörfler 2011) 367. I owe the focus on this sentence to Vivian Liska.

Therefore, in a more general manner, the sovereign should not be perceived as a position within the legal, let alone a particular person occupying this position. Neither does it 'own' the exception. *The sovereign is rather a dynamic correlate of the exception*, its other side within the quilting point between the legal and the political.

The use of the exception displaces both exceptionality and sovereignty: the sovereign is no longer in the same situation after applying exceptional measures. Such a 'use' is not a safe execution of a stable entitlement, but rather an irruption of forces within the legal that re-arrange the sovereign's binding as well. If exceptional measures cannot contain them, as is often the case, exceptionality and sovereignty are let loose to a peculiar form of a state of nature. Bare confrontation of forces, as well as resilience and determination, will decide the real sovereign as the position from which the exception *has already been decided*.

If the sovereign is indeed a dynamic correlate of the exception, we can try to perceive the centrality of the sovereign and the exception *only as a particular constellation of the political vis-à-vis the legal*. Meanwhile, previous considerations demonstrated that the exception and the sovereign are central by nature but rather as local stabilisations of two dynamic forms of energy: exceptionality and sovereignty. Both the sovereign and the exception as legal constructs are meant to suck out exceptionality from all parts of the legal system and concentrate it within one bulwarked central point. Thus, they aim at *maximally reducing the visibility of the political within the legal*. Metaphorically speaking, it is the drain that evacuates the political as much as possible from the legal. Naturally, it cannot disappear since it is the point where the legal draws its ultimate power from the political and *always gains the upper hand vis-à-vis reality, which is the mark of sovereignty*. But its firm reduction to the seemingly well-demarcated boundaries of the state of exception gives the legal an appearance of complete autonomisation.

To sum up, the legal system—which we saw previously as developing within the field of a truce—can be seen as a distribution of the energetic fields of both sovereignty and exceptionality. Most crucially, a well-functioning legal system should be able to dissociate exceptionality contained at its bottom—by compartmentalising it within exceptional measures, such as the state of exception or martial law—from its tiny quanta that appear at the end of the capillaries of the normative system. To this end, legal systems establish their inner distinctions between normality and exception, making the latter explicitly temporary, limited and subject to additional conditions. In other words, driving through the legal system a distinction between what is normal and what is exceptional is part and parcel of the process of normalisation as management of exceptionality. There is, consequently, a strict link between how a legal system evacuates exceptionality from the day-to-day application of the law—that should appear as legal as possible—and the concentration of exceptionality in special institutions.

4.5 Exceptionalisation between the Legal and the Political

Fixing exceptionality in its cathexes—which delineate a particular territory of the exception in a given legal order—aims at sucking it out of the legal system and thus reducing the visibility of the political in the legal. In a nutshell, the firmer isolation of exceptionality in legal devices—such as the state of exception—the more autonomous legality presents itself in its relation to the political. But what dynamics does exceptionalisation bring to these relations?

The intuitive answer would be that exceptionalisation increases the presence of the political within the legal. This presence is not easily translatable on the visibility of the political, given that legal ideology may deform it with illusions of normality. In such cases, the political is obfuscated in the law but discernible in mounting social tensions and generalised feelings of exceptionality behind apparent normality. But, what we also need to take into account is the paradox described previously by Dyzenhaus: some legality may be worse than none. Exceptionalisation does not just precipitate the political out of the legal, setting unbridled political power free. It rather reorganises the way in which the political and the legal are intertwined. *Exceptionalisation is the process in which the quilting point between the political and the legal can be extended over the entire legal system.*

Together with the dispersion of exceptionality throughout the legal system, the position of the sovereign begins to change. Just as exceptionality quits the exception, so does sovereignty quit, in exceptionalisation, the locus of the sovereign. As we said previously, the law is marked by *a permanent struggle to bind the political with the legal through a map of exceptions correlative to the sovereign position(s)*. The uniqueness and centrality of the sovereign are guaranteed by a well-circumscribed area of exceptionality. Whenever the sovereign corresponds to one central device, such as the state of exception, its position shares the features of the exception: stability, overriding position vis-à-vis the legal, identification with one office or even one person. Still, if exceptionalisation destabilises the central legal embedding of exceptionality within a legal device, then the sovereign is no longer one stable position. It is rather a changing map of positions dynamically determined by shifting exceptionality. Whenever exceptionality leaves the safe bulwarks of the state of exception and begins to permeate the entire legal system, sovereignty is no longer concentrated within the figure of the sovereign but rather disperses throughout the legal. If so, *the sovereign would be a particular constellation of sovereignty as such, which might equally be more scattered, flexible and changing if not countered by a firm fixing of the exception by a legal device*. In other words, if exceptionality flows out of the boundaries determined by the state of exception, the position of the sovereign accordingly dissolves into a changing map of positions of sovereignty. The crucial feature of exceptionalisation is that they no longer need to be concentrated in one institution, office or person, but can become a field of contestation.

Schmitt rightly recognises in his famous theorem that even though the sovereign seems primary vis-à-vis the exception, as its 'decision-maker', *it is the relation to the exception that partakes in constituting the sovereign*. If so, whenever the exception is in flux, so is the sovereign. It is then erroneous to seek primacy or causal relations in detecting where the shifts in exceptionality come from: the exception or the sovereign. It might be enough to say that both—in their specific three-dimensional relation binding the political with the legal—change their positions simultaneously, in a close binding. *The triad sovereign—exception—state of exception is just a particular stable incarnation of the two more general concepts: sovereignty and exceptionality*. The process of their destabilisation is precisely exceptionalisation.

If the sovereign decides on the exception—or, to be more precise, on the use of the form of exceptionality already circumscribed within the legal system—it is no longer the 'decision' of the sovereign how exceptionality determines the very position of the exception. The sovereign itself is fixed by this process. As I claimed in Chapter 2, exceptionality 'precedes' the sovereign and the exception by determining the map of their particular incarnations in a given system. This, in turn, means that every particular form of sovereignty is dependent on how exceptionality defines its borders. If exceptionalisation destabilises the exception as the quilting point between the legal and the political, then *sovereignty is evacuated from the solid position of the sovereign and begins to permeate the entire legal system*. It ceases to be fixed to one position within the system; there is no longer a singular bearer of sovereignty. Instead, other actors might find themselves locally and temporally exercising sovereignty.

Thus understood, sovereignty takes a turn from the sovereign-centred paradigm hallowed by Schmitt and Agamben towards a more flexible and processual understanding. Admittedly, if exceptionality is firmly embedded in the state of exception of which the sovereign is a correlate, then exercising sovereignty is solely in its hands. Yet such a conjectural overlap should not mislead us as to the relation between sovereignty and the sovereign. The former might be concentrated in the position of the latter, thus producing well-known aporias of the centralised locus of power always having the upper hand. But it may be equally dissolved into a more flexible set of positions, where sovereignty is exercised momentarily and—to use Foucault's term—capillarily.[84]

The spread of exceptionalisation means that more actors decide on particular exceptions than just one central sovereign. As a result, each of these actions becomes a quilting point between the legal and the political. From the

84 Michel Foucault, 'Power and Strategies' in Colin Gordon (ed), *Power/Knowledge: Selected Interviews and Other Writings 1972–1977* (Vintage 1980) 142.

perspective of the legal, exceptionalisation is nothing less than a systematic collapse of the law at its key feature: applicability. The fundamental grasp that the legal has over reality—analysed by Kelsen in relation to *Grundnorm* and effectiveness[85]—begins to dissolve into a map of positions where each time, its applicability invokes the political in a direct and explicit way. Cases are not decided with reference to the content of the law (even if with the irreducible jump over the abyss between the general and the particular) but through a fundamentally sovereign decision on what law is at all applicable. What, therefore, separates an exceptionalised legal system from the 'ordinary' functioning of the law—firmly embedded in the state of exception and the position of the sovereign—is the fact that *decisions are not taken within a space determined by the law, but outside of the law, in relation to its very applicability*. In an exceptionalised legal system, particular actors make the decision whether the law applies or not. To reiterate: this decision does not concern the applicability of one norm or another; it is not about whether one norm takes precedence over another or repeals it, which is the daily bread of every law-applying institution. After exceptionalisation, *the law as such is the subject of the decision*, which, for this reason, has a fundamentally political character.

This form of the legal in an obvious manner, eats away at legal certainty. Even more importantly, it eats away at the autonomy of the law, which becomes permeated by exceptionality not within the well-isolated realm of the state of exception but in its full extension. Contrary to the Schmittean account of the state of exception, the sovereign does not reconfirm here its own position, let alone suspend the legal through its own actions. Exceptionalisation dissolves the sovereign itself, dispersing it into a set of variable positions from which sovereignty is exercised locally and without formal authorisation of the legal.[86] If the quilting point between the legal and the political spills over the realm of the law in an uncontrolled way, then sovereignty exceeds any provisional fixes through which the legal attempted to embed it within its structure and give it formal legitimacy. *One no longer exercises sovereignty in reference to the formal position that the law strives to ascribe to the sovereign; it is exercised in the most basic sense just because it emerges from the quilting point of the legal and the political.* Local actors of sovereignty are not designated as such; they might draw legitimacy from the legal system, but the true role that they exercise is factual and correlative to the current map of relations between the legal and the political.

To wrap up these considerations, it should be reiterated that exceptionalisation does not necessarily open up an abyss of the political within the legal

85 See Sections 2.4 and 2.5 in this volume.

86 On the interpretation of Schmitt which perceives sovereignty as dispersed, see Burles, 'Exception and Governmentality', 251.

but rather makes the abyss already circumscribed—within institutions like the state of exception—spread over the entire legal system. In this lies the value of distinguishing the state of exception as a particular legal device, a form of exceptionality, from exceptionalisation as a metaconcept describing the process in which the distribution of exceptionality within a legal system is transformed. Agamben seems to confuse the two, adding the third understanding: the state of exception as a *status* in which the exception begins to govern the law (in this sense, it is close to exceptionality).[87]

Mounting exceptionalisation conflates the factual and the legal, making the very applicability of a rule each time dependent on a decision of the actor that exercises sovereignty at a given point. From the intra-legal ideological point of view, this process appears to be a collapse of legal autonomy and an unacceptable intrusion of the political into the legal. Yet, when perceived from a meta-level, increasing exceptionalisation is just a reconfiguration of the inherent binding between the political and the legal which is necessitated by the effectiveness of the law. It is perhaps this binding that sheds light on the otherwise obscure moment in Hans Kelsen's thinking, in which he attempts to determine what makes the law work. Kelsen felt compelled to make a concession for effectiveness as part of the validity of a legal norm. 'A minimum of effectiveness is a condition of validity',[88] Kelsen claims, noticing at the same time that the norm must preserve the possibility of being violated because a norm which acts like a law of nature is 'senseless'.[89]

> Just as the norm . . . as the meaning of an act is not identical with the act . . ., is the validity of a legal norm not identical with its effectiveness; the effectiveness of a legal order as a whole and the effectiveness of a single legal norm are—just as the norm-creating act—the condition for the validity; effectiveness is the condition in the sense that a legal order as a whole, and a single legal norm, can no longer be regarded as valid when they cease to be effective.[90]

Validity is a feature of the norm within the legal itself. But its effectiveness, which assumes *applicability*, must be based on an entanglement with the political—and, thus, require exceptionality. Therefore, *exceptionality—be it bulwarked in a legal device, be it spread over the entire legal system—is the price that the law pays for its effectiveness.*

Exceptionalisation means that the legal and the political cannot escape their entanglement but only change the way in which it is organised.

87 Agamben, *State of Exception*, 18–19.
88 Kelsen, *Pure Theory of Law*, 11.
89 Kelsen, *Pure Theory of Law*.
90 Kelsen, *Pure Theory of Law*, 211–212.

These two dimensions are intertwined through the 'shaft' of the two paired instances, the sovereign and the exception. Applicability of the law demands that it be quilted to the political somewhere. Yet, if exceptionalisation is dispersed too broadly over the realm of the law, to the point when it begins to cover the entire system, the political slowly takes over the legal. It consumes it from within: all decisions previously issued in the name of the law and bearing a trace of relation to the normative descend into the abyss of political arbitrariness. Alongside this process, the legal loses its fundamental grip on reality, not being able to decide a case without an explicit sovereign act that belongs to the political. In this way, the political underpinning of the legal becomes visible. *Yet, it is now an element that must intervene in the fundamental undecidability of the law opened by exceptionalisation.*

4.6 Law as Suspension: Infinite Deferral of the Law and the Exceptional Discharge

The preceding considerations allow us to make one last step towards the general theory of the exception. The question to be answered is ponderous: what—in the light of exceptionalisation—does modern law bring to political power?

In his *Philosophy of Right*, Hegel interprets (modern) sovereignty in a surprisingly fruitful way:

> Sovereignty, at first only the universal thought of this ideality, exists merely as a subjectivity assured of itself, and as the abstract and so far groundless self-direction and ultimate decision of the will; by virtue of this quality the state is individual and one. But in the next place subjectivity exists in its truth only as a subject, and personality as a person. In the constitution, which has matured into rational reality, each of the three elements of the conception has its own independent, real, and separate embodiment.[91]

Hegel's crucial discovery consists in identifying the structural triality of sovereignty. First, it is an abstract, groundless self-direction of the will, which decides 'ultimately'. Second, it is a subject and thus a part of the symbolic system—in Hegel's parlance, a constitution—on which a subject's position depends. Third, it is located somewhere. Hegel believes it needs to reside in an individual, preferably a constitutional monarch. Yet, in the light of our previous discoveries, we know that sovereignty can be dispersed throughout the system. Whichever option applies, sovereignty needs to reside somewhere;

91 G. W. F. Hegel, *Philosophy of Right* S. W. Dyde transl. (Batoche Books 2001) 225.

it is always *located* (just as consciousness is inseparable from intentionality in Husserl's phenomenology).[92]

The link and tension between sovereignty as the groundless potency to decide ultimately and its symbolic subjectivity has been a paradox ruminated upon by philosophers at least since Hobbes. But what Hegel grasps here is that sovereignty appears both as constructed within a legal system and as a force that founded it. It is a superposition of two loci that, from the side of the law, make it a full system and, from the side of reality, make it effective. As if bringing Schmitt's and Agamben's positions to the end, in this interpretation, sovereignty and exceptionality appear as two incarnations of the same position. This unique place is an excellent vantage point.

Seen from the side of the sovereign, the law is dispersion and deferral of political power. What it provides is *a great detour in the relation between power and reality*: a detour that takes place in a symbolic system and requires sovereignty as its cap. Therefore, modern law and modern sovereignty are inseparably intertwined. Sovereignty makes sense only in the relationship between ultimate decision-making and a deferral of a decision. The law reproduces reality in a symbolic order so that political power may operate on it, but in itself, it cannot cross the boundary with reality, requiring sovereignty as its quilting point. If we agree with Alain Supiot that the law historically precedes the state,[93] the great transformation brought forward by modernity is that the law becomes trapped by and within sovereignty, as its framework of distribution and deferral, which is structurally paralysed vis-à-vis reality until sovereignty intervenes.

Modern law is unique in so far as it does not pretend to just direct the execution of power or reproduce a natural order of justice: it creates a seemingly self-sufficient symbolic reproduction of the world based on the sovereign root. Sovereignty—based on the conviction of always having the upper hand vis-à-vis reality, as we saw previously—offers a foothold for modern law to *grasp* the world with its normative reproduction. In other words, without this sovereign grip, modern law would not be able to impose itself upon reality as a full symbolic world. At the same time, sovereignty would not have its meaning if the law did not offer a totalising normative grounding of reality.[94] Classic Marxist critiques of the law, focusing on the fact that it universalises and obfuscates exploitation through artificial equality,[95] in fact,

92 Edmund Husserl, *Ideas Pertaining to a Pure Phenomenology and to a Phenomenological Philosophy. First Book: General Introduction to a Pure Philosophy* (F. Kersten, Martinus Nijhoff 1983) 200.

93 Alain Supiot, *Homo juridicus. Essai sur la fonction antropologique du Droit* (Seuil 2005) 226.

94 See Carl Schmitt, *On the Three Types of Juristic Thought*, Joseph W. Bendersky transl. (Praeger 2004) 76.

95 Christopher M. J. Boyd, 'Can a Marxist Believe in Human Rights?' (2009) 37 *Critique* 579, 594; Alan Hunt, 'Law, State and Class Struggle' 20 (1976) *Marxism Today* 178–182; Edgar Bodenheimer, 'Impasse of Soviet Legal Philosophy' (1952) 38 *Cornell LR* 51, 66.

aim at this fundamental binding. Modern law does not organise and regulate the existing world; *it strives to create the world normatively from scratch*. In this context, human rights appear as the ultimate attempt not only to replace the human being with a legal subject[96] but also to give it a fully naturalised foothold, a legally defined nature.

Consequently, it would be impossible to imagine a 'truly' pure sovereign power in modernity without an admixture of the law, and vice versa. It seems that the ontological emergence of modern sovereignty contains within itself a modicum of legality. Kant grasped this paradox in his *Critique of Practical Reason*, noticing that modern will is born already in relation to its inherent universalisation, which happens through the law.[97] In other words, legality is the language in relation to which the modern sovereign appears as a speaking subject. Sovereignty does not appear symbolically otherwise than through 'speaking' legality, that is, distributing itself through the capillaries of the law. Only when legality becomes a full language, closing its determination of reality, sovereignty and exception, two dimensions of the same, appear in their proper forms.[98]

The relation between legality and sovereignty, as soon as internally defined by the law, establishes itself as the normality/exception distinction. In turn, this distinction delineates the area which is the projection of *the subject of the law onto the law*. Using Lacan's conceptuality, we can say that exceptionality fixed by the law corresponds to the 'I' of the law: a murky area that represents and covers the abyss of this part of sovereignty that exists outside of the law. In this respect, exceptionality represents self-identification and survival of the law. Through the invocation of exceptional devices, the law

96 See Bernard Edelman, *Le droit saisi par la photographie* (Flammarion 2001) 22.

97 'If a rational being is to think of his maxims as practical universal laws, then he can think of them only as principles that contain the determining basis of the will not by their matter but merely by their form.

The matter of a practical principle is the object of the will. This object either is the determining basis of the will or it is not. If it [were to] be the will's determining basis, then the rule of the will would be subject to an empirical condition (viz., to the determining presentation's relation to the feeling of pleasure and displeasure) and consequently would not be a practical law. Now if from a law all the matter, i.e., every object of the will, is separated (as determining basis), nothing remains of the law but the mere *form* of a universal legislation. Therefore a rational being either cannot think of *his* subjectively practical principles, i.e., maxims, at the same time as universal laws at all, or he must assume that the principles' mere form by itself alone, whereby they *are fitting for universal legislation*, makes them practical laws'. Immanuel Kant, *The Critique of Practical Reason* Werner S. Pluhar transl. (Hackett 2002) 40.

98 This observation is corroborated by the French example: Until 1789, it was not clear how the king related to sovereignty-related norms of public law. In particular, it was undetermined whether he could infringe them, as if they had been just its own derogable self-limitation, or not, in which case they would constitute properly constitutional provisions. The moment when the law determines this position, exceptionality appears in its proper form. See Saint-Bonnet, *L'état d'exception*, 237.

re-establishes its own identity as something that can exist through time.[99] In this consists the fundamental paradox of legalised exceptionality: *invoking the state of exception re-affirms the purely formal, fetishist and sovereign identity of the state and its law, precisely at the same time when exceptionalisation modifies its content.*[100]

The use of exceptional devices is, therefore, a structurally identitarian gesture through which the legal system reconfirms its formal continuity against material transformations. The proper question that exceptionality studies should ask is thus not 'Can the end of the state of exception re-establish the normal *status quo ante*?' (materially it cannot),[101] but 'How does the use of the state of exception produce a formal illusion of continuity against material change?' Using exceptional devices produces a performative effect on the identity of the legal system itself: although these devices are gates to acting exceptionality, they at the same time reuptake it in order to assert the identity of the legal system. This identity is expressed through the sovereign 'I' of the legal system that speaks and reasserts itself as 'still the same'. Therefore, binding exceptionality in and through the law is essential in building the law's own temporality—as periods of normalisation separated by the performances of exceptional acts by the sovereign 'I'. Moreover, the very fact that these devices remain within the system has not only a normative, but also prophetic-identitarian logic: *as long as there is a state of exception within a legal order, there continues to exist somebody who is to be defended and somebody who will defend.*

In contrast, *ongoing exceptionalisation muddles both the identity of the legal system and its internal arrow of time.* Performances of exceptionality cease to mark the periods of normalisation. There is no proper *status quo ante*, as there are no temporal marks. The presence of sovereignty becomes dispersed but ubiquitous. And just as in Lacan's *Seminar X*, its veiled closeness produces anxiety.[102]

Given all the previous considerations, exceptionalisation sheds new light on the legal system. First of all, it allows us to reconstruct conceptually the pre-ontological scene in which sovereignty and legality emerge in an intertwined bundle. While legality develops into a web of channels and capillaries distributing power, sovereignty remains as a short circuit of the legal system that gives it the upper hand over reality and, therefore, in contact with

99 As Saint-Bonnet notices, 'exception est l'invocation tendant à rattacher l'ordre juridique nouveau à l'ancien en vertu de la fonction légitimante de la continuité'. Saint-Bonnet, *L'état d'exception*, 314. See also Barczak, *Der nervöse Staat*, 206–207.

100 See Grangé, *L'urgence et l'effroi*, 321–323.

101 See Steffen Augsberg, 'Denken von Ausnahmezustand her. Über die Unzulässigkeit der anormalen Konstruktion und Destruktion der Normativen' in *Freiheit—Sicherheit—Öffentlichkeit* (Nomos 2009) 29.

102 Jacques Lacan, *Le Séminaire. Livre X—L'angoisse* (Seuil 2004) 91–105.

it. Precisely because of this sovereign grasp, there needs to be a minimum distance between the sovereign point and reality, which is filled out by normativity. The upper hand of sovereignty is based on establishing an unconquerable, almost fetishist place vis-à-vis reality: from this point, normativity performs a redoubling of the real world. But normativity in itself is impotent if it does not serve as a channel for the discharge of power contained in sovereignty.

In other words, the law begins in the sovereign foothold and develops in the space delimited by the curvature of exceptionality (which, as we know, is another incarnation of sovereignty). Exceptionality links legality both to the original grasp that sovereignty offers over reality (and in this function, it appears in exceptional devices) and to reality accessible in the day-to-day application of norms. In this sense, the law never *touches* reality other than through its outer limit, assured by exceptionality. The decision is, in this light, a discharge of sovereignty through the exceptional membrane between the law and reality. Exceptionality cuts through the inherent deferral of the law to reach its outside.

The general theory of exception can be thus concluded by noticing that the law is the suspension of the exception as much as the exception is the suspension of the law. Both are entangled in the sovereign structures of grasp-through-suspension. Without exceptionality, the law would be just an intraversable infinite space from Kafka's *Kaiserische Botschaft*,[103] an Agambenian object of interminable study, but never a working machinery. Ontogenetically, the law arises as the suspension of the exception and returns to it when the distance between sovereignty and reality needs to be contracted.

4.7 Conclusions

The general theory of exception offers a theoretical framework in which both exceptionality and sovereignty are conceived of as *fields of energy* rather than stable loci. This move allows for analysis of particular legal systems in which these two concepts are concretised as pairs, 'the sovereign—the exception', through the lens of ongoing transformations, migrations and spillovers that happen around such designated places.

The concept of exceptionality allows for grasping each legal system as *a palimpsest of normalisations and exceptionalisations*. Modern legal orders need to be seen as resulting from a specific truce: roughly speaking, a permanently shifting compromise between the legal and sovereignty. Normalisations and exceptionalisations correspond to the patterns of expansions and contractions of the legal vis-à-vis sovereignty. Moreover, exceptionality

103 Franz Kafka, 'An Imperial Message' in *The Complete Stories*, N. N. Glatzer ed. (Schocken Books 1976) 4–5.

gives a proper foothold for a genealogical analysis of a legal system. From its perspective, the distinction between normality and exception is a fleeting constellation established by the legal system itself. What it assures is the distribution of exceptionality—most importantly, by separating its work in relation to the entire legal order from its role in day-to-day law application.

Consequently, the general theory of the exception develops two strategic theorems by Schmitt and Agamben. First, in Schmitt, the sovereign is designated by its ability to decide on the exception. Here we will rather say that sovereignty and exceptionality are both two names of the same field of energy, which, when concretised in a given legal order, breaks down into the pair 'the sovereign—the exception' with *agency* as their link. In other words, the sovereign is the name of the subject of potency whose concrete boundaries and entitlements represent the exception. Second, in Agamben, there is a link between 'special' or 'emergency' exceptionality, such as the state of exception, and the day-to-day application of legal norms. Within the general theory of exception, this link is equivalent to the presence of exceptionality at two 'ends' of the legal system. Exceptionality/sovereignty is both a strategic supplement to law application, giving it its future, and the foothold of survival in cases when *salut public* is at stake.

Ultimately, exceptionality remains engrained in the very construction of modern sovereignty. The upper hand of the latter—the permanent possibility of a definitive intervention—defines normality as a truce. And it is this truce that exceptionality both permeates with its deferred potential presence and offers channels to leap from the law to reality. Deferral remains the very structure of how modern sovereignty and legality interact: they are both locked, with legality distributing and deferring the application of sovereign power and sovereignty intervening as a deferred force. Nowhere is it better discernible than in exceptional devices, which—like symptoms—offer an insight into the throbbing heart of negativity underneath the legal system. Exceptionality, present in legality like dregs in a coffee cup, is a reminder that normality that we know in the modern era is a construct based on suspension. The biopolitical logic which can grasp at any difference, manipulating it to rekindle the sovereign fight for survival and against the survival of the 'enemy', remains. Thus, exceptionality within the law remains a *temporal and existential substratum of modern statality.*

Chapter 5

Liberal Legalism and the Normalisation of the Exception

Gian-Giacomo Fusco

5.1 Introduction

The epistemological framework against which the state of exception has been construed in theory and devised in law is structured upon the dichotomy 'normality-exception'—where the latter cannot but be a temporary deviation from the first. Traditionally, its paradigmatic legal form evolved around three main elements: a legally legitimised authorisation to deviate from an order of norm (expressed in a constitutional provision or legislative instruments), stated circumstances in which such deviation is considered necessary and a clear temporal limit of the deviation. According to this paradigm, when specific threatening circumstances are defined as 'in place', an agent is authorised to deviate from the law and to take all the necessary measures to bring normality back in a limited period.[1] The framing of exceptional/emergency law according to this structure is a response to the worry about the perpetration *ad infinitum* of the exception—with the logical consequence of the destruction of normality and the arbitrary establishment of a new normative order. History is constellated by episodes of abuse of the discretion to deviate from the rule of law based on powers legally granted: embedded in any crises is the risk of exceptional and, therefore, illegitimate changes to legal and political systems. For this reason, emergency laws should operate both towards the containment of threatening events and of the broader powers they usually afford.

There is little doubt that, over the past few decades, the state of exception has steadily been normalised.[2] A close succession of emergencies, from

1 Bernard Manin, 'The Emergency Paradigm and the New Terrorism: What If the End of Terrorism Was Not in Sight?', in Sandrine Baume, Biancamaria Fontana (eds), *Les usages de la s´eparation des pouvoirs* (Paris: Michel Houdiard, 2008) 136–171.

2 On the normalisation of the state of exception, see Mark Neocleous, 'The Problem with Normality: Taking Exception to "Permanent Emergency"', *Alternatives* (2006): 31; Jean-Claude Paye, *Global War on Liberty* (New York: Telos Press, 2007); Günter Frankenberg, *Political Technology and the Erosion of the Rule of Law: Normalizing the State of Exception*

DOI: 10.4324/9781003490449-6

the never-ending terrorist threat to natural disasters and pandemics, had a decisive impact on governmental systems around the world, which have predictably reacted by implementing exceptional security measures aimed at strengthening police powers and limiting civil and political liberties. Traditionally equipped with emergency (constitutional) provisions originally intended to tackle extreme social and political crises, such as wars and insurrections, liberal democracies found themselves somehow legally unprepared to manage the multiplicity of critical events populating the current global scenario. The necessity to contain emergencies that do not conform to the 'classic' war-like form saw the proliferation of a plethora of ordinary and non-ordinary legislative measures tailored to fit the crisis of the day, making emergencies into moments of intense norm-production, juridification and institutional contestations. As Gunter Frankenberg poignantly argued, such a dynamic of normalisation implies that 'the instruments and ideology of emergency law are step by step wrapped in a cloak of regular normativity', becoming 'part of everyday life through their juridification, their emergence as *topoi* under emergency law as well as their inclusion in the doctrines of regular law'.[3]

Considering such a tendency, the framework of normality/exception that has underpinned the common sense of emergency powers seems to lose its epistemic function. When crises are no more occasions for a simple suspension of rights and delegation to the executive of broad extra-legal powers but become a field of normopoietic interventions, the exception seems to become a category of normality and as a concept loses its heuristic potential in accounting for the administration of emergencies. This is the kernel of a narrative of emergency that has been gradually established in the last two decades, especially in the field of (liberally oriented) legal theory, which has shifted the focus from the nature and scope of the growing network of legal instruments and institutions involved in the management of emergencies to the normative and political means for the containment of the transformative potential always present in exceptional circumstances.

The liberal mind seems to have 'made its peace with the state of exception',[4] by reducing its paradoxes to simple procedural questions of legitimate control and judicial oversight. As Nomi Claire Lazar put it, 'Normal and emergency values are continuous. Normal and exceptional institutions also have important elements of continuity. By decentring the norm/exception dichotomy, we can see how liberal democracies might remain such, even as they derogate

(Cheltenham: Edward Elgar, 2014); Ryan Patrick Alford, *Permanent State of Emergency: Unchecked Executive Power and the Demise of the Rule of Law* (Montreal: McGill-Queen's University Press, 2017); Alan Greene, *Permanent States of Emergency and the Rule of Law: Constitutions in an Age of Crisis* (London: Bloomsbury, 2018).

3 Frankenberg, *Political Technology and the Erosion of the Rule of Law*, 27.

4 Frankenberg, *Political Technology and the Erosion of the Rule of Law*, 100.

rights and the rule of law'.[5] According to such a viewpoint, the exceptional nature of emergency laws is somehow denied based on the fact that they are informed by the same principles underpinning legal operations in normal times. 'Order', Lazar claims, is a value that 'animates the day-to-day life of the state alongside liberal values, for instance in the workings of the criminal justice system, which every liberal democratic state requires. Rights are derogated for the sake of order every day'.[6] Emergency law, with its derogation/suspension of rights, is therefore not at all exceptional: it is a special variant of legal regulation emanating and sustaining the core funding values (order, common good, etc.) of liberal democracies but with different means. Lazar's strategy, here, is that of shadowing exceptionality behind the curtain of legality and principled justification. Leaving aside this theoretical strategy, which in light of what we have argued in Chapter 1 is a rather dubious one, the relevant question here is: what kind of liberal democracies and liberal law are the ones that suspend rights and the normal rule of the law, keeping at the same time their liberal essence? What are the theoretical implications of shifting or decentring the dichotomy normality exception from the perspective of the conception of the dominant liberal legalism?

The answer to these questions is complicated by the fact that for the liberal (political and legal) paradigm, the question of exceptionality has always been rather elusive to handle. And this is because the acknowledgement of the ultimate utility of loosening the ties of the law (or suspending them altogether) in times of crises does not fit well with the liberal aspirations to program state practices through law and to replace all those extra-legal—arbitrary—powers (typical of monarchical/absolutist tradition) with sets of regulated and controlled authorities. The outcome of such contrasting factors took the form of an accommodation of the exceptional and the legal. As Jules Lobel wrote, classic Liberal constitutionalism resolved the 'tension between law and necessity through a third approach, one that preserved the dichotomy between ordinary and emergency power by positing a boundary line separating and protecting the normal constitutional order from the dark world of crisis government'.[7] The sphere of emergency was delimited into a specific legal regime structured over a rationality opposed to that of normal times. While 'normalcy permitted a governmental structure based on separation of powers, respect for civil liberties and the rule of law', the emergency regime allowed 'for a strong executive rule, premised not on law and respect for civil liberties, but rather on discretion to take a wide

5 Nomi Claire Lazar, *States of Emergency in Liberal Democracies* (Cambridge: Cambridge University Press, 2009) 5.

6 Lazar, *States of Emergency in Liberal Democracies*, 5.

7 Jules Lobel, 'Emergency Power and the Decline of Liberalism', *Yale Law Journal* 98 (1988): 1388.

range of actions to preserve the government'.[8] Such a strategy, Loebel goes on, reflected a core philosophical viewpoint of liberal constitutional vision: the liberal paradigm 'premises constitutional democracy upon the tension between polar opposites: between law and politics, public and private, state and civil society, universal and particular, reason and desire, self and other'; these bifurcations 'attempt to separate the areas of our existence that can be governed by universal, collectively-derived and reasoned rules, from those areas that we want to preserve for particularized decisionmaking'.[9] For the same token, the legal delimitation of emergency powers reflects a set of dualities consistent with the liberal framework, such as crisis versus normalcy, war versus peace and constitutional versus unconstitutional actions.[10]

The legal encoding of the separation between normality and exception served to shelter the Constitution's normal ordering from the unconstitutional executive operations that are required in cases of emergency, giving at the same time ex-post control of such operations to specific authorities (normally the judiciary). By acknowledging that the normal administration of the law could be a hindrance in abnormal times, classic liberal thought considered exceptional regimes as the more appropriate instrument to preserve the normal universal rule of the law. However, pressured by the growing complexity of society and the widespread juridification of political and social life, the evolution of the liberal legal paradigm contravened such a classical approach by enshrining multi-layered exceptions into the legal system first through constitutional law, then incorporating them into normal statute law and finally providing a further layer of legalisation of the exception through international law. Such a gradual growing diversification of legal regimes of exceptionality is, in the end, the product of a cult of constitutional legality, part of the constant process of juridification of contemporary societies. By giving the exception, the feature of normal law, the liberal state aimed at controlling and limiting the potential authoritarian deviation of government, without realising that a legal cover is ultimately a further legitimate invitation to make use of exceptionalities.

~

The liberal political paradigm assigns the law the challenging task of acting as the primary tool for organising and integrating the full spectrum of social life. Norm creation, policy formulation and the dynamics of individual-group relationships are shaped and sanctioned by 'sovereign' rules. The imagery of the rule of law—whatever specific form it may take—provides the backdrop against which the liberal way of life establishes itself as a regime dedicated

8 Lobel, 'Emergency Power and the Decline of Liberalism'.
9 Lobel, 'Emergency Power and the Decline of Liberalism', 1389.
10 Lobel, 'Emergency Power and the Decline of Liberalism'.

to the protection of liberty and rights. From the prioritisation of individual rights as the supreme common good to the value placed on social membership defined by citizenship, juridical language is a substantive component of liberal political ideology. For the liberal tradition, legalism[11] (the ideology that restrains state power within legal procedures) is reassuring, as it conceives of the law as the sole mechanism capable of ensuring fairness, justice and equality. No other aspect of civilized life is seen to offer comparable potential for justice as the law. Though this ideal is seldom fully achieved, liberals hold that politics rooted in law is the sole one that truly merits standing for.

The portrayal of the law as a neutral, disinterested device—as the last universal in an increasingly relativist world—is part of that rhetorical strategy that systematically covers the law's dark side: its intimate relationship with violence and anomy or being dependent on specific social antagonistic practices, the always present 'necessity' to act outside or against the norms and the banal fact, never disproved by history, that the law can be used in the political commerce with destruction and death. Faced with its own authoritarian moments, the liberal legal mind—as Frankenberg claims—enters into a denial mode: 'as silence' or 'semantics of defence that argues away authoritarian structures (and sins) or justify them as inevitable, necessary or at least practical'.[12] Such sets of repressed experiences (the non-democratic and illegal establishment of liberal democracies by elites, executive and legislative prerogative, the codification/normalisation of the state of exception and the multifarious forms of administrative and judicial discretion) form, for Frankenberg, a 'gallery of shame'.[13]

Although, here, the reference to shame seems more rhetorical move rather than a point for theoretical reflection, the dynamic of such an emotion—shame—is perhaps the best metaphor for understanding the relationship the liberal mind entertains with its own authoritarian moments. In its common (and unproblematic) definition (in psychoanalysis and psychology), shame seems tied to the perception of the subject's self-image and manifests itself as a reaction to a supposed inadequacy, flaw or excess of the individual existence in comparison to an ideal conception of the self. As Slavoj Žižek claims, 'I am ashamed when I am confronted with the excess of my body'; when the reality of my existent being resists the subsumption of what I am asked to be. 'Shame', he goes on, 'enacts a desperate attempt to

11 Here, the label 'liberal legalism' is used unambiguously in its accepted sense as the attempt at structuring politics and the basic structure of social life according to a set of rules. On this issue, see John Gray, *Enlightenment's Wake: Politics and Culture at the Close of the Modern Age* (London: Routledge, 1995); Martin Loughlin, *Sword and Scales. An Examination of the Relationship Between Law and Politics* (Oxford: Hart Publishing, 2000).

12 Günter Frankenber, *Authoritarianism. Constitutional Perspectives* (Cheltenham: Edward Elgar, 2020) 76.

13 Frankenber, *Authoritarianism.*

keep up the appearance: although I know the truth . . . let us pretend that it hasn't happened'.[14] In the context of our theoretical intervention, shame points to the operation of tacit acceptance/normalisation of liberalism's reliance on authoritarian practices (repressed, rationalised within the legal and political discursive order) as if they are part of a normal business as usual and not as a crack in the mirror of its self-image. But this shameful veiling of its dark side is, somehow, 'deeply ambiguous: it enhances, constitutes even, what it purports to conceal'; it 'fixates our attention' on traumatic elements as something that ultimately 'legitimises' the need for the rule of law.[15] In this light, the (traumatic) consciousness of the ultimate impossibility of excluding exceptionality, constitute the rationale for its normalization, and a fundamental validation of the necessity of the rule of law.

A theoretical understanding of the normalisation of the state of exception from the point of view of liberal legalism must pass; therefore, through an analysis of the strategies with which the self-professed image liberalism built of itself has allowed it to bear and internalise its excesses. That is with that set of narratives with which the idea of law as a totalising regulative instrument has been made to accommodate its negation: that paradoxical view according to which the unconditional universal ruling of the law could be established only with the support of a power which reserves for itself the legitimate authority to suspend the rule of law—for the rule of law's sake.

5.2 Imaginaries of Emergency and Law

The conceptualisation of the troubled relationship liberal legalism entertains with its exceptional excess is not a hard task; it is enough to consider how in times of crisis, the necessity to expand and concentrate power, especially in the executive branch, to respond quickly and effectively to threats, does not go along very well with the principle of a government of laws and not of men. The liberal democratic paradigm, according to which power is limited and encased into rigid legal-sovereign structures, is challenged in its basic tenets by the shift of emergency laws intended to protect national security, by frequently reducing individual rights and freedoms, with the executive branch assuming a dominant role, sometimes sidelining legislative and judicial branches, produces. While this trend toward centralisation isn't exclusive to emergencies, crises significantly accelerate it, prompting a temporary yet substantial departure from traditional legal liberal forms. The dilemma of the exception is of easy formulation (but

14 Slavoj Žižek, *The Parallax View* (Cambridge, London: The MIT Press) 119–120.

15 Slavoj Žižek, 'Invisible Ideology: Political Violence between Fiction and Fantasy', *Journal of Political Ideologies* 1, no. 1 (1996): 16.

of difficult solution): liberal legality is construed on the idea that the best form of government is that of the law, for which individual rights are constraints on legitimate powers and where actors are constantly accountable for their actions; yet the very existence of emergency regulations is an acknowledgement that national/collective safety can justify broader, often unchecked government powers to preserve the state. For the liberal state, the question is, therefore, to what extent can a government justify temporary violations of its core principles without crossing the line into authoritarianism.

To address this tension, the legal and political discourse around emergency powers in democratic societies has been dominated by references to 'models'—that is, different forms of accommodating legality with the need to respond effectively to crises, sometimes by relaxing legal requirements. These models aim to balance crisis responses with democratic values, preserving the rule of law while equipping the state with tools to withstand exceptional challenges. This approach reflects a fundamental compromise: a temporary recalibration of democratic principles in service of the greater goal of preserving both state and constitutional integrity through the crisis.

In their *Law in Times of Crisis*[16]—perhaps the more comprehensive investigation into the question of emergency laws—Oren Gross and Fionnuala Ní Aoláin grouped the different models of emergency regulations into three broad categories. The first, 'models of accommodation', which includes all the major historical constitutional regulations of exceptional powers (from the Roman dictatorship to the French state of siege and legislative models), is based on the idea that 'when a nation is faced with emergencies its legal, and even constitutional, structure must be somewhat relaxed (and perhaps even suspended in parts)'.[17] The second group of models, which they termed 'law for all seasons', is developed on the premise that 'a state of emergency does not justify a deviation from the "normal" legal system'; and this is based on the conviction that the 'ordinary legal system already provides the necessary answers to any crisis without the legislative or executive assertion of new or additional governmental powers'.[18] The third 'Extra-legal model of emergency powers' assumes that 'public officials may act extra-legally when they believe that such action is necessary for protecting the nation and the public in the face of calamity, provided that they openly and publicly acknowledge the nature of their actions'; according to this model, the possibility to act outside and against the normal legal constraint is legitimised by the fact that

16 Oren Gross, Fionnuala Ní Aoláin, *Law in Times of Crisis: Emergency Powers in Theory and Practice* (Cambridge: Cambridge University Press, 2006).

17 Gross, Aoláin, *Law in Times of Crisis*, 17.

18 Gross, Aoláin, *Law in Times of Crisis*, 86.

the actions are aimed at the common good, are made public and are subject to ex-post political evaluation/adjudication.[19]

On the jurisprudential level, these models are all grounded on what Gross and Ní Aoláin define as 'assumption of separation', which is the belief in the 'ability to separate emergencies and crises from normalcy.[20] The validity of each model is determined by its capacity to 'contain'[21] emergencies and the always present possibility of abuse of exceptional powers. From the historical and historiographical point of view, instead, the models they proposed offers also a very broad schematisation of a rather long history, that of modern state and law, with the whole apparatus of ideas, narratives and myths that accompanied its birth and growth. The model operates a rather stringent and functional synthesis of broad and composed imagery that constitutes the grounding discourses for the very idea of the limits of the law. Such imagery aggregates concepts, principles and stories, whose persistence and re-sematisation operated by the European legal (and political) imagination make them assume the guise of foundational myths for emergency legal institutions.

5.2.1 The Myth of Roman Dictatorship

The Roman dictatorship represents somewhat the archetypical model for the modern regimes of emergency powers.[22] The legal form of such an institute of Republican Rome presents the basic structural elements of pretty much all emergency laws; that is: when specific threatening circumstances are 'defined' as in place, an agent is 'authorised' to deviate from the law and to take all the necessary measures to bring normality back, in a 'limited period'. In times of emergencies, the Roman Senate had the faculty to direct the consuls to nominate [*dictio*] a dictator for up to six months. After the appointment, the dictator acquired the fullness of power [*summum imperium*] normally vested in the consuls, which involved the authority to suspend normal administration of the law, mobilise the army and do all that it takes to protect the Republic from threats such as invasions and rebellion. After having resolved the crisis—or normally before the six-month time limit—the dictator was expected to step down, at which point his orders ceased to have effect, with the subsequent restoration of the normal political and legal situation. The operation of

19 Gross, Aoláin, *Law in Times of Crisis*, 112.
20 Gross, Aoláin, *Law in Times of Crisis*, 117.
21 Karin Loevy, *Emergencies in Public Law. The Legal Politics of Containment* (Cambridge: Cambridge University Press, 2016) Ch 1.
22 John Ferejohn, Pasquale Pasquino, 'The Law of the Exception: A Typology of Emergency Powers', *International Journal of Constitutional Law* 2, no. 2 (April 2004): 210–239.

the Roman dictatorship is, in its essence, conservative, as its goal is the preservation of the status quo.[23]

How the Roman dictatorship constituted a fundamental influence on the modern conception of emergency powers is as complex as it is peculiarly interesting. Decisive was the rediscovery of Roman practices by early modern thinkers and the subsequent developers of Republican ideas. As Schmitt put it, the concept of dictatorship was something humanists in the Renaissance 'encountered in the study of Roman history and their classical authors . . . Cicero, Livy, Tacitus, Plutarch, Dionysius of Halicarnassus, Suetonius, and so on'.[24] The reception and interpretation of such an institute were, therefore, influenced by the spirit with which Roman history was looked at and considered. The political and juridical ordering of ancient Rome was envisaged as offering specific *exempla* to get inspiration to read and critique the present.[25] A sense of superiority and fundamental utility was what early modern authors sought in antiquity. Machiavelli, for instance, opens his *Discourses on Livy* by acknowledging

> how much honour is awarded to antiquity' and by clearly stating that he has written about the Roman historian because 'who read these statements of mine can more easily draw from them that utility for which one should seek knowledge of histories.[26]

And it was the same Machiavelli who paved the way to the modern understanding of the concept of dictatorship—laying in this way the groundwork for a broader conception of emergency powers. In his *Discourses on Livy*, he dedicated substantial discussion to the role of dictatorship in Rome, highlighting its crucial function in the structural organisation of political-juridical powers of the Republic. After having praised its temporary nature, overall legality and utility, Machiavelli elaborated on a discourse on the necessity for emergency powers that has been repeated for

23 On dictatorship in Roman law and history, see David Cohen, 'The Origin of Roman Dictatorship', *Mnemosyne* 10, no. Fasc. 4 (1957): 300–318; Ronald Ridley, 'The Origin of the Roman Dictatorship: An Overlooked Opinion', *Rheinisches Museum für Philologie* 122, no. H. 3–4 (1979): 303–309; Marc de Wilde, 'The Dictatorship and the Fall of the Roman Republic', *Zeitschrift der Savigny-Stiftung für Rechtsgeschichte: Romanistische Abteilung* 130, no. 1 (2013): 1–39; Mark Wilson, *Dictator: The Evolution of the Roman Dictatorship* (Ann Harbor: University of Michigan Press, 2021); Luigi Garofalo (ed), *La dittatura romana*, Vol. 2 (Napoli: Jovene, 2022).

24 Carl Schmitt, *Dictatorship. From the Origin of the Modern Concept of Sovereignty to Proletarian Class Struggle* (Cambridge: Polity, 2014) 1.

25 Aldo Mazzacane, 'Profilo breve dell'umanesimo giuridico', in Cosimo Cascione, Carla Masi Doria (a cura di), *Fides Humanitas Ius. Studi in onore di Luigi Labruna*, Vol. VI (Napoli: Editoriale Scientifica, 2007) 3441–3452.

26 Niccolò Machiavelli, *Discourses on Livy* (Chicago: The University of Chicago Press, 1996) 1.

centuries without essential changes.[27] 'Among the other Roman orders', Machiavelli writes, dictatorship

> deserves to be considered and numbered among those that were the cause of the greatness of so great an empire, for without such an order cities escape from extraordinary accidents with difficulty. Because the customary orders in republics have a slow motion (since no council and no magistrate can work anything by itself, but in many things one has need of another, and because it takes time to add these wills together), their remedies are very dangerous when they have to remedy a thing that time does not wait for. So republics should have a like mode among their orders . . . . For when a like mode is lacking in a republic, it is necessary either that it be ruined by observing the orders or that it break them so as not to be ruined . . . . So a republic will never be perfect unless it has provided for everything with its laws and has established a remedy for every accident and given the mode to govern it. So, concluding, I say that those republics that in urgent dangers do not take refuge either in the dictator or in similar authorities will always come to ruin in grave accidents.[28]

The Roman model of emergency powers is here depicted as an 'order', that is a legal element in the constitutional system of the Roman Republic, which has allowed to protect the pluralist Republican orders from threats when the normal pace of the law becomes a hindrance to the self-standing of the state. For Machiavelli, a 'perfect republic' constitutes its structures through law, including emergency powers.

And in the development of modern political thought, such a narrative has been taken on and reframed innumerable times, ending up constituting the foundational discourse for the very existence of legally recognised emergency powers. Algernon Sidney, in his *Discourses Concerning Government*, for instance, wrote:

> I do therefore grant that a power like to the dictatorian, limited in time, circumscribed by law, and kept perpetually under the supreme authority of the people, may, by virtuous and well-disciplin'd nations, upon some occasions, be prudently granted to a virtuous man.[29]

27 On Machiavelli's reading of the Roman dictatorship, see Marco Geuna, 'Machiavelli e il problema della dittatura', *Consonanze* 13 (2021): 81–132.

28 Machiavelli, *Discourses on Livy*, book 1, 34-2.

29 Algernon Sidney, *Discourses Concerning Government (1698)*, T. G. West ed. (Indianapolis: Liberty Classics, 1990), II, 13.

In the same guise, James Harrington, in his utopian vision of *The Commonwealth of Oceana*, considered the best option a dictatorship embodied of a 'junta' taking on 'the whole administration of the commonwealth for the term of the said three months' and provided that it

> shall have no power to do anything that tends not to his proper end and institution, but all to the preservation of the commonwealth as it is established, and for the sudden restitution of the same to the natural channel and common course of government.[30]

Jean-Jaques Rousseau, in his *Contract Social*, espoused such a narrative in a chapter dedicated to dictatorship, where he wrote that the 'inflexibility of laws, which prevents them from being swayed by events, can in certain cases render them harmful, and this, in a crisis, can cause the ruin of a state'; there are eventualities 'for which the legislator has not provided', which when assuming the form of dangerous events that are making 'the apparatus of law' into an 'obstacle', then

> a supreme chief is appointed, who puts all laws to silence, and suspends, for a while, the authority of the sovereign. In these cases, the general will is not in doubt, and it is obvious that the people's principal aim is that the state should not perish.[31]

The Roman dictatorship came to influence the theory and practices of emergency powers[32] in the form of the uneven story of writing and re-writing

30 James Harrington, *The Commonwealth of Oceana and A System of Politics*, J. G. A. Pocock ed. (Cambridge: Cambridge University Press, 1992) 10.

31 Jean-Jacques Rousseau, *The Social Contract* (Oxford: OUP, 1994) 153.

32 Indicative in this sense is the direct reference to Rome and the dictatorship in Alexander Hamilton's *The Federalist Papers*, Clinton Rossiter ed. (New York: New American Library, 1961) 70: 'there is an idea, which is not without its advocates, that a vigorous Executive is inconsistent with the genius of republican government. The enlightened well-wishers to this species of government must at least hope that the supposition is destitute of foundation; since they can never admit its truth, without at the same time admitting the condemnation of their own principles. Energy in the Executive is a leading character in the definition of good government. It is essential to the protection of the community against foreign attacks; it is not less essential to the steady administration of the laws; to the protection of property against those irregular and high-handed combinations which sometimes interrupt the ordinary course of justice; to the security of liberty against the enterprises and assaults of ambition, of faction, and of anarchy. Every man the least conversant in Roman story, knows how often that republic was obliged to take refuge in the absolute power of a single man, under the formidable title of Dictator, as well against the intrigues of ambitious individuals who aspired to the tyranny, and the seditions of whole classes of the community whose conduct threatened the existence of all government, as against the invasions of external enemies who menaced the conquest and destruction of Rome. There can be no need, however, to multiply

of an antique institution in order to justify the narrative for which, in cases of peril, the suspension of the law and the delegation of powers to an agent for a limited amount of time is the wisest thing to do. While the relevance of such a narrative is out of doubt, it is interesting to note what, in the end, survived of the Roman dictatorship in the forming of the 'models of accommodation' of emergency powers. To put it in other words, in what form could an institute of antiquity—of a society and political community that is radically alien from ours—have had an impact on modern forms of emergency powers? This question becomes even more pressing given that while a considerable number of sources on the Roman dictatorship exist, their historical reliability is limited. No contemporary accounts from the period preceding the 2nd century have survived. Instead, we are left with late Republican and Imperial sources, which contain significant gaps in knowledge and interpolations, often employing late Roman terminology as well as literary and narrative tropes that obscure the original meanings.[33] One of the core sources for the understanding of the Roman dictatorship is Livy's *Ab Urbe Condita*. Such a work of history was not meant principally to give an account of facts but more 'to illustrate a system of values'. However, if we 'discarded these sources as historically unreliable, we would be left with little at all'.[34] In dealing with the Roman dictatorship, thus, modern authors eventually incurred into anachronistic reinterpreting and reading back into the institution the concerns of their own time,[35] and perhaps these concerns are what have allowed the dictatorship to survive—in a selectively mutated way—in our modern conception of emergency powers.

Thus, the Roman dictatorship had a decisive influence on modern political and legal thought in the form of a myth; better, it has been constituted by its re-imagination in the form of a myth. Far from being a simple fabricated narration, here, myth must be considered as an intricated net of discursive structures derived and developed from an object that cannot be known in and of itself.[36] The myth is a substance whose ontological status is that of absence. It is a constant (technical) formation and reformation of truths capable of legitimising a specific image of the real. In other words, as Furio

arguments or examples on this head. A feeble Executive implies a feeble execution of the government. A feeble execution is but another phrase for a bad execution; and a government ill executed, whatever it may be in theory, must be, in practice, a bad government. Taking it for granted, therefore, that all men of sense will agree in the necessity of an energetic Executive, it will only remain to inquire, what are the ingredients which constitute this energy'. See Hamilton, *The Federalist Papers*.

33 Marc de Wilde, 'The Dictator's Trust: Regulating and Constraining Emergency Powers in the Roman Republic', *History of Political Thought* 33, no. 4 (2012): 558.

34 de Wilde, 'The Dictator's Trust'.

35 Manin, 'The Emergency Paradigm and the New Terrorism'.

36 Enrico Manera, *Furio Jesi. Mito, Violenza, Memoria* (Roma: Carocci, 2018) 10.

Jesi has suggested in his very original interpretation of mythology, the myth is a way of producing meanings by moulding specific materials (texts, images, scriptures), which rest on a substance that lives in a fundamental state of absence.[37] In the case of a dictatorship, an institute of Roman law, which cannot be 'experienced' as such since it long disappeared and buried in the past but survived in the form of a literary product, has been made the vacuous core of a solid narrative that has legitimated our current understanding of exceptional powers, transmitting to the modern legal mind the paradigmatic forms of emergency laws.

5.2.2 *Necessity*

In his *Introduction to the Study of the Law of the Constitution*, Albert Venn Dicey identified the 'right' of the Crown to restore peace with all means necessary to what he calls Martial law. Contrary to the common understanding of the term, in the case of the English constitution, Martial law does not refer to a military ruling in a time of acute emergency but

> means the power, right, or duty of the Crown and its servants, or, in other words, of the Government, to maintain public order, or, in technical language, the King's peace, at whatever cost of blood or property may be in strictness necessary for that purpose.[38]

Such a capacity, Dicey claims, is shared by the government and by all citizens in the form of a 'common law right to repel force by force in the case of invasion, insurrection, riot, or generally of any violent resistance to the law'.[39] In his analysis of the nature of martial law, Dicey is at pains to distinguish the emergency legal provisions the English constitutions provide to the government from the actual rule of the army as in the French *état de siege*. In so doing, he intended to expose the ultimate 'permanent supremacy of the law'[40] under the English constitution while at the same time lying down a specific, separate 'common law' legal tradition to deal with emergencies.

However, in analysing the causes that could lead to the legitimate use of the powers the doctrine of martial law grants, Dicey seems to revolve around traditional arguments: 'The justification and the source of the exercise in England of extraordinary or, as it may be termed, extra-legal power, is always

37 See Furio Jesi, *Mito* (Macerata: Quodlibet, 2023).
38 Albert V. Dicey, *Introduction to the Study of the Law of the Constitution* (Indianapolis: Liberty Classic, 1982) 398.
39 Dicey, *Introduction to the Study of the Law of the Constitution*, 183.
40 Dicey, *Introduction to the Study of the Law of the Constitution*.

the necessity for the preservation or restoration of the King's peace'.[41] In the end, only necessity justifies the introduction of Martial law, and if the conditions that necessarily require a suspension/breaching of the normal law do not subsist anymore, it becomes a simple exercise of lawless violence. In the case of the not organically written English constitution, the right to suspend the normal administration of the law in a case of emergency belongs to the prerogative of the Crown and can be legally implemented only in a case of necessity. And this is because, for Dicey, necessity is the only principle that could make an illegal act into a legal one for both the government and the individual citizens: it must be noted, he writes, the

> striking analogy between the right of an individual to exercise force, even to the extent of causing death, in self-defence, and the right of a general or other loyal citizen to exercise any force whatever necessary for the defence of the realm. In either case the right arises from necessity.[42]

Necessity, here, becomes the ground shared by both government and citizens on which a 'right' to infringe the law can be factually established.

Surely, such a reference to the principle of necessity in the context of a discussion on martial law does not come as a surprise. Necessity is, indeed, part of the foundational discourse of exceptionality in law, and this is because of the 'tenaciously repeated Latin adage'[43] *necessitas legem non habet*. Although the precursor of such a maxim could be found in Roman law,[44] it is only with medieval jurisprudence that 'necessity' becomes a stable part of the European legal mind.[45] The principle that necessity has no law appears twice in Gratian's *Decretum*—the foundational text of canon law compiled in the 12th century; first, in a glossa, we could read that if 'something is done out of necessity, it is done licitly, since what is not licit in law necessity makes licit. Likewise, necessity has no law';[46] then, in the main body of the text, we could see the same principle applied to the opportunity to celebrate the mass in places that are not apt to it: 'It is preferable', Gratian states, 'not to sing or listen to the mass than to celebrate it in places where it should not

41 Dicey, *Introduction to the Study of the Law of the Constitution*, 404.

42 Dicey, *Introduction to the Study of the Law of the Constitution*, 402.

43 Giorgio Agamben, *State of Exception (Homo Sacer II, 1)* Kevin Attell transl. (The University of Chicago Press, 2005) 24.

44 See on this point Tomasz Giaro, *Excusatio necessitatis nel diritto romano* (Warszawa: Studia Antiqua Wydawnictwa Uniwersytetu Warszawskiego, 1982).

45 Franck Roumy, 'L'origine et la diffusion de l'adage canonique Necessitas non habet legem (VIIIe-XIIIe s.)', in Wolfgang Müller, Mary E. Sommar (eds), *Medieval Church Law and the Origins of the Western Legal Tradition: A Tribute to Kenneth Pennington* (Washington, DC: Catholic University of America Press, 2006) 301–319.

46 *Pars I. dist. 48: Si propter necessitatem aliquid fit, illud licite fit: quia quod non est licitum in lege, necessitas facit licitum. Item necessitas legem non habet.*

be celebrated, unless it happens because of a supreme necessity, for necessity has no law' [*nisi pro summa necessitate contingat, quoniam necessitas legem non habet*].[47] These early formulations already include the core idea that has been bequeathed to the modern legal tradition of necessity as a legal-factual operator that allows one to legally act illegally.

Starting with Gratian *Decretum*, necessity became widely discussed by Scholasticism in the Middle Ages, becoming a key term in the philosophical vocabulary of medieval conceptualisation of law. Aquinas, in this regard, developed a proper argument of necessity in the context of public law when, in *Summa Theologica* [*Prima secundae, q. 96, art. 6: utrum ei qui subditur legi, liceat praeter verba legis agree*], he applied such principle to the capacity to 'derogate' from the law in a case of emergency:

> every law is directed to the common weal of men and derives the force and nature of law accordingly . . . . Now it happens often that the observance of some point of law conduces to the common good in the majority of instances, and yet, in some cases, is very hurtful. Since then the lawgiver cannot have in view every single case, he shapes the law according to what happens most frequently, by directing his attention to the common good. Wherefore if a case arises wherein the observance of that law would be hurtful to the general welfare, it should not be observed. For instance, suppose that in a besieged city it be an established law that the gates of the city are to be kept closed, this is good for public welfare as a general rule: but, it were to happen that the enemy are in pursuit of certain citizens, who are defenders of the city, it would be a great loss to the city, if the gates were not opened to them: and so in that case the gates ought to be opened, contrary to the letter of the law, in order to maintain the common good, which the lawgiver had in view. Nevertheless it must be noted, that if the observance of the law according to the letter does not involve any sudden risk needing instant remedy, it is not competent for everyone to expound what is useful and what is not useful to the state: those alone can do this who are in authority, and who, on account of such like cases, have the power to dispense from the laws. If, however, the peril be so sudden as not to allow of the delay involved by referring the matter to authority, the mere necessity brings with it a dispensation, since necessity knows no law.[48]

Aquinas acknowledges that there are cases (of necessity) in which it is wise not to apply the law and that there are (sovereign) authorities appointed to do this. His strategy is here to complement the argument of equity, according

47 Agamben, *State of Exception*, 24.
48 Thomas Aquinas, *Summa Theologica* (Benziger Brothers Edition, 1947) 1368.

to which an exception to the law is legitimated by the fact that a strict application of a norm to specific facts would produce unfair/inequitable results, with that of necessity. In this passage, 'necessity' defines an exceptional facts that render the application of the law troublesome. Necessity, for Aquinas, represents a practice of granting exceptions when the strict application of the law goes against the superior principle according to which 'every law is ordained for the common well-being of men, and only for this does it have the force and reason of law'.[49]

Necessity also played a central role in the debate—so dear to the emerging theory of Natural Law—on poverty, where it was invoked to justify the infringement of private property whenever circumstances deemed it necessary. The early authority here is the usual Gratian who formulated this principle as follows: *In casu necessitatis omnia sunt communia, id est communicanda* [In the case of necessity, all things are common, that means are to be made common]. Such an argument was then developed as a question of whether, for the poor, accessing somebody else's property was allowed in order to survive. As we read in Albertus Magnus, the use of things, against property rights, for the poor is not a crime as long as it is restricted to a situation of succour and necessity, since 'what is given to the poor it is ours and it is theirs: ours because of dominium [positive right] theirs because of a natural law [iuris naturalis], which put in common all good in case of necessity'.[50] In the same vein, Aquinas argues that theft is licit for a starving family since: 'in a condition of necessity, all things are in common'; and, thus, it is not a sin if someone takes something of another that necessity has made.[51] In the case of private property, the state of necessity that characterises the existential/factual dimension of living in poverty allows for an exceptional infringement of property: since the necessity in which the poor live opens up a space to access a different legal realm (that of natural law) in which the *dominium* over things takes the form of use and never that of property.

From the early Medieval formulations, 'necessity' has become a stable part of legal vocabulary, either in the form of defence (in tort or criminal law) or as a doctrine pertaining to the sphere of public law. But what is 'necessity'? Or, to put it in other words: What is the signified of the legal word necessity? The *casu necessitatis* is that factual condition which allows for deviation/suspension of a norm—we often speak of a 'state' of necessity. It appears,

49 Agamben, *State of Exception,* 25.

50 'Illud quod exhibemus miseris, et nostrum est, et suum est: nostrum per dominium, et suum per rationem debiti iuris naturalis, quod in necessitate communicat bona' in Albertus Magnus, *Atisbonensis Episcopi, Ordinis Praedicatorum, Opera Omnia, Volumen XXX Commentarii n IV Sententiarum* (Paris: Ludovicus Vivès, 1894) 611.

51 'In necessitate sunt omnia communia, et ita non videtur esse peccatum, si alicuis rem alterius accipiat propter necessitate sibi factam commune', Aquinas q.66 art. 7, *Summa Theologiae.*

therefore, as fact—or a series of facts—which, in a sense, stimulate a specific legal reaction (an exception). However, as Agamben poignantly wrote, the legal status of necessity is nothing but easy to determine. If indeed necessity is a fact, decisions taken out of it are immediately juridical and do not necessitate any form of validation by legal institutions to be legally legitimate. Much like other forms of exceptionality, also necessity 'clearly entails a subjective judgment, and that obviously the only circumstances that are necessary and objective are those that are declared to be so'.[52] Necessity—what allows the possibility of 'legally' infringing the positive law—is an operator internal to legality that allows the capture of the possibility of making exceptions in law. In this sense, necessity is a purely formal/narrative element, which tells us that on certain occasions, it is perfectly legal to make an exception; its signified cannot but be the very institutional practice of making exceptions when it is deemed as the fairer, rightful thing to do.

5.2.3 Prerogative and the Law-Rule

The tension between the Liberal legal predicament for a pervasive and sustained legalisation of the whole political life of the state and the exceptional nature of emergencies is particularly evident in the theorisation of prerogative power (which stands symbolically as the archetype for the extra-legal model of emergency powers). Developed in the context of English political history, prerogative power came to signify, in the words of William Blackstone, 'the discretionary power of acting for the public good, where the positive laws are silent'.[53] Its nature is somehow ambiguous, as it could be considered either an extra-legal element standing side by side with the legal order or a constitutional element in its own right.

Let us now turn to perhaps the most renowned formulation of prerogative powers—the one offered by Locke. As we can read in his *Second Treaty*, the prerogative is that form of power 'in the hands of the prince' to 'act according to discretion, for the public good, without the prescription of the Law, and sometimes even against it'; and this is because

> for the legislators not being able to foresee, and provide by laws, for all that may be useful to the community, the executor of the laws having the power in his hands, has by the common law of nature a right to make use of it for the good of the society, in many cases, where the municipal law has given no direction, till the legislative can conveniently be assembled to provide for it. Many things there are, which the law can by no means

52 Agamben, *State of Exception*, 30.
53 William Blackstone, *Commentaries on the Laws of England: A Facsimile of the First Edition of 1765–1769*, Vol. 1 (Chicago: University of Chicago Press, 1979) 243–244.

> provide for; and those must necessarily be left to the discretion of him that has the executive power in his hands, to be ordered by him as the public good and advantage shall require.[54]

As it is evident from this passage, Locke's theorisation of the prerogative is based on the fundamental assumption that the political life of Nations is constantly constellated by unpredictable events and that the eminent task of politics is to govern them. Prerogative is the name of all those instruments in the hands of governing authorities to deal with the whole spectrum of contingency. The capacity to act outside and, at times, against the law, therefore, is something that belongs immediately to the office of the Monarch. And this means that differently than the 'Roman institution of dictatorship, Locke's Prince comes to the exception already holding the prerogative powers'.[55] What is at stake here is, therefore, not only the positioning of the authority to overcome the law's constraints but also the political (and somehow also moral) duty to overcome the law for the common good. Governing through law, for Locke, is not the only form of good and legitimate government: 'legitimacy is not reducible to legality', and indeed, the law rule must not exclude other modalities of exceptional government legitimised by the fundamental principles *Salus populi suprema lex*.[56] All in all, this insight into the function of prerogative power appears as one of the many contradictions one can find in Locke's admittedly radical support for the rule of law. However, as Clement Fatovic claims, if we put this in the context in which he was writing when liberalism had not yet become a 'legalistic and jurisprudential'[57] political philosophy, this image of the prerogative aligns with the general theory of the state of early Modernity.

When discussing the origin of this form of discretionary power, Locke very clearly denies any form of natural/divine ground: prerogative power does not belong to the order of God's creation, but it is historically established as an extra-legal power by the relationship of trust between the subjects and the King (executive)—who has the right, and in a sense the duty, to exercise his power for the common good. And the people, for the same token, retain the power and right to limit the prerogative when it deems necessary (in the form of an ex-post right to resistance/revolution). In line with classical Modern natural law tradition, Locke's text expresses these points through a sort of

54 John Locke, *Second Treatise of Government* (Indianapolis: Hackett Publishing Company, 1980) §159.

55 Karin Loevy, *Emergencies in Public Law* (Cambridge: Cambridge University Press, 2016) 25.

56 Pasquale Pasquino, 'Locke on King's Prerogative', *Political Theory* 26, no. 2 (1998): 201–202.

57 Clement Fatovic, 'Constitutionalism and Contingency: Locke's Theory of Prerogative', *History of Political Thought* 25, no. 2 (2004): 278.

'natural history of government'[58] that explains vividly the nature of the prerogative and its relationship with the law:

> when commonwealths differed little from families in number of people, they differed from them too but little in number of laws: and the governors being as the fathers of them, watching over them for their good, the government was almost all prerogative. A few established laws served the turn, and the discretion and care of the ruler supplied the rest. But when mistake or flattery prevailed with weak princes to make use of this power for private ends of their own, and not for the public good, the people were fain by express laws to get prerogative determined in those points wherein they found disadvantage from it: and thus declared limitations of prerogative were by the people found necessary in cases which they and their ancestors had left, in the utmost latitude, to the wisdom of those princes who made no other but a right use of it; that is, for the good of their people.[59]

The history of political associations begins here with the family and the authority of the father, then developing into a proper political community with the emergence of the modern state, under the drive of growing social complexity.[60] Prerogative emerges here as both a natural and historical phenomenon: natural because 'it invokes the authority of the father', historical since it refers to the concrete 'beginning of society' and not to the analytical and theological concept of the state of nature'.[61]

Locke's historicisation of the question of prerogative is construed upon three fundamental claims: (1) prerogative, that authority emerging in the relationship of trust (and duty) between the governing institutions and the subjects, is the ultimate source of exceptionality, (2) it is an inalienable right of the people to regulate and constraints the power of the executive 'in virtually any manner they see fit' (something that Locke advice not to do, since it would limit the ability of the government to resolve emergencies) and (3) the normative capacity of law to guarantee people's 'Peace, Quiet, and property'[62] operates, historically, by limiting the prerogative as a source of exceptionality and arbitrariness—indeed in the history of civilisation exceptionality turns out to be the ground of intervention of the law. The rule of law, in this sense, is the counterpart of the prerogative, which in turn is something

58 Pasquino, 'Locke on King's Prerogative', 203.
59 Locke, *Second Treatise of Government*, §162.
60 Pasquino, 'Locke on King's Prerogative', 204
61 Pasquino, 'Locke on King's Prerogative', 204.
62 Locke, *Second Treatise of Government*, §136.

always open to normalisation but which should remain not legally codified in its entirety to allow better governmental handling of contingency.

~

In the imagery supporting the theory and legal structure of emergency powers, the exceptional excesses of the law exist beyond the usual boundaries of the legal form as something that can nevertheless be regulated—either as a product of the legal system itself or as the object of legal normalisation. In the case of dictatorship, for instance, the legal emergency break assumes the form of a proper institution: a product of the legal system itself. Necessity, instead, is essentially a legal operator that allows the legalisation of what would otherwise be an infringement of the rule of law. And the theory of prerogative illustrates very effectively how exceptionality, although essentially extra-legal, can be the object of legal intervention. The possibility to identify and separate normality from exceptionality stands surely as the epistemic ground of our conception of emergency law; however, such a principle goes hand in hand with the idea that exceptionality is still in tight relationship with the law's ruling as something that can be limited and governed. In its varied typology exceptionality is always a consequence of general laws and principles (legal or political) that authorise governmental agencies to act in violation of other laws. And the possibility of its normalisation has always been implicit in the legal narratives that have accompanied and sustained its evolution.

5.3 The Meaning of the Constitution of Exceptionality

Historically, the state of exception emerges as a distinct legal issue only with the rise of the modern conception of the state as a system of governmental institutions whose functions are both regulated and constrained by law and rights. As banal as it might seem, no proper legal instrument for crisis management existed in ancient regimes, since, as Clinton Rossiter claimed, it 'is unnecessary to suspend rights that do not exist or augment powers that are already absolute'.[63]

As a legal construct rooted in public law, emergency law appears alongside the first constitutional texts of early democratic states. It has since evolved in tandem with the broader trend of intense juridification that characterises modern society, embedding itself ever more deeply into legal systems. The entrenchment of exceptionality within the law is, therefore, intrinsically tied to the expanding bureaucratisation of society, a process set in motion by the rise of the modern bourgeois state, and the expansion and diversification of its form is part of the whole process of the widening of law's grip over

63 Clinton Rossiter, *Constitutional Dictatorship: Crisis Government in the Modern Democracies* (Princeton: Princeton University Press, 1948) 80.

reality. 'In the era of the total constitution', Martin Loughlin argues, when the law regulates the totality of the procedures for enacting and overseeing the emergency governmentality, exceptionality 'is no longer simply a matter of the ruler's conscience': it is rather a matter of procedural conformity and broad discretion conferred by legislations.[64] It follows, then, that 'governments make no claim to act by virtue of necessity, emergency, or higher good; they invoke an already existing lawfully conferred power. In the total Constitution, the exception, being constitutionalized, is normalized'.[65] Through its encoding into law and subsequent normalisation, exceptionality gradually becomes disembedded from the executive (sovereign) office, evolving into an autonomous body of doctrines and legal principles in its own right. And the frequent and often hyperbolic references to national security threats, the use of war metaphors and the appeals to the nation staged and broadcast on a mass scale during times of emergency can be seen as discursive strategies that serve to legitimise powers governments possess within the legal definition of their emergency systems.[66]

Even from a strictly jurisprudential point of view, this process of normalisation of exceptionality is distinctly modern. It would be indeed complicated to conceive and situate legal emergency powers before the appearance of the concept of the modern Constitution in the 18th and 19th centuries; as crucial for the very standing of the legal essence of exceptional powers is the modern positivist conception of the law, according to which—as we have seen previously—the protection of the constituted order through exceptional means involves the possibility of a legitimate stepping outside the limits of the legal form. With the establishment of the bureaucratic state—structured around the legal-political demands for security, control and predictability—the question of discretion granted by exceptional powers can assume the form of a proper issue (revolving around a discourse over the reach of law's remit). However, the truth is that the imagery of emergency powers is much older and rooted in Medieval speculation over law and its limits. What kind of relationship does the modern encoding of the exception into the law entertain with these earlier legal speculations and political experiences?

The rules of the law are created to be applied in future cases but with an eye on the past. It is, in the end, the past that dictates and orients the future projection of the law, and this is essentially a feature of all normative systems. The emergence of specific legal formations (and doctrine) is, in a sense, an abstract generalisation grounded on the conception of a present,

64 Martin Loughlin, *Against Constitutionalism* (Cambridge, MA: Harvard University Press, 2022) 161.

65 Loughlin, *Against Constitutionalism.*

66 Gian-Giacomo Fusco, 'Exception Fiction Performativity', in C. Cercel, G. G. Fusco, S. Lavis (eds), *States of Exception. Law, History, Theory* (Abingdon: Routledge, 2020).

which is in turn influenced by the consciousness and knowledge of the past. The establishment of the law marks the moment in which normative entities become identifiable as separated from the background they are inevitably and inextricably tied to, going to form 'a way of knowing or an epistemology, which creates a rational reason to continue to act in a way that is consistent with that epistemology'.[67] In the case of the exception, we could see how the imagery of emergency constitutes the discursive (imaginative) ground on which the Modern European legal mind (or tradition) constituted its laws to deal with the exceptional. What survives of this past set of images and paradigms in the contemporary legal text are keywords shaping the form of the emergency paradigm and the semantic/epistemological structures with which legal systems perceive and react to critical events and conflicts.[68]

Law's operations, structures and categories are indeed constantly shaped as a form of knowledge (or memory) by reacting to events, demanding at the same time unlimited applications and control over the future. Legal systems are, Niklas Luhmann claims, ways 'to take an open future into society and bind it there'; and this makes them akin to an immune system of society.[69] Leaving onside the peculiar idiosyncrasies of his system theory, the consideration of law as an immune system captures law's functions in their relationship to the social environment as few other theories do. For Luhmann, the immunitary function of law is revealed in its ability to regulate and inform conflicts:

> it fits in with the theory of the immune system to say that law learns from conflicts. Without conflicts law would not develop, would not be reproduced, and would then be forgotten . . . . At any rate, law does not spring up from the nature of matter or from human nature, as assumed earlier, but it emerges and develops during the search for solutions to conflicts as soon as these solutions are not just ad hoc (like and including the use of violence), but are intended to apply to more than just the case in hand. The immunity answer uses the time-binding effect of normative rules. Accordingly, the formulation of rules is like the generation of antibodies for specific cases. If no demands are made on the immune system of society, it cannot learn and consequently cannot generate disturbance-related defence mechanisms. In other words, the immune system stores its own system history.[70]

67 L. Smith, 'Fusion and Tradition', in S. Degeling, J. Edelman (eds), *Equity in Commercial Law* (Lawbook Co, 2005) 20.

68 Rafał Mańko, 'Legal Survivals and the Resilience of Juridical Form', *Law and Critique* (2023): 1–23.

69 Niklas Luhmann, *Law as Social System* (Oxford: Oxford University Press, 2004) 475.

70 Luhmann, *Law as Social System*, 477.

From this perspective, legal systems exert a regulative influence on conflicts by transposing, or even elevating, them into a distinct domain, one of norms and legal operations. This domain functions much like antibodies, preserving the memory of past conflicts from which it emerged. However, the law should not be understood as merely suppressing the inherent nature of conflict itself but rather as a means of managing and transforming it within a framework of regulation and order. Indeed, as Luhman claims, the law 'does not serve to avoid conflicts' but it 'merely seeks to avoid the violent resolution of conflicts and to make suitable forms of communication available for every conflict'; when the law steps in

> communicative material is sorted. Texts become relevant, other cases are consulted, the opinions of specific authorities become important. One can go back hundreds, even thousands of years-all from the point of view that information can be acquired from the facts of these cases that is relevant to and consistent for the case of conflict at hand. Law serves to continue communication by other means. It is societally adequate not only when it tackles emerging conflicts but especially when it creates conflicts and can provide adequate complexity of its own to handle them.[71]

To paraphrase a famous dictum, the law is the continuation of conflicts with other means. When legal norms acknowledge rights and duties, place conflicts around these rules, rights and duties, according to a specific, legal and, to a certain extent, abstract image of society they produce. It follows then the autonomous and autopoietic functionality of legal systems, which, by keeping the memory of its own operations (and to a certain extent of the conflicts from which generated), sustains itself through its cumulative expansion. Therefore, to the extent that it lives in its own autonomy, the legal immunity system, Luhman writes,

> does not adapt to its environment. There is no 'similarity' between trigger and defence. On the contrary, the legal rule is not a conflict. When it is a trigger for further conflicts—which is typical in the legal system—new rules develop or at the very least new interpretations of the rule to be preserved in a text.[72]

From this point of view, the normalisation of exceptionality, its encoding into the law, by taking as its own object and target of intervention the legal system itself represents a form of systemic immunity—or a second-degree immunity of the law. The expansion and diversification of exceptionality

71 Niklas Luhmann, *Social Systems* (Stanford: Stanford University Press, 1996) 375.
72 Luhmann, *Law as a Social System*, 477.

in the legal text is, in this sense, the product of an adaptive process of an ever-growing legal system to different social and political events. The legal form of emergency powers are, indeed, the outcome of specific events and emerged as a specific generalisation of rules depending on the history and social and political conditions on which a legal system is grounded. When encoded and granted by the law, and when implemented in particular circumstances, exceptionality creates 'precedents for future exigencies as well as for "normalcy"'—since it is part of regular law. As Gross and Ní Aoláin maintain:

> Whereas in the 'original' crisis, the situation and powers of reference were those of normalcy and regularity, in any future crisis government will take as its starting point the experience of extraordinary powers and authority granted and exercised during previous emergencies. What might have been seen as sufficient 'emergency' measures in the past (judged against the ordinary situation) may not be deemed enough to deal with further crises as they arise. Much like the need gradually to increase the dosage of a heavily used medication in order to experience the same level of relief, so too with respect to emergency powers: the perception may be that new, more radical powers are needed to fight impending crises. In turn, new extraordinary emergency measures confer an added degree of ex post legitimacy and respectability, as well as a sense of normality, to previously used, less drastic emergency measures. What were deemed exceptional emergency actions in the past may now come to be regarded as normal, routine, and ordinary, in light of more recent and more dramatic emergency powers. As our understanding of normalcy shifts and expands to include measures, powers, and authorities that had previously been considered special, exceptional, and extraordinary yet necessary to deal with emergency, the boundaries of new exceptions are pushed further to include new and more expansive powers and authorities.[73]

The outcome of this process of normalisation here is not only the growing and diversification of emergency regimes—where the old ones are replaced by the new ones—but also the getting used to them, which in turn produces an increased systemic tolerance. Such a dynamic represents, in a sense, a distortion (if not a proper backfiring) of the very aim of the legal regulation of emergency, which is the ultimate control of exceptionality. Truly unforeseeable critical events can never be eliminated by any legal order, no matter how meticulously they are built. However, as the receptive capacity of the legal system increases, through the expansion and diversification of normalised emergency regimes, the unforeseeable—and with it, the need

73 Gross, Aoláin, *Law in Times of Crisis*, 228.

for legal exceptionalism—shrinks, but the normal application of the exceptional widens.

5.4 Liberal Legalism and Exceptionality

Judith Shklar, in a book that after more than half a century has lost none of its relevance, defined legalism as 'the ethical attitude that holds moral conduct to be a matter of rule following and moral relationships to consist of duties and rights determined by rules'; which in the case of the liberal tradition is translated into the idea that 'the court of law and the trial according to law are the social paradigms, the perfection, the very epitome of legalistic morality'.[74] For Shklar, liberal legalism is first of all, an ideology which assumes political significance because of a fear of the arbitrary use of power. Highlighting the ultimate ideological nature of such a disposition is a way for her to criticise those liberals who 'belief that law is not only separate from political life but that it is a mode of social action superior to mere politics'.[75] To consider law as a separate entity different from morality and law is an ideology that has its roots in 'the legal profession's view of its own function'.[76]

All in all, Shklar's classic work is a defence of legalism itself. The target of her critique is mostly directed to that form of liberalism that 'cultivates the project or illusion of *abolishing politics*, or of so constraining it by legal and constitutional formulae that it no longer matters what are the outcomes of political deliberation'.[77] Underpinning such an idea is, as Martin Loughlin put it, a somewhat pessimistic view of politics,

> conceived as an activity in which the passions hold sway. The political sphere, being one of power conflicts, is dangerous and potentially destructive. Constraints are therefore required to ensure that passions are channelled towards right conduct. Law thus presents itself as a set of foundational principles providing the framework within which politics is to be conducted. Politics must be tamed and placed within bounds so that its energies can be harnessed positively, that is, in accordance with the dictates of reason and justice. No longer is law a conventional medium of the relationship between ruler and ruled or the pliant instrument of the ruling authority. Instead, law expresses the rational foundation of

74 Judith Shklar, *Legalism: Law, Morals, and Political Trials* (Cambridge, MA: Harvard University Press, 1964) 1–2.

75 Shklar, *Legalism*, 8.

76 Shklar, *Legalism*, 9.

77 John Gray, *Enlightenment's Wake: Politics and Culture at the Close of the Modern Age* (London: Routledge, 1996) 77.

> the governing relationship; it establishes the preconditions for the conduct of politics.[78]

For liberal legalism, the juridification of social and political life becomes an instrument for neutralising the politics' antagonistic potential; to bridle into the supposed rational-technical framework of the law, channelling clashes of values and worldviews into specifically regulated conducts. But, Loughlin continues, the 'legalisation of politics has led primarily to a politicisation of law'.[79] Since the shaping of political and social life is inherently a political act, the law, when wielded as the primary tool to neutralise politics, inevitably becomes politicised itself.

This sense of legalism was already present in the Schmittian critique of liberalism, which is something worth looking at here. In the 1929 essay *The Age of Neutralizations and Depoliticisation*, Schmitt suggests that liberalism and the liberal state are a 'symptom of general cultural neutrality . . . characteristic of the age of technology'.[80] The large diffusion, if not triumph to liberalism, as a political doctrine came to represent, in his view, one of the utmost manifestations of an epoch dominated by 'economic-technical' thought. The liberal state and liberal institutions, more generally, are devised to exclude political antagonism and to secure the integrity of private interests from the intrusion of political power. The liberal state is, indeed, a neutral state vis-à-vis society's most intimate components: the private interests of the individual, from property rights to religious freedom. For the liberal ethos, Schmitt claims, 'politics is confined to securing the conditions for liberty and eliminating infringements on freedom'.[81] The state and law, from this perspective, must first and foremost attain the goal of insulating the private economic sphere from the interference of politics; put in other words, to depoliticise large sectors of social life. This position is ultimately sustained, Daniel McLoughlin maintains, by the

> antipolitical fantasy in which things manage themselves, the ideal of the marketplace as an objective and impersonal mechanism, in which the pursuit of private interest will, guided by the free hand, add up to the public good, rendering politics and the state unnecessary.[82]

78 Loughlin, *Sword and Scales*, 223.
79 Loughlin, *Sword and Scales*, 233.
80 Carl Schmitt, '*The Age of Neutralizations and Depoliticisation*', in Carl Schmitt, *The Concept of the Political* (Chicago, IL: University of Chicago Press, 2007) 88.
81 Schmitt, '*The Age of Neutralizations and Depoliticisation*', 71.
82 Daniel McLoughlin, 'Crisis, Modernity, Authority: Carl Schmitt on Order and the State', *Australian Feminist Law Journal* 31 (2009): 142.

As Heiner Bielefeldt observes, Schmitt considered the rule of law (*Rechtsstaat*)—understood as a rule-by-law state—as one of liberalism's key strategies for neutralising the political. The idea of the rule of law is an expression of a historical process of increasing rationalisation, also manifested in the dogmas of legal positivism (which Schmitt calls normativism—of which Hans Kelsen is the utmost exponent). Modern jurisprudence's hyper-formalist approach, Schmitt contends, rests on a rigid separation between sociology and law, whereby any element irreducible to the formal structure of norms is excluded from legal consideration.[83] Liberal legalism is, in this sense, a product of such an approach to conceiving the law, which ultimately conduces to a degeneration of law into mere technicism and a purely instrumental conception of legal normativity.[84] By prioritising abstract norms and principles over concrete political stances and decisions, the rule of law seeks to purge legal and political judgements of personal or subjective influences, which are by definition the nest of arbitrariness, to ensure (albeit often illusorily) ultimate control and command. In this vision, political orders are inseparable from their legal architectures, and decisions emerge as rational byproducts of formal procedures. Yet, crucially, this conception of law and state, so central to the liberal bourgeois tradition, offers no inherent safeguard against the risk of tyranny it aims to exclude. As Schmitt argues, a

> merely formal concept of law, such as that law is anything the lawmaking bodies ordain via the legislative process, would transform the rule of law into an absolutism of legislative offices, and any distinction of legislation, administration, and adjudication would be eliminated.[85]

~

Overall, for liberal legalism, the law is an instrument to govern through depoliticisation, by channelling and constraining politics to legal form. By aiming to subsume political decisions, and ultimately the entire structure of the state, into the juridical sphere, legalism transforms politics and political struggle into a matter of procedure and rational-technical administration. In this perspective, the normalisation of exceptionality, its encoding and expansion, is in line with the general aim of expanding control over the potential political use of exceptional laws. However, the strict and, at times, pervasive regulation of emergency powers—which we have categorised as 'normalisation of exceptionality'—while trying to constraint the political misuse of

83 See Carl Schmitt, *Political Theology. Four Chapters on the Concept of Sovereignty* George Schwab transl. (Chicago, IL: The University of Chicago Press, 2005).

84 John P. McCormick, *Carl Schmitt's Critique of Liberalism: Against Politics as Technology* (Cambridge: Cambridge, 1997) 206.

85 Carl Schmitt, *Constitutional Theory* (Durham, NC: Duke University Press, 2008) 191.

the exception is at the same time a legitimisation of its use—in the form of a legally determined instrument. As Oren Gross has argued, in times of acute crises, governments 'tend to do whatever is necessary to neutralise the threat'; however, 'it is extremely dangerous to provide for such eventualities within the framework of the legal system . . . because of the large risks of contaminating and manipulating that system, and the deleterious message involved in legalizing such actions'.[86]

From the standpoint of liberal legalism, the legal incorporation of exceptionality is not an anomaly but rather a logical extension of its core objective: the continual empowerment and expansion of legal applicability. As we have observed, exceptions allow the law to extend its reach over cases that lie beyond its formal scope, effectively stretching the boundaries of law. The progressive codification and systematic integration of exceptions within legal frameworks not only amplify the law's domain but also reinforce its authority, adaptability and capacity to absorb and regulate unforeseen circumstances under its ever-expanding reach.

Moreover, the order predicated by the liberal mind is essentially structured on the separation through insulation and depoliticisation of social fields (principally the social/economic sphere) from political intervention. Nothing prevents exceptional measures from being used to protect a political order structured on the separation of social domains; on the contrary, the state of exception is—as the history of the last century has demonstrated—a rather appropriate instrument to restore and shelter the autonomy of the economic sphere from politicised (legal or extra-legal) social demands. In other words, as Marie Goupy suggested, Schmitt—who devised his theory against the liberal order—may have paradoxically provided a theory of exceptionality that is adapted to safeguarding the liberal order by its capacity to *integrate* the crisis.[87]

86 Oren Gross, 'Chaos and Rules: Should Responses to Violent Crisis Always Be Constitutional?', *Yale Law Journal* 112 (2003): 1132–1133.

87 Marie Goupy, 'The State of Exception Theory of Carl Schmitt and the Ambivalent Criticism of Liberalism', *Z Politikwiss* 28 (2018): 395–408.

Chapter 6

State Form and Liberalism Authoritarian Drives

Gian-Giacomo Fusco

6.1 Introduction

The elective affinity between liberalism and democracy, which we often take as a natural datum, conceals the uneasy fact that the two are not identical and frequently pursue conflicting goals.

As Carl Schmitt has observed, while the first is fundamentally predicated on a conflict of different individual interests, the latter instead requires 'first homogeneity and second—if the need arises—elimination or eradication of heterogeneity'.[1] Perhaps there is no better explanation for this distinction than the one offered by Friedrich Hayek: '[L]iberalism and democracy', he claims,

> although compatible, are not the same. The first is concerned with the extent of governmental power, the second with who holds power. The difference is best seen if we consider their opposites: the opposite of liberalism is totalitarianism, while the opposite of democracy is authoritarianism.[2]

It follows that 'it is at least possible in principle that a democratic government may be totalitarian and that an authoritarian government may act on liberal principles'.[3] Not surprisingly, then, in light of the evolution of the institutional, political and economic function of the state's power (at a global level), marked by a gradual democratic decay[4] alongside the simultaneous rise of strong governmental practices and market expansion, the idea of a synthesis of authoritarianism and liberalism has become a meaningful one.

Risen to prominence in the context of the economic and political crises that have invested Europe in the last two decades, the notion of 'authoritarian

1 Carl Schmitt, *The Crisis of Parliamentary Democracy* (Cambridge, MA: MIT Press 1988) 9.
2 Friedrich Hayek, 'The Principles of a Liberal Social Order', *Il Politico* 31.4 (1966): 601.
3 Hayek, 'The Principles of a Liberal Social Order'.
4 Tom Gerald Daly, 'Democratic Decay: Conceptualising an Emerging Research Field', *Hague J Rule Law* 11 (2019): 9–36.

DOI: 10.4324/9781003490449-7

liberalism' captures the coupling of economic liberalism with the strengthening of governmental practices characteristic of the contemporary phase of capitalism. It reveals, in this sense, how the supposed optimisation of the political management of the economic sphere has assumed authoritarian traits. Authoritarian liberalism, in the words of Michael Wilkinson, 'expresses a standard classical liberal animosity towards irrational interference in the economy', especially in the form of threats of 'bottom-up social democratic pressure'.[5] Indeed, for the liberal mind, the market and the economic sphere more broadly must be protected from political and social interference and ultimately depoliticised; achieving this may sometimes require authoritarian measures.

The term authoritarian liberalism was coined by the German jurist Herman Heller in 1932 to define the trajectory of the institutional change of the late Weimar period, which saw, on the one hand, a move from a parliamentary system to a government by presidential degree (under the emergency powers granted by Article 48), and on the other hand the strengthening of the ideological defence of market liberalism and capitalist economy. In Heller's words: 'the substance of authoritarian liberalism appears to have been more or less adequately characterised: the retreat of the 'authoritarian' state from social policy, liberalisation (*Entstaatlichung*) of the economy and dictatorial control by the state of politico-intellectual functions'.[6] This definition is developed as a critique of a speech titled 'Strong State and Sound Economy' (*Starker Staat und gesunde Wirtschaft*), which Carl Schmitt gave at the general assembly of the 'Langnam-Verein' (the industrial employer's association of the Rhine-Rhur).[7] For Heller, this talk is significant as it synthesises two supposedly antithetical principles: a strong authoritarian state and a free-functioning economy.

In 'Strong State and Sound Economy', Schmitt, while addressing pressing political questions of the late Weimar period, further developed his critique of the liberal tradition. In his view, by prioritising the vision of social order as structured as an idealised market, liberalism ultimately aims to the depoliticisation of human interactions through a transformation of human antagonism into a market competition—that is, a conversion of the political into a conflict of economic interests. Liberalism, Schmitt claims, transforms 'the enemy from the viewpoint of economics into a competitor and from the intellectual point into a debating adversary'.[8] And accordingly, the state must, first and foremost, be limited to ensuring the conditions necessary for economic

5 Michael Wilkinson, 'Authoritarian Liberalism in the European Constitutional Imagination', *European Law Journal* 21.3 (2015): 315.

6 Herman Heller, 'Authoritarian Liberalism?', *European Law Journal* 21.3 (2015): 300.

7 Carl Schmitt, 'Sound Economy—Strong State', in Renato Cristi (ed), *Carl Schmitt and Authoritarian Liberalism* (Cardiff: University of Wales Press 1998).

8 Carl Schmitt, *The Concept of the Political* (Chicago, IL: University of Chicago Press 2007) 28.

freedoms to flourish, preventing all those interferences that might hinder them. The separation of politics from a market society can be established and effectively guaranteed only through a 'strong state', capable of putting a brake on political interferences in the economic and political spheres. Therefore, economic liberalism and liberal institutions are not fundamentally opposed to authoritarian governments. A strong state is essential to safeguarding a free and efficient market economy from the democratic pressures that arise within society.

'Qualitative total state' is the name that Schmitt, in his address to the Langnam-Verein, gave to that form of a strong state, which guarantees substantial autonomy to owners of private capital while at the same time suppressing the 'enemies' of the free economy. The qualitative total state combines the necessity of insulating the state's power and government from the democratic contestation of the exploited classes with the need for the capitalist economy to administer itself autonomously, avoiding social turbulences and uncertainties. The liberal-capitalist-state, in Schmitt's account, to eliminate the threat brought by its enemies—socialist and communist movements, unions, etc.—and to promote and consolidate the interests of capital, needs a state form characterised principally by the strength of its authority rather than by its democratic virtue. The realisation of liberal principles, Schmitt maintains, can be obtained only through the establishment of a normalised space in which private economic interests can thrive and the subsequent depoliticisation of specific sectors of human social life. 'Only a strong state', for Schmitt

> can depoliticise, only a strong state can openly and effectively decree that certain activities remain its privilege and as such ought to be administered by it, that other activities belong to the sphere of selfmanagement, and that all the rest be given to the demonian of a free economy.[9]

To the extent that markets are not a natural datum but something that must be socially construed and politically defended, a state power is ultimately necessary to institute it and shelter it from interferences coming from the outside. In other words, the depoliticised condition of the liberal vision of the economy needs a state strong enough to insulate the markets from its own influence. It follows, then, as Wolfgang Streeck claimed, that the '*liberal-authoritarian* state', that Schmitt had in mind is the liberal state in its pure form: 'strong and weak at the same time: strong in its role as protector of the market and the economy from democratic claims for redistribution'—to the extent of implementing all forms of actions to silence such claims—'and weak in its relationship to the market as the designated site of

9 Schmitt, 'Sound Economy—Strong State', 226–227.

autonomous capitalist profit-seeking, which government policy was to protect and if necessary expand without, however, entering it'.[10]

~

Although the concept of authoritarian liberalism emerged in the context of the crisis of the Weimar Republic, which eventually led to the establishment of the Nazi regime, it has become mainly used to describe the ideological underpinning and the institutional development of the European Union.[11] As Wilkinson maintains, the term authoritarian liberalism effectively captures two symptoms of the institutional evolution of Europe: 'first, there is an authoritarian aspect to EU, and especially Eurozone, governance, represented by a twofold process of de democratisation and de-legalisation', manifested into 'the regular bypassing of parliamentary authority and parliamentary debate as well as the violating or circumventing of normal guarantees associated with the rule of law, including the protection of social rights'; and second, 'is the material nature of this authoritarianism and its historical pedigree: its aim at the maintenance of a regime of economic liberalism'.[12]

What follows is an attempt to re-anchor the concept of authoritarian liberalism to its original domain, that of the state form, and to explore the question: What is the state form of authoritarian liberalism? Addressing this issue is instrumental in deepening our understanding of how contemporary liberal regimes have effectively sustained the normalisation of exceptionality.

6.2 The Dual State

Hauke Brunkhorst sustains that the authoritarian liberal institutional asset of Europe could be read as a form of 'dual state'. 'The technocratic system of executive federalism', he maintains, 'has the formal and (even more)

10 Wolfgang Streeck, *How Will Capitalism End?* (London: Verso 2016) 152.

11 Alexander Somek, 'Authoritarian Liberalism', *ALJ* (2015): 67; Alexander Somek, 'Delegation and Authority: Authoritarian Liberalism Today', *European Law Journal* 21.3 (2015): 340–360; Werner Bonefeld, 'Authoritarian Liberalism: From Schmitt via Ordoliberalism to the Euro', *Critical Sociology* 43.4–5 (2017): 747–761; Werner Bonefeld, *The Strong State and the Free Economy* (London: Rowman & Littlefield International 2017); Michael Wilkinson, 'The Specter of Authoritarian Liberalism: Reflections on the Constitutional Crisis of the European Union', *German Law Journal* 14.5 (2013): 527–560; Michael Wilkinson, 'Authoritarian Liberalism: The Conjuncture Behind the Crisis', in Eva Nanopoulos and Fotis Vergis (eds), *The Crisis Behind the Crisis: The European Crisis as a Multi-Dimensional Systemic Failure of the EU* (Cambridge: Cambridge University Press 2018); Michael Wilkinson, 'Authoritarian Liberalism as Authoritarian Constitutionalism', in *Authoritarian Constitutionalism* (Edward Elgar Publishing 2019) 317–337; Michael Wilkinson, *Authoritarian Liberalism and the Transformation of Modern Europe* (Oxford University Press 2021). See also: Grégoire Chamayou, *The Ungovernable Society: A Genealogy of Authoritarian Liberalism* (John Wiley & Sons 2021).

12 Wilkinson, 'Authoritarian Liberalism', 104.

informal power to shape Europe as well as national parliamentary legislation and governance', by frequently using 'exceptional measures (prerogative state/*Maßnahmestaat*), even if all its actions are regularly backed by the normative state (*Normstaat*)'.[13] Brunkhorst is not alone in proposing Ernest Fraenkel's concept of the dual state as a relevant instrument for the critique of political systems today,[14] and perhaps this is because it still is a heuristic instrument capable of explaining the combination of seemingly antithetic elements such as strong/anomic governmental practice and normal legal regimes.

Appeared in 1941, *The Dual State. A Contribution to the Theory of Dictatorship* is Ernest Fraenkel's contribution to the study of the nature and form of the Nazi state. The starting point and main purpose of his investigation are, as suggested in the introduction to the first edition, to demonstrate how the 'National-Socialist state is remarkable not only for its supreme arbitrary powers but also for the way in which it has succeeded in combining arbitrary powers with a capitalistic economic organization'.[15] The Third Reich effectively wielded arbitrary power while maintaining the 'rational legal system' that is 'indispensable for the operation of a capitalist economic order'; and this, Fraenkel argues, assumes the form of a paradox since 'rational calculation is not consistent with the rule of arbitrary police power which is characteristic of the Third Reich'.[16] Nazi Germany, therefore, is structured upon a fundamental institutionally hybrid system in which the normal rule and exceptionality are the two functioning poles of a dual political/legal machinery.

His experience in legal practices, Fraenkel claims, allowed him to find a 'key to understanding the National Socialist system of rule in the duality or concurrent existence of a normative state (*Normenstaat*) that generally respects its own laws, and a "prerogative state" (*Maßnahmenstaat*) that violates the very same laws'.[17] In this dissociated institutional formation, the prerogative state is a 'governmental system which exercises unlimited arbitrariness and violence unchecked by any legal guarantees', while

13 Hauke Brunkhorst, 'The European Dual State: The Double Structural Transformation of the Public Sphere and the Need for Repoliticization', in Jiří Přibáň (ed), *Self-Constitution of European Society. Beyond EU Politics, Law and Governance* (Abingdon: Routledge 2016) 250.

14 Jan Christoph Suntrup, 'Between Prerogative Power and Legality—Reading Ernst Fraenkel's *The Dual State* as an Analytical Tool for Present Authoritarian Rule', *Jurisprudence* 11.3 (2020): 335–359; Serdar Tekin, 'The Dual State in Turkey', *European Journal of Turkish Studies* 34 (2022); Eva Pils, 'China's Dual State Revival Under Xi Jinping', *Fordham Int'l LJ* 46 (2022): 339; Richard Sakwa, 'The Dual State in Russia', *Post-Soviet Affairs* 26.3 (2010): 185–206.

15 Ernest Fraenkel, *The Dual State. A Contribution to the Theory of Dictatorship* (Oxford: Oxford University Press 2017) xxiv.

16 Fraenkel, *The Dual State.*

17 Fraenkel, *The Dual State*, xxiii.

the normative state is composed of 'an administrative body endowed with elaborate powers for safeguarding the legal order as expressed in statutes, decisions of the courts, and activities of the administrative agencies'.[18] To the extent that, as Fraenkel bluntly claims, the 'Martial law provides the constitution of the Third Reich, the constitutional charter of the Third Reich is the Emergency Decree of February 28, 1933'.[19] The precondition of the emergence of the Nazi dual state is the implementation of an indefinite state of exception. Although essentially different in their functioning and aims, the two 'states' composing the institutional structure of Nazi Germany were tied in a relation of symbiosis, which nevertheless did not exclude regular frictions between the two. In their self-constitutive relationships, the Normative State is a pawn at the disposal of the Prerogative State, but it is still one fundamental component of the system.

Why, then, did the new *Führerstaat* need to resort to general law? Fraenkel's answer is rather straightforward. The German economic system still had a purely capitalist character and was, therefore, in need of a state enforcing rights and basic legal forms necessary to make a capitalist economy work:

> The late-capitalism of the post-war Germany used only one method to overcome the crisis which threatened its existence, the armament boom. Early liberal capitalism sought to reduce the functions of the state to a minimum because it had faith in its own inherent laws. Contemporary German capitalism, however, needs a state which removes its socialist opponent, proves that 'private benefit is public benefit' and provides it with the external enemies against whom it must arm itself as a sine qua non for its preservation . . . . German capitalism today requires state aid in two respects: (a) against the social enemies in order to guarantee its existence, and (b) in its role as guarantor of that legal order which is the pre-condition of exact calculability without which capitalist enterprise cannot exist. German capitalism requires for its salvation a dual, not a unitary state, based on arbitrariness in the political sphere and on rational law in the economic sphere. Contemporary German capitalism is dependent on the Dual State for its existence.[20]

For Fraenkel, the social and material conditions that led to the establishment of the Third Reich necessitated, therefore, both violence and law: the first, to depoliticise the economic sphere, the latter to sustain it in its capitalist form.

18 Fraenkel, *The Dual State*.
19 Fraenkel, *The Dual State*, 3.
20 Fraenkel, *The Dual State*, 205–206.

At least since Max Weber's theory of law, the pursuit of legal predictability in the economic sphere has been tied to the existence and enforcement of legal rationality. In the dual Nazi state, remnants of formally rational law—embedded within its normative half—provided a stable institutional framework. This predictability gave economic actors enough confidence in the protection of their private property rights so that they tacitly supported the regime. Through an unspoken quid pro quo, they facilitated the expansion of a fundamentally violent system, even as they might have otherwise disavowed its irrational ideology. This paradoxically implies that the dual state is a schizophrenic construct: a framework where rationality is irrationally preserved, as an expression of material conditions that it aims to protect. Fraenkel is rather clear on this point when he wrote that the

> legal order of the Reich is thoroughly rationalized in a functional sense for the regulation of production and exchange in accordance with capitalistic methods. But late capitalistic economic activity is not substantially rational. For this reason, it has had recourse to political methods, while giving to these methods the contentlessness of irrational activity.[21]

'Capital', Mark Neocleous in this regard argues,

> will happily cast its vote for the irrationality of arbitrary prerogative so long as it is granted the rationality of functional regulation, thereby accommodating itself to the irrationality of an arbitrary power which maintains the conditions of rationality and the rule of law.[22]

It is worth noting that Fraenkel is eager to distinguish his vision of the dual state from the concept of a 'totalitarian state' and Schmitt's version of it: the 'qualitative total state'.[23] The image Schmitt aimed to promote with that concept is that of a situation in which the state possesses control of all the major means of mass influence, which grants the right to free business enterprise and where the public sphere remains a relatively autonomous space. Nazi Germany, Fraenkel claims, 'cannot be called totalitarian state in the broader sense' as the very existence of private enterprise in the Third Reich is a barrier and a limit to the scope of the prerogative state—and for this reason, 'dual state' is a preferable definition.[24] While this theoretically is a correct analysis, it is ultimately very hard to deny the substantial similarity between the Schmittian idea of the strong state and free economy and the

21 Fraenkel, *The Dual State.*
22 Mark Neocleous, *Critique of Security* (Edinburgh: Edinburgh University Press 2008) 37.
23 Fraenkel, *The Dual State*, 60–62.
24 Fraenkel, *The Dual State*, 61.

concept of the dual state. In both cases, the strengthening of governmental power is functional to the protection of the capitalist economy and liberal economic freedoms. In a sense, the Nazi dual-state realised the vision of the 'strong state, free economy'.

All in all, Fraenkel's theory of the dual state, brings to the fore the fundamental internal tension within the structure of the modern state—only partially resolved by a sustained legalism and the doctrine of the separation of power—the one that persists between the rule of the law and raw governmental power. In his introduction to the Italian translation of *The Dual State*, Norberto Bobbio questioned whether it would have been more effective to frame the discussion in terms of the classic antithesis between the rule of law and the rule of men, rather than referring to a 'dual state': that is the two faces of state's power, one regulated by law and the other open to the exercise of power, which is present (in different forms and structures) in all political systems.[25] Such a question is also made relevant by the fact that Fraenkel constantly seeks to posit the exception of the Nazi rule in the historical continuum. This becomes evident in his definition of the prerogative state, which he presents as a product of the historical evolution of German legal and political culture.[26] In so doing, Fraenkel tries to historicise the disruptive innovation of the Nazi regime by placing it within the broader trajectory of the modern state. However, if (as we have already had the chance to observe) the dualism between norm and exception, law and government, is characteristic of the Modern political experience, electing dualism as the distinctive character of Nazi Germany does not make it essentially something new. Perhaps this is precisely Fraenkel's point: what sets the dual state apart is the extent to which one pole, the prerogative, has come to dominate the entire state structure. By framing Nazi rule as an extreme manifestation of the modern state rather than an exceptional anomaly, Fraenkel avoids an uncritical portrayal of its uniqueness while simultaneously highlighting its break from the past.

~

In a compelling passage, Fraenkel clearly warns that what he has called Normative State, should 'by no means' be considered identical with the rule of law—the *Rechtsstaat* of the liberal period': the Normative State is a 'necessary complement to the Prerogative State and can be understood only in that light. Since the Prerogative and Normative States constitute an interdependent whole, the consideration of the Normative State in isolation is not permissible'.[27] As far as the state of exception represents the constitutional

25 Norberto Bobbio, '"Introduzione" a Ernest Fraenkel', in *Il Doppio Stato. Contributo alla Teoria della Dittatura* (Torino: Einaudi 1983) xxiii–xxiv.

26 Fraenkel, *The Dual State*, 6.

27 Fraenkel, *The Dual State*, 71.

charter of the Third Reich, the splitting between prerogative and normative state, is, in the end, the product of a legal operation. Exceptionality is, therefore, what allows the separation between the irrationality and anomy of power and the rationality of a stable law. And given it was the same law that provides the original source of exceptionality, it follows logically that the two sides of the dual state are present in a state of latency in the same *Rechtsstaat*. But what does keep these two ontologically different elements together? What is the modality of their articulation?

6.3 Bipolar Machine

In *The Kingdom and the Glory*, Agamben, adopting political theology as a method, exposed how the 'economic-governmental vocation of contemporary democracies', in which the executive dominates over the other forms of power, 'is not something that has happened accidentally but is a constitutive part of the theological legacy of which they are the depositaries'.[28] In this work, he has explored the theological influence on the evolving structuring of political power within the Western Tradition; that is, its operating, on the one hand, as a form of a centralised authority commanding according to general rules, while on the other hand appearing as diffuse and immanent techniques for shaping individual social life. Or, to put it in other words, how political power manifests itself in the distinct poles of sovereignty and government.[29]

By tracing the theological roots of the modern and contemporary governmental vocation of state power back to the early Church Fathers, Agamben both complements and, to some extent, revises Michel Foucault's claim that governmentality (and the whole spectrum of phenomena associated with biopolitics) is essentially a modern phenomenon, the outcome of a departure from the traditional paradigms of power based on sovereignty and law. Central to the Foucauldian predicament is that governmental rationality is manifested in the passage from the old-sovereign power configured as 'right to *take* life or to *let* live', to the modern bio-power 'to *foster* life or *disallow* it to the point of death'.[30] From this perspective, sovereignty is defined negatively, primarily as the power to impose death. Its formal expression lies in the juridical order, structured around legal rules and their corresponding punishments. Within the paradigm of sovereignty, life is merely what remains when power is inactive—when the sword of the law stays sheathed. Governmentality, by contrast, represents a positive capture of life within political

28 Giorgio Agamben, *The Kingdom and the Glory* (Stanford: Stanford University Press 2011) 143.

29 Devin Singh, 'Anarchy, Void, Signature: Agamben's Trinity Among Orthodoxy's Remains', *Political Theology* 17.1 (2016): 29.

30 Michel Foucault, *The History of Sexuality*, Vol. 1 (New York: Penguin 1998) 138.

calculation, where the living substance—biological, social and cultural—is the object of power. Here, the administration of life's flourishing becomes the very purpose of political care.[31]

While agreeing with Foucault that sovereign power and biopolitics represent distinct paradigms, Agamben opts for a different genealogy and a somewhat different articulation of the two. Within his research path, theology represents the place in which the two models were elaborated. From Christian theology, he writes, derive two 'political paradigms, antinomical but functionally related to one another': political theology, 'which founds the transcendence of sovereign power on the single God' and the 'economic theology' which replaces this transcendence with the idea of an *oikonomia*, conceived as an immanent ordering of both divine and human life.[32] The first paradigm paved the way for the theory of sovereign power, while the second gave rise to the idea of government, from which modern biopolitics and dominion of economy over all aspects of social life derive.

For Agamben, the emergence of these two paradigms is rooted in theological debates over how an all-powerful God can function both as a transcendental creator, bringing all things into existence from nothing, and as an immanent force actively administering the world. This dilemma centres on the reconciliation of God's singular, omnipotent substance with its concrete manifestations in the three hypostases: Father, Son and Holy Spirit. To preserve monotheism and prevent the fragmentation of divine unity, the early Church Fathers adopted the Greek term *oikonomia* (originally referring to household management) to conceptualise God's government of the world without compromising his ontological unity. *Oikonomia* becomes, without any substantial semantic alteration, the operator that granted the conciliation of the Trinity with the divine unity: the monarch-like absolute and transcendent God is one in its substance, but its administration [*oikonomia*] of the world is manifested as a trinity. And, as Agamben maintains, the divine being 'is not split, since the triplicity of which the Fathers speak is located on the level of the *oikonomia*' and not on the level of being or substance.[33]

31 Gian-Giacomo Fusco, *Form of Life. Agamben and the Destitution of Rules* (Edinburgh: Edinburgh University Press 2023) 177. On Agamben's reception of Foucault, see Mika Ojakangas, 'Impossible Dialogue on Bio-Power: Agamben and Foucault', *Foucault Studies* (2005): 5–28; Anke Snoek, 'Agamben's Foucault: An Overview', *Foucault Studies* (2010): 44–67; Jessica Whyte, 'The King Reigns but He Doesn't Govern': Thinking Sovereignty and Government with Agamben, Foucault and Rousseau', in Tom Frost (ed), *Giorgio Agamben: Legal, Political and Philosophical Perspectives* (Abingdon: Routledge 2013) 143–161; Tom Frost, 'Agamben's Sovereign Legalization of Foucault', *Oxford Journal of Legal Studies* 30.3 (2010): 545–577; Katia Genel, Craig Carson, 'The Question of Biopower: Foucault and Agamben', in *Rethinking Marxism* (Routledge 2023) 43–62.

32 Agamben, *The Kingdom and the Glory*, 1.

33 Agamben, *The Kingdom and the Glory*, 53.

However, as Agamben claims, this strategy of excluding the fracturing of God's essence into the three figures brought about another fundamental separation: the one between God and his action, between 'ontology and praxis', as the separation between a unitarian substance and its economy 'amounts to instituting within God a separation between being and acting, substance and praxis'.[34] Since the Trinity pertains to the economic and administrative sphere, the praxis through which God governs the world is fundamentally distinct from his substantive being and cannot be inferred from it. The two are ontologically alien and, therefore, God's economic government of the world does not derive its foundation from divine almighty substance. For this reason, Agamben could claim that divine government is without foundation—anarchic.

The ontological fractures that separate God the almighty creator from God's practical administration of the world are logically formed over a differentiation between a pole of transcendent sovereignty and one of governmental immanent actualisation. The two poles, Agamben argues, although irreconcilable, are functionally interconnected in a governmental machine. If being and praxis, absolute sovereign power and its concrete execution 'are separated in God by a clear opposition then no government of the world is actually possible'; there would be, 'on the one hand, an impotent sovereignty and, on the other, the infinite and chaotic series of particular (and violent) acts'. God can, in the end, govern the world only 'if Kingdom and the Government are correlated in a bipolar machine', the centre of which is, however, empty.[35] This tension positions sovereignty as the source of legitimacy for government, while government, in turn, embodies the actual existence of sovereignty. What makes possible the exercise of power is, therefore, other than the exercise of power itself, but—at the same time—the other of the exercise of power can assume its most proper transcendental sovereign substance only through its actualisation (concretisation). There is no sovereignty without government and vice-versa: a government with no kingdom is just a series of acts—inherently purposeless—unable to create order, that is to say, unable to govern.

'As a matter of fact', Agamben writes,

> the modern State inherits both aspects of the theological machine of the government of the world . . . [t]hrough the distinction between legislative or sovereign power and executive or governmental power, the modern State acquires the double structure of the governmental machine.[36]

34 Agamben, *The Kingdom and the Glory*, 53.
35 Agamben, *The Kingdom and the Glory*, 114.
36 Agamben, *The Kingdom and the Glory*, 142.

Indeed, it assumes on itself the role of the transcendental sovereign that can legislate universally; while at the same time wearing the 'ministerial clothes' through which the administrators—those who de facto are constituting and operating the governmental machine—are authorised to act, following the rule of the law but hardly constrained by it. In this bipolar governmental machine, the legitimate manifestation of power is trapped in the dialectical articulation between the two poles of (1) sovereign power, speaking the language of the law, which works as a legitimate foundational authority and (2) the immanent government, which gives a reality and an operativity to the sovereign transcendental pole. The sovereign law and the executive are, thus, separated on the plane of their essence (in the sense that government is not sovereignty—and vice-versa) but are functionally linked on the plane of their existence (where the government is the actualisation of a transcendent, external cause). The modern rule of law, Agamben claims, represents the ultimate figure of the perfect articulation of the two antithetical poles of the bipolar machine, as 'the law regulates the administration and the administrative apparatus applies and implements the law'.[37]

~

We are here in a position to answer the questions with which the previous section terminated, that is, what keeps the two halves of Fraenkel's dual state together? And what might be the modality of their articulation? As Agamben's theological genealogy of sovereignty and government exhibits, the answer to the first question is rather clear: nothing. The relation between the sphere of the sovereign law and the executive is an anarchic one: the centre of the bipolar machine is empty. Composed of interconnected elements that lack an ontological foundation for their relationship, the administration of power in the West is ultimately groundless and anarchic—that is not necessarily tied to the general sovereign law that legitimates its existence. The articulation between the two poles of the bipolar machine—we now move to the second question—is based on a relationship of vicariate. The governmental praxis is vicarious since it is an effective action 'in the name' of a sovereign principle. To act vicariously, however, implies the absence of the agent on whose behalf the action is taken. It follows logically that the legitimacy of the government lies in a sovereign legal transcendental absence, made real only through the government praxis. The reality of sovereignty and law, and their ultimate conservation as something that exists, consists of their execution, which is anarchic and absolutely free. And exactly because of this groundlessness governmental institutions are constantly in need of affirming their legitimacy, either by (often violent) security mechanisms (that is, by sustaining the health and wealth of the

37 Agamben, *The Kingdom and the Glory*, 143.

population) or by the consent of their subjects. Concepts like divine transcendence, the general will, constituent power and practices like elections, for Agamben, form a set of strategies that have helped conceal the constitutive anarchy of power under the veil of legitimacy.[38]

The dual state Fraenkel had in mind while observing the Nazi state, therefore, represents the moment of maxim divarication of the two poles: when an anarchic government assumes the guise of a prerogative state, which can dispose of the law at its own will (making the law as a pure instrument to reach economic efficiency). Radically different from the dual state is the legislative state, structured upon the principle of the rule of law (*Rechtsstaat*), in which 'every activity of government presents itself as an application and execution of a law enforced impersonally'.[39] In this latter case, the sphere of sovereign law and its concrete execution coincide. All in all, what Agamben seems to suggest through his genealogical speculations in *The Kingdom and the Glory* is that the different forms the Modern state assumed are structured over a specific relationship between the two poles of the bipolar governmental machine. And the critique of state power should begin with the tension inherent in the dialectical interaction between government/oikonomia and sovereignty/law.

6.4 Authoritarian Statism

Western democracies are caught in the middle of what has been defined as 'democratic decay'[40] or 'democratic recession'.[41] The rise of neoliberal governmentality, marked by the retreat of sovereign majoritarian institutions and the growing centrality of the executive administration, has reshaped the image liberal democracies build of themselves[42] (into what we have defined earlier as 'authoritarian liberalism'). The form of the liberal state, in the present phase of capitalism, seems to be undergoing a shift in the relationship between sovereignty/law and government. Power today has taken on the form of management and administration, marking a 'new state in the union of capital and the state, of sovereignty and the market'; in which the liberal state 'centralises and multiplies authoritarian government techniques, rivalling the politics of the

38 Gian-Giacomo Fusco, *Form of Life*, 180.
39 Agamben, *The Kingdom and the Glory*, 133–134.
40 Daly, 'Democratic Decay'.
41 Larry Diamond, 'Facing Up to the Democratic Recession', *Journal of Democracy* 26.1 (2015): 141.
42 On this issue, see Ian Bruff, 'The Rise of Authoritarian Neoliberalism', *Rethinking Marxism* 26.1 (2013): 113–129; Cemal Burak Tansel (ed), *States of Discipline Authoritarian Neoliberalism and the Contested Reproduction of Capitalist Order* (London: Rowman and Littlefield 2017); Ernesto Gallo, Three Varieties of Authoritarian Neoliberalism: Rule by the Experts, the People, the Leader', *Competition & Change* 26.5 (2022): 554–574.

so-called totalitarian states'.[43] It is right now clear that contrary to its standard predicament, the current dominant version of liberalism has no reason to get rid of the state's power and control. What we are witnessing is indeed a functional integration of state sovereignty, with its administrative and legal functions, into a strong governmental machine, which 'relies upon coercive state practices that discipline, marginalize and criminalize oppositional social forces and the judicial and administrative state apparatuses which limit the avenues in which neoliberal policies can be challenged'.[44]

The deployment of authoritarian tactics and coercive apparatuses to safeguard capital accumulation is hardly a novel phenomenon. The use of anti-democratic disciplinary measures to dismantle barriers to accumulation has long been a focal point of social and political critiques of the state for a while.[45] For the modern liberal mind, liberty consisted principally of equal economic opportunity and non-interference of government in the pursuit of them. In the historical development of modernity, liberal ideology fostered the illusion of a virtuous circle between capitalism and democracy; whereas the latter, instead of being a political system made of institutions capable of allowing the 'people' to rule, was essentially programmed to separate the sphere of politics and that of the economy.[46] The compromise that came about is that of the minimisation of state interference in the economy by channelling and limiting political participation in electoral procedures. Liberal democracy became, though, synonymous with free and transparent elections, while the liberal state functions as the enforcer and guardian of the freedom to act in pursuit of profit, making private property the sanctified site of capitalist accumulation. This separation of the economic and political spheres is considered the only functioning strategy to enable economic actors to operate with minimal constraints, accumulating vast power and wealth at the expense of other social domains. When, in times of crises, social demands start interfering with the economic sphere, the task of the liberal state is that of strengthening its coercive function and limiting the possibility of democratic corrections of the capitalist economy—even if this means essentially constraining democracy.[47]

43 Maurizio Lazzarato, *Governing by Debt* (South Pasadena: Semiotext(e) 2015) 95.

44 Cemal Burak Tansel, 'Authoritarian Neoliberalism. Towards a New Research Agenda', in Cemal Burak Tansel (ed), *States of Discipline Authoritarian Neoliberalism and the Contested Reproduction of Capitalist Order* (Rowman and Littlefield 2017).

45 On this issue, see Bob Jessop, *State. Past, Present, Future* (Cambridge: Polity 2016) 211–237.

46 Michelle Williams, 'The Crisis of Democracy: Neoliberal Capitalism, Authoritarianism and Reclaiming Democracy', in Michelle Williams, Vishwas Satgar (eds), *Destroying Democracy Neoliberal Capitalism and the Rise of Authoritarian Politics* (Johannesburg: Wits University Press 2021).

47 This is, of course, one of the basic tenets of both Hayek's (neo)liberalism and the idea of a strong state predicated by Ordoliberals; see on this point Werner Bonefeld, *The Strong State and the Free Economy* (London: Rowman and Littlefield 2017) Ch 1; Peter Nedergaard,

Writing in the shadow of the economic (and political) crisis that invested the Western capitalist world in the 1970s, Nikos Poulantzas identified the emergence of a new state form, imposed as a normal structure of the liberal capitalist state, which he called 'authoritarian statism'. Such a new form of state involves an 'intensified state control over every sphere of socio-economic life *combined with* the radical decline of the institutions of political democracy and with draconian and multiform curtailment of so-called "formal" liberties'.[48] Authoritarian statism manifests itself in an evident 'decline of parliament, the strengthening of the Executive, the political role currently assumed by the state administration',[49] and this implies a shift of power from the legislature to the executive and administrative apparatus, where real authority becomes concentrated and insulated from the influence of parties and parliaments—nominally the people's representatives.[50] This renewed pre-eminence of the administrative apparatuses made the relative separation between legislative and executive power less sharp, producing a sort of fusion between the powers of the state that has led to a decline in the rule of law. For authoritarian statism, parliaments and parties are reduced to mere electoral registration chambers with minimal authority.[51] As a result, state administration has emerged as the primary political actor and lawmaker with a consequent change in legislative functions and law's normativity. Poulantzas maintains:

> [T]hrough a process correlative with changes in the nature of such regulation, the power to fix norms and enact rules is shifting towards the Executive and the state administration. That legitimacy embodied by parliament which had as its frame of reference a universal rationality is gradually passing over into a legitimacy characterized by the instrumental rationality of efficiency and embodied by the Executive-administration. Indeed, the general and universal laws still enacted by parliament—which are, at bottom, merely framework-laws—are applied only after the Executive has passed them through a process of concretization and particularization. This is the stage of decrees, judicial interpretation and civil service adjustment, without which the norms enacted by parliament do not enter into the practice of the law . . . . What is more, the initiative in proposing laws has almost entirely shifted from parliament to the Executive, new bills being directly

'An Ordoliberal Theory of the State', *German Politics* 28.1 (2018): 20–34; Andrew Farrant, Edward McPhail, Sebastian Berger, 'Preventing the 'Abuses' of Democracy: Hayek, the 'Military Usurper' and Transitional Dictatorship in Chile?', *American Journal of Economics and Sociology* 71.3 (2012): 513–538.

48 Nikos Poulantzas, *State Power Socialism* (London: Verso 2001) 204.

49 Poulantzas, *State Power Socialism*, 217.

50 Jessop, *State*, 225.

51 Jessop, *State*, 226.

> elaborated by the civil service. Such laws are no longer inscribed in the formal logic of the juridical system—a logic based on norm-universality and on the rationality of the General Will represented by the Enactor—but are entered in the quite different account-book of concrete, day-to-day economic policy embodied by the administrative apparatus.[52]

In this reconfiguration of power structures, the law undergoes a fundamental transformation, shifting from a universal guiding principle to a tool that frames and legitimises executive action. As legal normativity adapts to this new role, its once-universal rationality is hollowed out, reduced to little more than a procedural preamble to the substantive authority of the executive-administrative apparatus.

True to his Marxist method, Poulantzas' vision of the state must be placed in strict relation to the material conditions and the specific phase of capitalism in which they emerge. Authoritarian statism, he claims, grew out of a phase '*permanently and structurally characterized by a peculiar sharpening of the generic elements of political crisis and state crisis*—a sharpening which is itself articulated to the economic crisis of capitalism'.[53] In many ways, this state form reflected the deepening structural crisis of capitalism that characterised the 1970s. Driven by deteriorating living conditions, declining job security, the erosion of traditional privileges and the overall destabilisation of the labour force, this crisis intensified class struggle and fuelled the political militancy of unionists, subaltern groups and new social movements.[54] And when factors of crisis intensify, Poulantzas claims, 'fascistic elements or tendencies appear in the democratic form of State to a much more marked degree than previously'.[55] By mixing democratic institutions and fascistic elements, authoritarian statism appears as an antidote to the crisis of capital through the formation of an 'entire institutional structure serving to prevent a rise in popular struggles and the dangers which that holds for class hegemony' and accumulation.[56]

But, authoritarian statism, for Poulantzas, should not be identified with a fascist order. 'The present-day State', he claims, 'is neither the new form of a genuine exceptional State nor, in itself, a transitional form on the road to such a State: *it rather represents the new "democratic" form of the bourgeois republic in the current phase of capitalism*'.[57] Poulantzas firmly maintained that liberal

52 Jessop, *State*, 218–219.
53 Jessop, *State*, 206.
54 On this issue, see Duco Hellema, *The Global 1970s: Radicalism, Reform, and Crisis* (London: Routledge 2018).
55 Poulantzas, *State Power Socialism*, 210.
56 Poulantzas, *State Power Socialism*.
57 Poulantzas, *State Power Socialism*, 208. Exceptional states (of which fascism is a variant) are characterised by a suspension of elections and the regulation of power transfer, an integration

democracy was the normal state form of advanced capitalism.[58] Liberal democracy has some basic 'normal' institutional arrangements and legally recognised rights: freedom of association and speech, free elections and a competitive party system. It also presupposes (parliamentary) oversight of the executive and state administration, as well as a degree of accountability from both legislators and the executive to the electorate and public opinion. However, if political crises cannot be resolved through normal democratic procedures, the tendency is to recur to the exceptional instruments that are normally provided by the legal system, which suspend the normal functioning of democratic institutions. And when crises become 'normalised', elements of the exceptional state are injected into the normal one. This is the kernel of Poulantzas' argument: to the extent that the contradiction of capital and the tendency of crisis to become a stable part of global contingency 'features of the political order that were previously exceptional and temporary were more and more becoming normalised' in the form of authoritarian statism.[59] This implies that significant 'exceptional' measures not only coexist with but actively reshape the 'normal' characteristics of the capitalist state, through a continuous accommodation and functional integration of ordinary and exceptional structures, all operating under the strategic control of the state's commanding heights.

~

The theory of authoritarian statism is a crisis theory of the state which effectively accounts for the authoritarian drive of the current dominant form of the liberal state. And not surprisingly, it has garnered some recognition.[60] From our perspective, the theorisation of such a state form complements the previous discussion over the normalisation of exceptionality, providing a materialist and historical account of how the exceptional state has been embedded within the liberal normality of the state. Since Poulantzas' original theorisation, authoritarian statism has remained

---

of ideological apparatuses inside state's institutions and concentrated powers altering the standard division of powers; on this point, see Nikos Poulantzas, *Political Power and Social Classes* (London: NLB 1973); Nikos Poulantzas, *Fascism and Dictatorship* (London: NLB 1974).

58 Jessop, *State*, 220.

59 Jessop, *State*, 224.

60 Jamey Essex, 'Getting What You Pay for: Authoritarian Statism and the Geographies of US Trade Liberalization Strategies', *Studies in Political Economy* 80.1 (2007): 75–103; Sune Sandbeck, Etienne Schneider, 'From the Sovereign Debt Crisis to Authoritarian Statism: Contradictions of the European State Project', *New Political Economy* 19.6 (2014): 847–871; Kanishka Jayasuriya, 'Authoritarian Statism and the New Right in Asia's Conservative Democracies', *Journal of Contemporary Asia* 48.4 (2018): 584–604; Lukas Oberndorfer, 'Between the Normal State and an Exceptional State Form: Authoritarian Competitive Statism and the Crisis of Democracy in Europe', in *The State of the European Union: Fault Lines in European Integration* (Springer VS 2020) 23–44.

the dominant state form within Western liberal democracies, adapting to crises that periodically reshape its contours.[61] The escalating securitisation of the social and biological body, driven by ongoing global emergencies, has further accelerated the normalisation of exceptionality. Ultimately, this process remains the more effective strategy to adapt the state's structural evolution to systemic crises and to protect and sustain capital accumulation.

6.5 The Administrative State

In his *Legality and Legitimacy*, published in 1932, amid the social and political turmoil that eventually led to the collapse of the Weimar Republic, Carl Schmitt offered a penetrating critique of Germany's unfolding constitutional crisis. Faced with substantial changes in the institutional assets of the Reich, he felt the need to reassess the typology of state forms, abandoning the classical categorisation of regimes—democracy, aristocracy and monarchy—in favour of a new framework. He identified four different types of regimes (or states): legislative, jurisdiction, governmental and administrative. Essentially, he replaced a categorisation-based 'concrete authority' of the ruler (the subject at the top of the institutional hierarchy) with a new determined 'by the manner' in which the law is applied. The legislative state, Schmitt argues, is a political system in which norms, 'the highest expression of the community will' regulate the whole institutional apparatus and the society it aims to rule—this is the parliamentary *Rechtsstaat*.[62] Similarly, the jurisdiction state is a rule-based system in which judges directly generate 'legal doctrines and also applies this law to the norm-setting legislature and its law'.[63] The governmental state, instead, 'finds its characteristic expression in the exalted personal will' and 'commands' of the ruling head of state. In the last type of regime, the administrative state, 'command and will do not appear authoritarian and personal'; in this kind of system, 'men do not rule, nor are norms valid as something higher. Instead, the famous formula "things administer themselves" holds true'.[64]

To a certain degree, Schmitt claims these four regimes are all present in every political system, as in every state there are lawmaking processes, authoritative commands, administration and judicial apparatuses, which are all normally 'reunited in the sovereign'.[65] However, he also claimed that 'our state form is undergoing a transformation' turning 'toward the administrative state'. The German *Sozialstaat* or welfare state, which Schmitt defined

61 Christos Boukalas, 'No Exceptions: Authoritarian Statism. Agamben, Poulantzas and Homeland Security', *Critical Studies on Terrorism* 7.1 (2014): 112–130.
62 Carl Schmitt, *Legality and legitimacy* (Duke University Press 2004) 3.
63 Schmitt, *Legality and legitimacy*, 5.
64 Schmitt, *Legality and legitimacy*, 5.
65 Schmitt, *Legality and legitimacy*, 5.

(as we have seen in the first section) as a quantitative total state, is by nature an administrative state, since by intervening in all spheres of social life, under the political demands for redistributive policies, it cannot but expand significantly the administration apparatus. That such an economic state, Schmitt claims, 'cannot possibly also work as a legislative state and must become an administrative state is already almost universally known today'.[66]

The administrative state rules somewhat impersonally, taking into consideration only the functional effectiveness of the system according to a technical-instrumental logic, the pursuit of which is the perpetuation and self-preservation of the administrative machine itself. Much like the legislative, also the administrative state is devoid of a personal will, but unlike it, it does not operate by following general law from which to deduce particular rules. Its ultimate purpose is to adapt efficiently to circumstances and its most specific instrument is the decree. As Schmitt puts it:

> The administrative state can call on factual necessity, the condition of things, the force of circumstances, the necessity of the moment, and other non-normative, situation-specific justifications. Correspondingly, the administrative state finds its existential justification in the purposefulness, the usefulness, and, in contrast to the conformity to norms of the normatively grounded legislative state, the directly concrete, factual appropriateness of its administrative measures, orders, and commands. Both the governmental and the administrative states perceive a distinctive quality in concrete commands, which are directly executable or easily obeyed, and they make an end of the advocate's pleas accompanying the jurisdiction state as well as of the parliamentary legislative state's tendency toward endless discussion, recognizing already in decisionism the immediately executable directive as a legal value in itself. In this regard, it still holds true: 'The best thing in the world is a command'.[67]

In 1944, in the middle of the German tragic defeat, Schmitt expanded on such arguments in the lecture *The Situation of European Jurisprudence*. One of the core points he has advanced is that jurisprudence—as a somewhat scientific practice of reflecting on the meaning of the law—is undergoing an existential crisis. This is because with the triumph of positive law (according to which only stately produced law should be considered as laws) legislative activities became ultimately the prerogative of the state, which could change laws whenever it deems it necessary. In the 20th century, Schmitt observed, the norms production accelerated under the pressure of social and political

66 Schmitt, *Legality and legitimacy*, 6–7.
67 Schmitt, *Legality and legitimacy*, 8–9.

instances, making the pondered reflection jurisprudence necessitate basically impossible. 'The passing of new legislation', Schmitt argues,

> became faster and more streamlined, the road to legal regulation shorter, and the role of jurisprudence accordingly smaller. War and its aftermath, mobilisation and demobilisation, revolution and dictatorship, inflation and deflation have, despite all other differences, led in all European countries to the same result—that the passing of new legislation has become simplified and accelerated. The trend consisted in ever new and broader authorisations, through which legislative bodies delegated authority to issue legally binding 'decrees' and 'directives' which displaced the law.[68]

Under the pressure of urgent social and economic issues that characterised the interwar period, all major European states started making use of decrees to intervene more effectively in society—speeding up the legislative action. But this, of course, produced a normalisation of what is by definition exceptional, that is, the law decree. The decree, Schmitt notes, has also been defined as 'motorised law', the normalisation of which cannot but produce a generalised motorisation of law. Here, the emergence of the administrative state, announced in *Legality and Legitimacy*, is explained as a reaction to the acceleration of political and social life, to which the state adapted by speeding up legislative procedures by adopting the exceptionality of enacting decrees as a modus operandi. In such a situation, Schmitt maintains, the law 'became a means of planning, an administrative act, a directive', often not publicly announced and communicated to those interested in it and subject to rapid changes and adaptations to new circumstances.[69] And this tendency cannot but produce a decline in the legislative authority of the democratic institution par excellence, that is, the parliament.

William Scheuermann, in his *Liberal Democracy and the Social Acceleration of Time*, developed further Schmitt's speculations over the 'motorisation of law', by looking at the contemporary status of liberal democracy. The hypothesis from which his book moves is that, at the turn of the new millennium, social acceleration, fostered by intense technological innovation, is having an impact on the structure and functioning of liberal democracies. Social acceleration, he writes, consists of a

> decrease in the amount of measurable units of time necessary for a particular activity or experience (e.g., goods produced, messages transmitted, or kilometres covered via automobile). It also refers to a decline in the

68 Carl Schmitt, 'The Situation of European Jurisprudence', in *Carl Schmitt's European Jurisprudence* (Nomos Verlagsgesellschaft mbH & Co. KG 2022) 26.
69 Schmitt, 'The Situation of European Jurisprudence', 29.

amount of quantifiable time necessary for what one observer has dubbed 'socially relevant' changes.[70]

Social acceleration of time, Scheuermann argues, is manifested and sustained by three interrelated processes: technological acceleration in communications, movement and production; the speeding up of the paces of social change and transformation; the *heightened tempo of everyday life*.[71] Scheuerman, to explain the sources of such acceleration of time, accepts David Harvey's analysis, which identifies the immanent dynamics of capitalist production as determining a 'time and space compression'. Capitalism has always operated by attempting to accelerate production and consumption; acceleration is indeed a way to maximise accumulation and profitability. 'The history of capitalism', Harvey writes, 'has been characterized by a speed-up in the pace of life, while so overcoming spatial barriers that the world seems to collapse inward upon us';[72] as Capitalism 'always restlessly searching out new organizational forms, new technologies, new lifestyles, new modalities of production and exploitation and, therefore, new objective social definitions of time and space'.[73]

Although liberal democracy is, for Scheuerman, the natural state form for capitalism, its structural formation seems to produce antiliberal and antidemocratic results paradoxically. The problem here is that the timing of liberal democratic institutions is out of joint with that of an intensified social acceleration. 'Amid the intensified tempo of modern social and economic existence', the traditional 'liberal temporal separation of powers' generates 'the rise of executive discretion and decay of parliamentary legality'.[74] Liberal constitutionalism, Scheuerman writes, involves a sustained separation of powers, which includes a decisive temporal subtext: legislation is prospective or future-oriented; judicial activity is fundamentally retrospective or past-oriented; and the executive is contemporaneous or present-oriented in its fundamental orientation.[75] By being concerned principally with solving the present, the executive is particularly suited to quick and efficient intervention. Scheuerman writes:

> High-speed society privileges high-speed institutions, and in the liberal democratic worldview it is typically the executive who is viewed as an

70 William E. Scheuerman, *Liberal Democracy and the Social Acceleration of Time* (Baltimore: John Hopkins University Press 2004) 9.

71 Scheuerman, *Liberal Democracy*, 9–13.

72 David Harvey, *The Condition of Postmodernity* (Cambridge: Blackwell 1989) 240.

73 David Harvey, *Justice, Nature and the Geography of Difference* (Oxford: Blackwell 1996) 241.

74 Scheuerman, *Liberal Democracy*, 26.

75 Scheuerman, *Liberal Democracy*, 29.

> especially energetic institutional agent. In contrast, deliberative representative legislatures risk getting left at the wayside, as the ever faster pace of social and economic life conflicts with the conventional emphasis on the legislature's necessary reliance on careful, wide-ranging, and time-consuming deliberative exchange.[76]

The accelerated pace of contemporary capitalist society has disrupted the temporal rhythm of liberal democracy, shifting the balance of power in favour of the executive and administrative apparatus. As Scheuerman observes, the relentless demands of a rapidly evolving capitalist economy increasingly necessitate swift and adaptive state intervention. In response, authority is progressively concentrated in executive and administrative bodies, widely regarded as the most capable of delivering immediate action.[77] Consequently, liberal democracy seems to be destined to inevitably move toward an executive-centred, administrative state; and the task, for Scheuerman, is to resist such tendency by reframing the meaning and function of liberal democracy in order to save its liberal essence.

~

For those apologists of the ultimate utility of a strong executive-centred government, the rise of the administrative state seems quite the natural evolution of liberal democracies in an increasingly unstable and interconnected world, where crisis mode has become the normality. Perhaps the most notorious of them, Adrian Vermeule, in several works (at times written with Cass Sustain and Eric Posner) focusing on the US constitutional settlement, defended the administrative state by affirming its legitimacy (and legality) and ultimate utility in protecting American democracy. Unflinchingly he has claimed, for instance, that 'we live in a regime of executive-centred government, in an age after the separation of powers, and the legally constrained executive', where 'the executive governs, subject to legal constraints that are shaky in normal times and weak or nonexistent in times of crises'.[78] For the administrative state, an executive-centered form of government appears inevitable, and the law can no longer be expected to constrain it.[79]

In the administrative state, governance extends beyond the traditional separation of powers, allowing the executive to wield its authority with minimal restraint, all in the name of the community's supposed well-being. The most

76 Scheuerman, *Liberal Democracy*, 45.

77 Scheuerman, *Liberal Democracy*, 124.

78 Eric A. Posner, Adrian Vermeule, *The Executive Unbound. After the Madisonian Republic* (New York: Oxford University Press 2010) 4.

79 Posner, Vermeule, *The Executive Unbound*, 14.

eminent victim of the rise of the administrative state is the law itself. Indeed, as Vermeule claims, the administrative state,

> threatens law's imperial sway. It threatens to relegate courts and judges to a lower status, as marginal officials who are stationed in the outlying provinces and are charged with patrolling the very outermost boundaries of executive authority, but who are no longer central actors—no longer the guardians of principle.[80]

Although the law is a constitutive part of this executive's empire—the administrative state is, in the end, a legal creation—its role is ancillary to that of the administration; it constitutes a marginal addendum to the growing power of the executive.[81] The law, in this sense, is reduced to a further layer of legitimation, integration and sustenance of the broad discretion of the executive.

The administrative state is essentially a variant of authoritarian statism—and, by extension, one of the institutional forms of authoritarian liberalism. From this perspective, the normalisation of emergency powers takes on a new significance, one that liberal legalism was never equipped to acknowledge openly. The perpetual invocation of the state of emergency amid the cascading global crises of recent decades is neither the result of a calculated political strategy nor a flaw in the law. Rather, it is a defining feature of the prevailing state model, where embedding exceptionality within the norm and expanding its reach is not a mark of failure or opportunism but a deliberate means of consolidating liberal executive authority.

80 Adrian Vermeule, *Law's Abnegation. From Law's Empire to the Administrative State* (Cambridge: Harvard University Press 2016) 4.
81 Vermeule, *Law's Abnegation*, 209.

Index

Kolibri 360 GmbH
Ferdinand-Jühlke-Straße 7
99095 Erfurt, Deutschland
produktsicherheit@kolibri360.de